THE PSYCHOLOGY OF RELIGION

THE PSYCHOLOGY OF RELIGION

AND ITS APPLICATION IN PREACHING AND TEACHING

BY

JAMES H. SNOWDEN, D.D., LL.D.

Professor of Systematic Theology in the Western Theological Seminary, Pittsburgh, Pa.
Author of " The World a Spiritual System : an Introduction to Metaphysics,"
" The Basal Beliefs of Christianity," " Scenes and Sayings
in the Life of Christ," etc.

FIFTH EDITION, REVISED

NEW YORK   CHICAGO   TORONTO

Fleming H. Revell Company

LONDON   AND   EDINBURGH

To

SAMUEL BLACK McCORMICK, D.D., LL.D.,

Chancellor of the University of Pittsburgh,

This Volume

Is Respectfully Dedicated

PREFACE

PSYCHOLOGY may approach the study of religion along either of two lines. It may come as a pure science to study religion in its cold white light, without religious presuppositions. It will then scrutinize the nature of religion and endeavour to discern its facts and deduce its laws. Such purely scientific and critical psychology of religion has a work to do, and it must be permitted to have a full and free right of way in its processes and conclusions. Much of this kind of work has been done, and it has its value. However, the scientific psychologist cannot, any more than any other thinker, wholly strip himself of presuppositions, but consciously or latently has in his mind some religious or philosophical system or assumptions which inevitably shape and colour his study of religion.

The other line of approach to this subject is that which is based on views of religion which are accepted by the psychologist as already established on their own grounds. He then comes to religion to clarify it of error and to confirm and illuminate it, as other psychologists approach the study of education or business as established fields of human activity and proceed to illuminate them with the light of their science.

The present volume follows the second of these two lines of approach. It takes up the study of religion on the accepted basis of philosophical theism and Christian faith, and its object is to throw the light of

7

psychological elucidation on such faith and life. It is
therefore of the nature of an exposition rather than of
a critical investigation. But such application of psychology is as legitimate as its similar application to
other fields of life.

In order to make the book available for readers that
have not formally studied psychology, it opens with
an elementary chapter in which the faculties and
activities of the soul are sketched as a background
or introduction to the special field of the psychology
of religion. The applications of the subject to preaching and teaching are necessarily limited to a few principal points, but these are suggestive of the practical
usefulness of this study. It is hoped that the volume
will be found helpful by ministers and Sunday-school
teachers and general readers in enabling them to
understand better the religious life and to be more
efficient in Christian service.

J. H. S.

PITTSBURGH, PA.

CONTENTS

Draw if thou canst the mystic line
Severing rightly His from thine,
Which is human, which Divine.
—EMERSON.

I say that man was made to grow, not stop;
That help, he needed once, and needs no more,
Having grown but an inch by, is withdrawn:
For he hath new needs, and new helps to these.
This imports solely, man should mount on each
New height in view; the help whereby he mounts,
The ladder-rung his foot has left, may fall,
Since all things suffer change save God the Truth.
Man apprehends him newly at each stage
Whereat earth's ladder drops, its service done;
And nothing shall prove twice what once was proved.
—BROWNING.

Till we all attain unto the unity of the faith, and of the knowledge of the Son of God, unto a full-grown man, unto the measure of the stature of the fulness of Christ.—PAUL.

CHAPTER I

INTRODUCTION

PSYCHOLOGY is the science of the soul; the study of its faculties and activities, of the modes and laws of its operations.

1. **Psychology a Late Science.**—As psychology is the knowledge of man's own mind and inmost self we might expect to find that it appeared early in the history of human thought as one of the first of the sciences: yet it is one of the latest. Man studied everything else before he studied himself. His own consciousness was the last thing of which he became conscious. At first he was absorbed in his senses and lived objectively in the outward world, and only long afterward did he become aware of himself and study his subjective states and processes. In this respect the experience of the race is recapitulated by the child, a fact which has been finely expressed by Tennyson:

> The baby new to earth and sky,
>   What time its tender palm is prest
>   Against the circle of the breast,
> Has never thought that "this is I:"
>
> But as he grows he gathers much,
>   And learns the use of "I" and "me,"
>   And finds "I am not what I see,
> And other than the things I touch."
>
> So rounds he to a separate mind
>   From whence clear memory may begin,
>   As thro' the frame that binds him in
> His isolation grows defined.

17

Of course man used his mind and unconsciously obeyed its laws long before he studied psychology. Practical experience always precedes systematic knowledge; art is older than science. Men did not first think about life and then begin to live, but they first lived and then began to think. Their instinctive impulses and practical needs pushed them into action before they reflected on what they were doing. For ages they lived in the sunlight before they studied solar physics, and practised agriculture before they developed the sciences of chemistry and botany. They used their bodies before they dreamed of physiology, and health did not wait on hygiene. So they have used their minds since the first man began to live, but psychology is a modern science. It is true that there were beginnings of this science in ancient times, as all our modern sciences have their ancient roots and germs. The Delphic oracle said, " Know thyself," and Plato and Aristotle were even profound psychologists; yet the scientific study of psychology is hardly a hundred years old. At first it was largely introspective and subjective and only recently has it entered the laboratory of accurate observation and measurement. But, now that it has gotten a start, it has grown rapidly and much progress has been made and a great literature on the subject has been produced.

2. The Application of Psychology.—Science first grows out of experience, as the flower out of the soil, and then goes back into experience to deepen and enrich it, as the petals of the flower fall back into the soil to fertilize it and bring forth finer blossoms. Science and art thus constantly react upon and mutually enrich each other. All our magic machines and marvellous multiplication of goods grow out of our science

which masters the forces of nature and turns them into
our nimble and mighty servants. The same result follows from the study of psychology. As it discloses the
laws of the mind it enables us to use these laws more
efficiently and fruitfully. The mind is the primary
agent with which men work in all their activities, and
therefore psychology should be one of the most practical of the sciences.

Psychologists were slow and late in beginning this
application, but now they are working it out in all directions. Recently some of the master psychologists
have been writing such practical books. Professor
Josiah Royce entitles his work on psychology *Outlines
of Psychology with Some Practical Applications,* and
such applications are suggested all through the book.
Professor William James delivered his helpful *Talks
to Teachers on Psychology.* More recently Professor
Münsterberg has written several works on the practical application of psychology, notably his *Psychology and Industrial Efficiency,* in which he applies this
science to the choice of a vocation, scientific manage-
ment, the electric railway service, the telephone ex-
change, advertising, buying and selling goods, and to
many other points in the field of business, in a most
illuminating and helpful way. There is a growing
literature of such books, and they bring psychology
down out of the clouds of theory and out of the
laboratory and hitch it to the wagons of the world's
work.

3. **Psychology in the Field of Religion.**—If psychology is of such practical importance in the fields of
education and art and even of business, how much
more so should it be in the field of religion. Religion
is the highest activity and interest of the soul, and

therefore it is of the most vital importance that we understand its psychology in order that we may develop it into its fullest power and finest fruitage. And it is specially important that ministers and religious teachers should understand it, for religious psychology is the very stuff with which they work. The psychologists have only recently entered this field. When they first broke into it they were immensely interested in and pleased with it as a rich " find " or mine in their domain, and they have been working it with uncommon diligence and delight. Professor Edwin D. Starbuck was one of the first to enter this field, and his *Psychology of Religion,* with its inductive gathering and tabulation and analysis of facts and results, is still one of the most useful books on the subject. Professor William James followed with his *Varieties of Religious Experience,* which on the whole holds its place as the most important contribution psychology has yet made to religion. Other books have followed in rapid succession, and the literature on the subject is already very large and rich.

4. Value of Work Done in this Field.—The value of the work done in this field widely varies. Some of it has been highly subjective and speculative and even characterized by wild vagaries; but much of it has been sound and sane and has yielded solid results of great value. The psychology of religion is a doubly subjective science in that it depends on both the psychology and the religion of the worker in this field. As some psychologists have tried to work out a psychology of the soul without any soul, so have some of them endeavoured to construct a psychology of religion without religion. Under their treatment of it religion has evaporated into a mere subjective feeling

or delusion without any objective reality, and such psychology of religion is baseless and worthless both as psychology and as religion. Any one's view of the psychology of religion will depend upon his philosophy lying back of both his psychology and his religion. If he is a materialist or pantheist or any kind of determinist, neither his psychology nor his religion will have much value to a theist, for such deterministic monism cuts the ground from under free agency and responsibility and lets all worthy and useful psychology and religion fall into a common ruin. The present book is based on theistic philosophy and Christian faith, and with such a soil this field of study has some root and substance and sap and can grow fruit that is worth while.

The psychology of religion has not made any revolutionary discoveries or introduced any radical changes in religion. As a rule advancing science does not upset the fundamental practical experience of the race, but confirms and illuminates it. Agricultural science has not driven wheat from the harvest field or displaced bread from the table, and astronomy has not blown out the sun. Psychology has not appeared as the foe of religion to destroy it or radically change it, but as its friend to help it. The facts of religion are independent of the theories of psychology, and they stand as some of the most solidly rooted and permanent facts in the world. Psychology searches into the nature and operation of religion, but it can no more uproot it than geology can uproot the mountains. Religion has so far not suffered at the hands of psychology: when some psychologists have explained religion away, it was not their psychology but their philosophy that did this destructive work. Psychology

simply throws new light on the old facts of religion
and thereby makes them more luminous and fruitful.
No doubt it does sweep away many shadows and
errors from religion, but this is the work, not of an
enemy, but of a friend. The psychology of religion
comes not to destroy but to fulfil.

5. **Sources and Methods.**—The original source of
all psychology is the mind itself, which is immediately
known to the psychologist only in his own mind. Introspection is therefore the first source of psychology
in general and of the psychology of religion in particular. The student of this science should learn to
observe the working of his own mind so as to discriminate all its various activities and note its modes
and laws. This is a difficult art because not only does
such introspection call for the trained skill required
in all scientific observation, but the mind itself, when
made the object of its own observation, is so changeable and elusive that it is hard to catch it and hold
it still. The very act of becoming conscious of a state
of one's own mind changes the state and may radically
modify if not wholly destroy it. Trying to catch and
see one's own mind is like trying to turn on the gas
or electric light quick enough to see the dark: the
state may vanish as we try to see it.

Nevertheless we can study our own mental states,
and such states are the original and only direct source
we can have of any kind of psychology. If therefore
we have no religious experience we can have no religious psychology. We see things not only as they
are but also as we are, and our own faculties and
affinities limit our possible experiences. The absence
of any religious experience in the soul is as fatal a
bar to religious psychology as blindness is to the sci-

ence of esthetics. In this study, then, we need to keep in close touch with the reality of our own experience and translate everything into its terms and bring it to this test.

The secondary and derived source of material for the psychology of religion is the experience of others as this is observed in their behaviour and is communicated to us orally or through written records. There are many special books which record the religious experience of others, and these are rich sources of religious psychology. The biographies of notable religious characters are especially valuable as materials for this study. But all literature is a secretion from the experience of the human soul and is a great mine containing rich veins of ore that can be worked in the interest of religious psychology. This science, like Cæsar, sends out a decree that all the world shall be taxed in its interest, and every field of human experience brings grist to its mill.

The great book and source for this subject, of course, is the Bible. This is a mass of religious experience from beginning to end; for it was all experienced before it was written, and after it was experienced it was expressed, after it was done it was said. The Hebrew people were endowed with religious genius, as the Greeks were with intellectual brilliance and the Romans with organizing power, and God could blow his breath and music through them more fully and richly than through less spiritually sensitive souls. Their prophets and apostles were mountain peaks that caught the light of God's unity and spirituality and righteousness earlier than other people and reflected it down upon the world. Their religious experiences were therefore deeper and loftier and richer than those of any other people and have become the classical ideal and inspiration for succeeding ages.

This religious experience of these wonderful people was secreted and crystallized in the Bible, which remains as the richest mine of religious psychology in the world. The divine revelations they received are recorded in it, their prayers and songs are embalmed in it, their growth and discipline in faith and righteousness, their doubts and fears, blind gropings and stumblings, trials and tears, mistakes and sins and shame, their penalties and repentance, the growing spirituality and beauty of their ideals, and all the tragedy and pathos of their history, are mirrored on these pages, the most immortal and incomparable book in the world. It is a masterpiece of psychology in its dissection of the human heart and disclosure of the interior workings of the soul and its religious experience. To this classical book and source we must ever go for the fullest and clearest illustration and illumination of the psychology of religion.

The method of our science is the general method of all psychology and of all science, which is the careful observation and interpretation of the facts in its field. Some sciences have an elaborate outfit of special instruments, but psychology has few: its laboratory, useful as it is, plays a subordinate part and has made few important contributions to the science, William James, the master psychologist of the day, being the witness on this point. The mind's own processes are the fundamental instruments of all science. Observation, comparison, discrimination, tracing of causal links and connections, deduction of general principles,—these are the methods of science. Science has no secret chamber in which it works and no patented process of discovering truth. It works in the open and uses the ordinary processes of human thinking. The greatest scientist or even the profoundest metaphysician does not differ in his essential processes of reasoning from the man on the street: he is only more careful.

The study of the psychology of religion calls for no other faculties and methods than those we use in the common fields of life. We need to strive to see clearly and accurately, to cleanse our minds of prejudices, to see reality as it is and interpret it into its true meaning, to be candid and humble and teachable, to have a passion for truth and to be obedient to every heavenly vision, and then we may hope to find the truth, at least as a practical guide in life.

As the psychology of religion is a special branch or application of general psychology, it may be well, in an elementary book like this, to introduce the subject with an outline sketch of the psychology of the soul. Such a sketch must be very rudimentary and little more than a skeleton or bundle of definitions, but it will furnish a background and framework for what is to follow.

CHAPTER II

THE PSYCHOLOGY OF THE SOUL

WE are now to observe the soul itself and take stock of its contents. It is not a far-off world, or one external to us, but is our inmost self in which we live and move and have our being. We might then think that we understand it perfectly, and we do understand it better than anything else, for we have immediate experience of it; and yet our knowledge of it may be vague and confused, or mistaken and perverted, and needs to be cleared and systematized by reflective thought.

We shall not stop to define or discuss the nature of the soul, or to consider whether or not we have or are souls, for these questions belong to philosophy rather than psychology. We accept the empirical intuitive fact, more certain than any other fact, that we think, therefore we are; we are conscious beings, and the conscious self is what we mean by the soul.

Consciousness is an infinite complex and may at first appear to be a scene of confusion; but, like the world of nature, it turns out to be a world of beautiful order, and its operations can be reduced to a few fundamental activities and laws.

I. The Fundamental Faculties of the Soul

An old and obvious and fundamental division of the faculties of the soul is the threefold division into intellect, sensibility, and will. We think, we feel, and we

will: these exhaust the activities of the soul, for we
never do anything more or less than these things. It
is not meant, of course, that the soul has three separate
faculties or parts that act in these ways, for the soul
has no spatial dimensions and parts and is not di-
visible, but the whole consciousness acts in these three
fundamental modes. Neither does the soul act in only
one of these ways at a time, but in all of them simultaneously, though they are combined and blended in
different ways and degrees. We never think that we do
not at the same time feel, and we never feel that we do
not at the same time will. Every state and activity of
consciousness is a complex exercise of thought, feeling,
and will. Yet one of these states may be and usually is
so predominant as to submerge and obscure the others.
We may seem to be thinking only, or feeling only, or
willing only, but closer inspection discloses all three in
simultaneous action. There are also logical relations
among these states, thought stirring up feelings and
feelings moving the will, and this fact is of the greatest
practical importance. However, while these three
fundamental activities are always interblended and
logically related, yet we can dissect them and study
them one at a time.

1. INTELLECT

The intellect comes first in order of our study. This
is the knowing power of the mind, and it resolves itself
into the faculties or activities of perception, concepts,
reasoning, association, memory, and imagination.

1. **Perception.**—Sense perception is the consciousness of external objects when the mind is stirred into
activity by the excitation of our senses. These are the
organs of sight, sound, smell, taste, and touch, which

are nerve ends differentiated and adapted to receive
different kinds of external impressions. By counting
our organic feelings as senses and breaking up the sense
of touch into various subsenses, such as contact, heat,
cold, and still others, we can have any number of senses
up to fifteen or twenty; but the classical number of
five stands in the usual description of our senses.

Each one of the sense organs is a wonderful arrangement for receiving external impressions and trans-
mitting them to the brain. Sound waves, which are
successive rarefactions and condensations of the air
caused by the vibrating body, impinge on the drum of
the ear and send a stream of molecular changes up to
the auditory centre in the brain; and the other senses
send their currents of distinctive changes up to their
special brain centres. These sense excitations arrive
in the brain as some form of molecular agitation, very
much as telegraphic messages arrive in a telegraph
office, or as telephone calls arrive in the central ex-
change.

And now the mind has the wonderful and quite mysterious power of interpreting or experiencing these
molecular changes as perceptions of the external objects producing them. How the mind does this is utterly beyond our inspection and knowledge and is one
of the ultimate mysteries of psychology.

It is to be noted, however, that the mind is not simply a blank and passive plate or mirror that receives
these impressions and contributes nothing to them itself. On the contrary, the mind is active and creative
in the process. It has a constitution of its own which
furnishes the moulds in which these sense materials are
cast and shaped. It has inherent general principles or
ideas of unity and difference, quantity and quality,

logical order and causation, and other "categories," as Kant, their great discoverer, called them, and by these the mind gives form and meaning to its sense materials. It would lead us over into the field of philosophy to discuss this point further, but it is fundamental in the constitution of the mind.

The sense of sight gives us a visual image of an object, the sense of sound an auditory image of it, and so on, each sense thus creating in our mind its appropriate sense perception or percept. When two or more of these percepts are caused by the same external object, they combine into a unitary compound percept, or construct, as it is called. These percepts and constructs are the immediate objects of our knowledge and are the only things we thus know. They are the only things in our mind and immediately present in its experience. We intuitively project these percepts and constructs into the outer world and think we see objects in external space; but this is a kind of mental illusion, and the real process of seeing and knowing takes place in the mind itself. This fact does not in the least deny or impair the reality of the outer world, but it does throw light on the process by which we know it.

In forming its sense perceptions the mind not only contributes to them its constitutional principles or categories, but it also pours into them the contents of its existing knowledge and thus colours and enriches them, or, it may be, perverts them with mistaken notions. We set every new fact or impression in the framework and light of our existing knowledge, and this "apperception," as it is called, is a large and vital factor in all our knowledge. We thus see things, not only as they are, but also as we are. The mind itself is an active and determining agent in forming our knowledge. Every one thus sees his own objects and creates his own world. It is these differences in minds that make the immense differences in the things men see. When Turner showed one of his sunsets to a friend and the friend remarked that he had never seen such a sunset, Turner replied, " Don't you wish you could? " Ruskin says that " the greatest thing a human soul ever does in this world is to see something, and tell what it saw in a plain way." We may think that he did not tell anything in a plain way in his pages that are cloth of gold emblazoned with gems, but then he did tell in a plain way what *he* saw.

These percepts and constructs are the representatives in our minds of the realities of the objective world, and therefore it is of the first importance that they represent them accurately. They are the constituent elements or cut stones or pressed bricks out of which we build our world. We then see the fundamental importance of forming correct percepts and constructs. Any inaccuracy or error in them, caused by inattention, ignorance, mental blindness, self-interest, prejudice, or passion, will throw us out of gear and right working relations with reality; it will ramify and pervert all our ideas and plans; and it may undermine and ruin our whole structure of thought and life.

We should then bring the most skilful training and give the greatest care to the forming of our percepts so that they will exactly fit and reproduce reality. In seeing things we should train our vision so that we shall see them clearly and correctly, and not see blurred and blotted, distorted and perverted images of them; and so with all the other senses. In seeing accurately the shape of a leaf or the colour of a bit of ribbon we may be determining something of immense importance.

If the tiny bricks in a building, or even one brick, is of the wrong size or shape, it may throw the whole building out of plumb and even endanger its stability. We should beware of mixing up our subjective opinions and prejudices and especially our own interests with objective reality and thus shaping and colouring it to suit our own ends. Of course we should and must interpret things in the light of our own knowledge, and this is a reason why we should be constantly stocking our minds with richer stores of knowledge that we may ever see a richer world. In a sense we make the things we see, for we contribute to them the contents of our own minds, as we have already seen. But this process does not justify us in contributing any false colour or element to our perceptions.

Just to perceive reality as it is: this is the foundation of truth and honesty; it goes deep into our character and life and destiny; and we should give to it our utmost training and care.

2. Concepts.—The next step in our mental processes is to turn an individual percept or construct into a general idea or concept. The mental image that reproduces an individual object, such as an apple, is released from its local context in consciousness and made to stand for and represent all apples, or the class or general idea of an apple; and in a similar way all individual percepts or constructs are generalized into concepts. These general classes, however, are not the same as the intuitional principles or categories of the mind of which we have spoken. Categories are inherent in the constitution of the mind and are not the product of experience, although experience is necessary to call them into action.

This process by which we generalize objects into

classes is a very high power of the mind. The lower animals do not have it. A horse or a dog knows individual things, but it does not have general ideas or concepts of things. The accuracy and fulness and richness of contents of our concepts depend upon the correctness and vividness and wealth of detail of our percepts; and so again we see the importance of accurate sense perceptions as the foundation and constituent elements of our general ideas.

3. Reasoning.—The process by which the mind works with its percepts and concepts is its reasoning power. This consists in comparing, discriminating, analyzing, and classifying its percepts and concepts, or its images of objects and its general ideas, so as to discern their relations, logically combine them into larger units, trace their connections and especially their causal links and deduce their consequences; and thus we build up our knowledge into judgments and propositions and systems and draw practical conclusions. It is this power of the mind that arranges and rules all the fields of life.

Thus starting with tiny visual images in his eyes and percepts and constructs in his mind the astronomer combines these into grand concepts and reasons out a sublime system for the whole stupendous heavens. Every other scientist in like manner perceives and constructs the facts in his field, and thus our knowledge grows from more to more. Each one of us thus reasons out his own purposes and plans and builds his own world.

4. Association.—Association of ideas is the power they have of clinging together so that when one comes up in the mind it brings others with it. It is our constant familiar experience that one object or idea sug-

gests another or many others.   The sight of a rain cloud
suggests the idea of an umbrella, and this idea may suggest the fact that it was borrowed from a neighbour,
possibly without his consent or knowledge.   The sight
of a little lock of hair or a glimpse of the old home
crowds the mind with a thousand fond recollections
too deep for tears.   When any idea enters the mind it
quickly draws to itself a cluster of associations, as when
a magnet is thrust into a keg of nails it comes out
thickly encrusted with the bits of iron.

Every one knows that any idea arising in the mind
may grow until it fills all the thoughts and absorbs
the whole life.   A striking illustration of this is seen
in Dr. J. G. Frazer's work on primitive religion entitled *The Golden Bough*.   It appeared in the first edition in two large volumes, but in the third edition
these had grown to twelve, and the bibliography, containing the titles of the works quoted in it, and the in-
dex fill the last volume.   "When I originally conceived
the idea of the work," he writes in the Preface of the
third edition, "my intention merely was to explain the
strange rule of the priesthood or sacred kingship of
Nemi and with it the legend of the Golden Bough,
immortalized by Virgil, and at first I thought that it
might be adequately set forth within the compass of a
small volume.   But I soon found that in attempting
to settle one question I had raised many more: wide
and wider prospects opened out before me; and thus
step by step I was lured on into far-spreading fields
of primitive thought which had been little explored by
my predecessors.   Thus the book grew on my hands,
and soon the projected essay became a ponderous
treatise."   The subject thus kept running its roots out
over the borders of the field until it encompassed and

enmeshed the globe. And even then Dr. Frazer probably felt that he had only begun his investigations. Association is an insatiable appetite that devours more and more, a fire that spreads from a centre in every direction, a banyan tree that keeps dropping branches that become roots and thus grows into a vast forest. A single seed may become a harvest that fills all the years of life. All knowledge is related, and from any centre association may run threads of relation and bind it into unity.

These associations often seem accidental and whimsical, but they are really governed by beautiful laws that spin threads and enable us to trace links of connection between associations that seem at first to have no possible relation. The most common of these laws are contiguity in time and place, similarity and contrast, and causal connection. Objects and ideas that have been experienced together once will tend to appear together again, and any object tends to suggest its likeness or contrast, or its cause or consequence. However fantastic or absurd seems the association there is always some connection, it may be through many intermediate links, by which the one term in such a relation suggests another.

Every object and idea and word is surrounded with a fringe or atmosphere of associations, and as every mind has its own stock of knowledge, words and ideas have very different meanings and suggestions for different minds. The idea of a prison has a vastly different connotation or meaning for a convict than for one who has never been inside prison walls, or the word music for the musician than for one without musical training or sense. These associations give breadth and depth and wealth of meaning to words and objects as the overtones in music give character and richness to musical notes.

It is the number and variety of the associations with which our minds are stored that constitute the width and wealth and power of our mental life. Every mind organizes around any idea its entire contents. It perceives every new truth in the light of and brings it into relation with its existing knowledge, in accordance with the process of apperception. One mark of a man of genius is the immense range and variety of his associations by which he calls the whole world to his aid to illustrate and illuminate his ideas; and the poverty and impotence of an ignorant or feeble mind is the meagreness of its associations. Multiply your associations, store your mind with facts and ideas through observation and reading, and you will thus have a reservoir in your mind that you can tap on any subject at any time and draw forth streams of thought and power. This is one result and value of education.

5. Memory.—Memory is the conserving power of the mind, its capacity to store up and retain and recall its experiences. It is the treasure house of life in which all its past is packed away and out of which our associations emerge; it is the thread of continuity that binds all our days together into conscious unity. Without the power of memory we would not have conscious knowledge of the past and would not even know ourselves as identical persons from day to day. It is thus the spinal column of personality. While it is not the highest power of the mind and is related to conservatism rather than to initiative and progress, yet memory is fundamental and enters vitally into our whole life. Its cardinal virtues are quick reception, tenacity of retention, and readiness of recall, and it thus puts our

whole stock of knowledge and experience at our fingers' ends.

6. **Imagination.**—Imagination is the picture-making power of the mind. It is sometimes thought of as a mere play of the mind, while observation and reasoning do its sober solid work. There is a kind of imagination, the fancy, which does move in an unreal world on a light gay wing, but imagination proper is one of the most fundamental and fruitful of our faculties. It begins with memory images, which are bits of imagination, and it constructs images or pictures of objects and scenes from the stores of memory. This is reproductive imagination, and it is a constituent element in all our thought.

A deeper use of the imagination is its power of realizing objects that lie beyond the immediate range of the senses and contact of the mind with reality. It is the mental tool by which we translate symbols, such as words and algebraic signs which only stand for things, into the meaning and power of the things themselves. Thus in studying geography and history the mind has certain information about places and events that are not immediately before it: imagination takes these statements which are little more than symbols and translates them into images which we see almost or altogether as vividly as though the realities themselves were present to us; it clothes these skeletons with flesh and blood so that they breathe and move. Knowledge is never digested and assimilated into our own thought and experience, it never becomes alive and moves us, until we thus turn it into pictures or vivid images that may be as vital and vigorous as the living realities. Imagination is an eye that sweeps the earth and the heavens and penetrates all space and time and sees facts face to face.

A still higher activity of this faculty is the creative imagination which constructs pictures, plans, ideals, visions of its own, and thus " bodies forth the forms of things unknown, turns them to shapes, and gives to airy nothing a local habitation and a name." It is this form of imagination that creates plans that improve our life at every point. A mother sees in her mind an ideal of a better home, and presently her own home begins to grow into new order and show new touches of taste and beauty until her ideal is realized. A farmer sees the vision of a better farm, more thorough in its cultivation and more fruitful in its fields and orchards, and his own farm soon shows improvement and approximates his ideal. A mechanic imagines a better piece of work, more strongly built or handsomely shaped or finely finished, and he makes a better engine or piece of furniture.

It is the creative imagination that produces all the glories of literature and art and all the great achievements of men. Men of genius are eminently the children of their imagination; they see visions that unveil the beauty of the world. A poet sees fairy fancies and grand cathedrals of poetic thought and, with his " eye in a fine frenzy rolling," he puts them into immortal lines. The painter sees in the gallery of his imagination a picture of fair features and glowing colours and deep meaning, and his brush copies it on canvas. A sculptor sees an angel in a block of marble, and his chisel sets it free until it begins to breathe. A musician hears in the chamber of his heart sweet strains and grand harmonies, and he flings them out through his voice and finger tips upon the air.

Every deed was first a thought, every victory was first a vision. Columbus saw in imagination a new path to the old world, and that vision, treated with scepticism and ridicule by the dull-eyed men of his day, led him out over the unknown mysterious Atlantic until he stood victorious upon a new shore. Four centuries later another man of creative imagination saw an electric cable running under that same ocean, and again the vision was ridiculed; but it held on its way and now enmeshes the globe with a network of cables that is constantly throbbing with the life of the world. Luther had a vision that shattered papal despotism and liberated Europe. Lincoln had a vision that wrote the Emancipation Proclamation and freed an enslaved race.

Imagination, then, is no light and fanciful exercise of the mind, but is its most powerful faculty. It is by this power that man dreams dreams and that over his path hover visions that coax and woo him on to larger and lovelier things. He follows their gleam, he hitches his wagons to their stars and rises starward from the dust. The world has learned to beware of how it stands in the way of imagination: that invisible impalpable power may have in it more might than ten thousand bayonets or a million tons of dynamite and may crush mountains, shape the centuries, and create a new world.

We have thus rapidly looked into the workshop of the intellect and noted the machinery by which it turns out the products of thought. It is by these faculties and processes that the human mind has written all the books and libraries in the world; that it perceives objects, evolves ideas and ideals, builds systems of science and philosophy, conquers nature, constructs the plans and paths along which life moves, and has thought out our whole vast civilization.

We may note, in leaving this part of our subject, the important distinction between knowledge and intelligence. Knowledge is information: intelligence is developed and disciplined mind. Knowledge is a possession: intelligence is a power. Knowledge does not necessarily produce or imply intelligence: intelligence produces knowledge. Knowledge is static and passive: intelligence is dynamic and active. Knowledge receives: intelligence creates. Knowledge handles the old and familiar and is disconcerted with the new: intelligence is stimulated by the new and meets and masters novel situations and problems. Knowledge drills, and intelligence thrills. Knowledge is useful and necessary, great widths and immense stocks of it in the mind by so much enlarge and enrich life, but intelligence is the principal thing, for only intelligence is power, and with all our getting we should develop intelligence.

2. SENSIBILITY

The sensibility is the power of the soul to experience feeling, or a state of excitement. The feelings are an infinite complex, shading into one another like the evanescent hues of a sunset, and they do not admit of such exact classification and analysis as do the faculties of the intellect. They fall, however, into some broad classes.

1. **Sensations.**—Sensations are feelings caused by direct physical action on the nerves. They include, first, the excitations of the senses. The degree of feeling in these senses varies. It is very slight in sight and hearing, except when the excitation is excessive, or when the organ is abnormally sensitive by reason of an

inflamed or diseased condition, and then the feeling may be intense. There is also but slight feeling in smell and little in taste. These four senses produce states of perception that are largely intellectual. "Knowledge and feeling, perception and sensation," says Sir William Hamilton, "though always coexistent, are always in the inverse ratio of each other."

In the sense of touch the feeling element becomes pronounced and often predominant. The sensation of resistance experienced in hard or rough substances or on sharp points or edges is almost purely a feeling. The nerves of feeling distributed over the entire surface of the body are really a complex sense. Temperature has special nerves for both heat and cold; and there are many special pain and pleasure points or nerves all over the body.

Besides the senses, there are numberless organic feelings throughout the body. The appetites are attended with a wide range and variety of feeling in tone and intensity. The movement of the muscles is accompanied with muscular feelings. The internal organs ordinarily carry on their activities without producing any feeling, but any derangement of their condition or operation reports itself in feeling that may range from dim discomfort to intense agony. There is always present a scarcely perceptible, quiet, comfortable mass or sense of feeling that is the background of our consciousness and whole life. Every sensory nerve in the body is sensitive to irritation and is ready to respond with its peculiar feeling.

2. Emotions.—A second general class of feelings are the emotions, which are feelings caused by the presentation to the mind of an object or idea. The sight of an enemy may throw the soul into a state of violent fear,

and of a friend may kindle it into a glow of love and
joy; and the idea of an enemy or of a friend will produce the same feelings, though in a much weaker degree. Every object and idea tends to produce its own
peculiar feeling and there may thus be as many kinds
or shades of emotion as there are objects and ideas;
but they fall into a few general classes, such as fear and
hope, hatred and love, joy and sorrow, antipathy and
sympathy, the sublime and the ridiculous, aspiration
and reverence, and these may range in degree from a
mere tendency or slight stir of feeling to the greatest
intensity.

When the intellectual element predominates over the
feeling and especially when it is a fixed system or disposition of ideas the emotion becomes a sentiment, such
as the sentiment of friendship or patriotism; and when
the feeling element predominates over the intellectual
the emotion becomes a passion.

3. Pain and Pleasure Tone.—Feelings have a pain
or pleasure tone, which is often their most distinctive
and compelling characteristic. Every feeling, whether
of sensation or emotion, has this quality. The physical
sensations are attended with the pains and pleasures
of the senses and appetites or organic feelings, and
emotions are characterized not less by the same tone.
A mere idea may flood the soul with pleasure or send
flames of agony leaping along the nerves. All of our
feelings may be arranged and marshalled under these
two captains of the soul.

> Love, Hope, and Joy, fair pleasure's smiling train,
> Hope, Fear, and Grief, the family of pain;
> These mixed with art and to due bounds confined,
> Make and maintain the balance of the mind.
> —POPE.

4. Temperaments.—Every person has a prevailing emotional tone or disposition which is a native inheritance and is persistent through life, though subject to some control and slow modification by the will. A temperament is the emotional pitch to which one is keyed and is the tonic note of all his music. It is the sounding-board which gives quality to all his moods. It is an emotional lens that gives character and colour to all his experiences. All his mental states sift through his temperament, as light through a stained glass window, and are tinged by its hues.

There are four temperaments, which have been known and named from ancient times: the sanguine, the phlegmatic, the choleric, and the melancholy. These names embody the ancient view that these temperaments were due to four humours of the body: blood, phlegm, bile, and a hypothetical black bile.

The sanguine temperament, implying fulness of blood, is a lively and hopeful disposition. It is marked by vivacity and effervescence, bubbling over with exuberant hopefulness and always seeing things through a rosy optimism. It looks at the bright side of objects and has great confidence in its own views and visions. It paints its plans and prospects in the colours of the imagination and wreathes them in rainbows. It may be correspondingly blind to the real difficulties in the way and meet with unseen obstructions and run into disaster. It infects language, and people of this temperament are apt to speak in glowing terms, unconsciously bordering on visionary unreality. They sometimes live in a " fool's Paradise," and often experience a rude awakening and shock. Yet they quickly recover their resiliency and are soon dreaming new dreams. The sanguine people furnish the lively element in life;

they radiate good cheer and are the optimists of the
world.

The opposite of the sanguine is the phlegmatic temperament. This is a dull passive disposition, slow in
its movements of thought and action. It is deficient in
initiative and progressiveness and jogs along in traditional grooves. It is not easily excited with hope on
the one hand, or on the other depressed with discouragement, but plods along with equal step through sunshine and storm. People of phlegmatic temperament
furnish the ballast in the ship of progress. They are
solid and immobile and give substance and stability to
the world.

The choleric temperament is impulsive and rash, hot
and violent, progressive and pushing, decisive and
domineering. It will brook no interference with its
desires and plans, but breaks through all opposition.
It is the progressive spring in human character, impatient of tradition and conservatism, and driving forward, it may be, recklessly and blindly. People of this
disposition are leaders and pioneers in the world, working under high pressure and sweeping all obstacles and
opposition out of their path.

The melancholic is the deep brooding temperament,
characterized by outward passivity but inward intensity. It is given to thought and meditation and strives
to see things as they are in their inmost natures. It
does not shrink from but rather is attracted to the dark
side of things and is veined and tinged with pessimism.
Its deep undertone is one of sadness in view of the
world. It weaves minor notes into all its chords. The
people of melancholic temperament are the philosophers
and prophets and poets, the thinkers and dreamers of
the race.

These four temperaments may be more or less mixed in the same person, with one of them the predominant strain. Some people alternate in their temperament so that at different times they seem like different persons. Moods are passing phases of temperament, and these are very changeable in the weather of the soul. One temperament may prevail at one age in life, and another at a later age. Childhood, it is said, is phlegmatic, youth is sanguine, maturity choleric, and old age melancholic. The female sex is prevailingly sanguine and phlegmatic, and the male choleric and melancholic. Nations and races may be characterized by dominant temperaments. The Hebrews were melancholic, the Greeks sanguine, and the Romans choleric. The Irish are sanguine, the English phlegmatic, and the Scotch choleric. The French are sanguine, and the Germans phlegmatic.

These temperaments go deep into character and life and give texture and tone to our virtues and vices, our temptations and triumphs; and they produce different types of religious life.

5. **The Uses of the Feelings.**—The uses or functions of the feelings is a subject much discussed by psychologists, but with varying results. The broad use of the feelings is to promote the volume and value of life and give it interest and motive. Pleasure as a rule attends and stimulates such activities of body and mind as are conducive to life, and pain attends such activities as injure or hinder it. As Herbert Spencer expresses this fact, " Pains are the correlatives of actions injurious to the organism, while pleasures are the correlatives of actions conducive to its welfare." He works this principle out at great length in his *Principles of Psychology,* and again in his *Principles of*

Ethics, unfolding the modifications and limitations that govern its application. It is evident that this view is true in a broad way. The bodily activities that sustain and promote life, such as eating and exercise, are usually attended with pleasure, and injurious activities and conditions, such as disease, produce pain. And the same fact is true of emotions, for they stimulate or depress life according as they are pleasurable or painful.

We at once think, however, of the pleasures, such as gluttony and intoxication, that are injurious and even deadly, and of the pains, such as those attending medicine and surgery, that may promote health and save life. But only the effect of pleasures and pains in the long run is to be considered. Activities that are permanently pleasurable promote life, and pains that ultimately bring good results are accepted as good. And further, when pleasures are taken to include satisfactions of the higher moral and spiritual sense, these higher satisfactions take precedence over and control sensual gratifications and are the greatest means of life.

It is not true that pleasures of the lower order are the means and guides of life and that we are to do all we can to get pleasure and avoid pain; but in the long run and up through the whole scale of life it is true that pleasure or satisfaction coincides with life and pain with death.

It is the feelings that give us a sense of the value of objects. Pure intellect perceives facts and relations, but not worths. One object is as truly a part of reality to it as another, and it thinks only in terms of reality and not of value. Its work is done when it determines the reality and relations of an object; some other power of the soul must evaluate its worth, and the heart does this. " Our judgments," says William James, " concerning the worth of things, big or little, depend on the *feelings* the things arouse in us. When we judge a thing to be precious in consequence of the *idea* we frame of it, this is only because the idea is itself associated already with a feeling. If we were radically feelingless, and if ideas were the only things our minds could entertain, we should lose all our likes and dislikes at a stroke, and be unable to point to any one situation of experience in life more valuable or significant than any other." [1]

The interest of life resides in our feelings. It is not until our ideas strike these mystic strings and wake them into music or discord that they excite our interest. The feelings are like the box of the violin or sounding-board of the piano: the strings would give forth thin and insignificant notes if they were not reënforced by these resonators which sympathetically catch up their vibrations and give them depth and complexity, richness and sweetness. And so out of our feelings arise the joys and sorrows, the triumphs and tragedies of our life.

The feelings also are the immediate motives that move the will. There is no tendency for the will to act until the feelings pour their flood upon it as a stream upon a wheel, or as steam into the cylinder upon the piston that drives the engine. Objects and ideas generate feelings of sensation and emotion, and these accumulate in volume and pressure until they overcome the inertia or indecision or opposition of the will and push it into action, or explode it as a spark explodes

[1] *Talks to Teachers on Psychology*, p. 229. See also *The Problem of Knowledge*, by D. C. Mackintosh, p. 348.

powder. Pain and pleasure especially are imperious
forces that move the will and guide and govern life.

3. THE WILL

The will is the power of the soul to control itself in
its thoughts and feelings, decisions and actions. We
have seen that through the senses a stream of sensations pours into the consciousness. The whole consciousness is a stream of activity, fluctuating in level
and volume and rapidity, sinking into the subconscious
deeps in sleep and then rising into a tumultuous tor-
rent and overflowing all the banks of the soul. This
stream, however, is not an ungovernable flood, sweeping everything before it, on which the will floats as a
helpless log or drifts in a boat without engine or rudder. The will has a large control over the stream and
flood; it has a rudder in its hand and an engine in its
boat by which it can steer and drive it in any direction to its own destination.

   1. **The Attention.**—The will first exercises its power
in attention. As the word means, this is a "stretch-
ing" or striving of the mind towards an object. The
field of consciousness swarms with impulses, sense perceptions, concepts, memories, feelings, desires, ideas,
and ideals. The mind is not indifferent and helpless in
the presence of this complex field, but has various affinities and interests and has the power of choosing the
object it will fasten upon and make the focus of its
attention. It then concentrates its powers on this object as the centre of consciousness, while other objects
are crowded into the background and margin of the
field. This act of attention is necessary to any normal
mental activity whatever. The simplest act of seeing a
light or hearing a sound involves the fixing and focus-

ing of the mind on the object. Consciousness cannot be diffused over a miscellaneous multitude of things. Such a mental field grows misty and loses all meaning and perception. Consciousness must concentrate itself on one principal object as the focus of attention, though many other objects lying around the central object on the margin of the mind may be dimly seen or felt.

This object of attention is forced on the mind in involuntary attention, which occurs when an object is thrust into the mind so violently as to overwhelm and exclude all other objects. A flash of lightning or a clap of thunder instantly compels attention and for the moment crowds everything else out of consciousness.

In voluntary attention, however, the mind exercises its own power in selecting the object on which it fixes its gaze and interest. Many objects, ideas, desires may be competing for the attention and crowding on the self with their vociferous and even violent claims and clamours, but the soul can itself decide which of these contestants it will choose as the object to which it will give its attention and thus enthrone it in the central place in its field.

Voluntary attention is the root of self-control and character, the power that compresses all the energies of the soul into one stream and the lack of which lets them divide and drift off into impotence, so that the soul is strong or weak according to its strength or weakness at this point. " Human nature," says Professor Hugo Münsterberg, " is indeed so arranged that the attention at first follows in an involuntary way all that is shining, loud, sensational, and surprising. The real development of mankind lies in the growth of the voluntary attention, which is not passively attracted, but which turns actively to that which is important and significant and valuable in itself. No one is born with such a power. It has to be trained and educated. Yes, perhaps the deepest meaning of education is to secure this mental energy which emancipates itself from haphazard stimulations of the world, and firmly holds that which conforms to our purpose and ideals. This great function of education is too much neglected." [1] Constant care and exercise should be given to this power, that it may be developed and disciplined into masterful self-control.

Once the attention is given to an object a wonderful process sets in. The associations of the mind begin to gravitate to the central object in an increasing mass. All the knowledge and experiences and memories in the mind having any affinity with the central object gather around it, swelling and enriching its volume and meaning and power. This process goes on until the total contents of the mind may be organized around this one idea.[2] At the same time these associated ideas kindle their appropriate emotions, and they add their fire to the central mass and turn it into a blazing heap. And thus the attention piles fuel on an idea and converts what at first may be a mere spark or pale cold image into the hot spot and burning focus of consciousness, which rages as a furnace in the soul and moves the will and masters the life.

These associated ideas embrace all the operations of the mind, such as tracing the nature and activities, the causes and consequences of an object, and these are attended with their appropriate feelings. When this process has accumulated a sufficient volume and pres-

[1] *Problems of To-day*, p. 17.　　　　　[2] See pp. 32-35.

sure of feeling, the will responds with the appropriate decision and action. The will is thus not a power external to the operations of the mind, which thrusts its arbitrary decision in upon them, but is inherent in the mind's constitution. The action of the will marks the point where thought and feeling have reached a sufficient degree of clearness and intensity to overcome any indifference and doubt and opposition and to effect choice and decision. At this point the feelings pour their stream upon the will and push it into action. Thus the will unconsciously works in involuntary attention and in all the operations of the mind, and in voluntary attention it consciously forms its choices and decisions.

2. Motives.—This brings us to the fact, familiar in our experience, that the will is not an arbitrary action of the mind, but a rational process, taking place under the play of motives. A motive is any influence tending to move the mind, and motives are of several kinds.

(a) The first motives are the instincts. An instinct is that which instigates or "stings" us into action, as the word means. It is an inherited constitutional tendency to act in a certain way when the appropriate condition or stimulus is present. It is a reflex response, a latent impulse or coiled-up spring waiting to be released. It is not the product of personal experience, but is prior to such experience and is at first involuntary and unconscious in its action.

Instincts are seen in beautiful purity and perfection in an infant, which at once begins to perform many complex and even difficult acts with perfect precision, such as suckling the breast and clasping objects, and then in rapid succession it begins to grasp at objects and carry them to its mouth, to cry and smile, to laugh and play, to creep and stand, to walk and talk, and so on through childhood. Some instincts serve their temporary purpose and then fade away, and others arise as they are needed. The appetites of hunger and of sex are two of the most powerful human instincts and are among the main masters of the world. The animal world is full of instincts, many of them marvels and mysteries of adaptation and perfection. Most animal instincts are also found in man, with many more that are peculiar to himself. Professor James, in his *Psychology*,[1] devotes a chapter to their study, enumerating and describing many of them, such as fear, anger, imitation, sympathy, acquisitiveness, constructiveness, play, curiosity, sociability, secretiveness, cleanliness, modesty, love, and parental love.

The important fact about instincts is that they express and satisfy the fundamental needs of life by their automatic action. They urge us into action along the line of these needs before we are able to reason them out and consciously supply them. They are reflex actions which do not pass through the higher centres of the brain but are short-circuited through the lower centres. The babe can do nothing as the result of reasoning, and if it had to act on conscious motives it would quickly perish. Even the mother could not keep it alive if it did not have an outfit of instincts that do necessary things automatically. It is imperative that we should eat and sleep and work and play, and nature does not wait for us to find out these needs and discover and supply the means of satisfying them, but it has put springs within us which are released at the touch of the proper stimuli and push us into action before we reflect on the process.

[1] Vol. II, Chapter XXIV.

It is important to observe, however, that instincts sooner or later emerge into the field of consciousness and reason, and then they often need enlightenment and control. They may fall out of adjustment by reason of changes in environment and advancing civilization, or become abnormal and perverted, or they may conflict with higher motives and need modification or inhibition or even suppression. In so far as they act as involuntary and blind impulses they are no more rational and ethical activities than the digestion of the stomach and the beating of the heart and are not motives in the proper sense. But as they emerge into the light of reason and conscience they become rational and ethical and are true motives.

There are not only instincts that relate to our bodily life, but also those that are intellectual and moral. The mind has as many instincts as the body, and the whole soul is full of them; or rather all instincts have mental roots and relations. Curiosity is a universal and powerful intellectual instinct, sprouting prolifically in every child and impelling savages to peer into caves and astronomers to explore the heavens. Religion is one of the profoundest and most universal instincts in our human world, building its temples and altars under every sky. Instincts thus cover the whole field of our activities and remain through life as fundamental springs and motives that push the will along the path of our primary needs.

(b) Ideas of action are incipient motives. They tend to slip by and short-circuit the processes of deliberation and decision and, like reflex actions, to discharge themselves immediately. The moment we think of an action we experience an inclination to do that thing. Thus when we look down from a height the idea of jumping

down that suggests itself makes us feel like giving way
to the impulse, and this feeling is so strong in some
persons that they fear and avoid such places. Then
why do not all our ideas pass directly into action?
Because they are inhibited by other ideas that counteract them. The idea that emerges in the centre of consciousness and tends to execute itself is surrounded
with other ideas in the margin of the field, ideas of
right or propriety or fear of consequences, and these
act as checks to curb it. Were it not for these inhibitory restraints every idea would immediately discharge itself, and this would destroy our deliberation
and free will and responsibility. This is the condition
of some insane minds. They rattle right off into instant action, as a locomotive runs wild and exhausts
itself when it starts with no engineer in its cab. The
normal mind is under the restraint of many inhibitory
ideas and these hold it in the balance until it can form
its decision. Ideas become proper motives only when
they are deliberative.

(c) A third class of motives are our conscious desires and ends. A desire is a complex mental state consisting of an idea and a feeling, an idea of an end or
object, and a feeling of an attitude towards it, such as
craving for it or antipathy to it. Desires cover the
whole field of life, embracing the infinite manifold of
our cravings. They are forward-looking in their attitude, whereas instincts push us on from behind. They
stand peering into the future to see what they can
seize that will further their satisfaction. They move
the workman to his toil, the merchant to his trade, the
gold seeker in his search, the statesman in his ambition, the prophet and preacher in the pursuit of their
ideals, and the philosopher and poet in their dreams of

truth and beauty. The two master desires are for the possession and enjoyment of good and for escape from evil, corresponding with the two primary feelings and forces of pleasure and pain.

These motives differ endlessly in nature and efficiency. A motive is effective according as it perceives reality correctly and clearly, seizes on ends that are realizable and adopts means that are suitable and efficient for them; and it is further effective as this idea or intellectual element is fired with intense feeling that gives it force to cut its way through opposition to attainment. The motive and the will at this point are fused into one activity and a powerful motive and a masterly will are one and the same thing. Men differ in their will power, then, according to their ability to perceive practicable ends clearly and to energize the ideas of these ends with vivid and unconquerable feelings of purpose and determination.

These motives are subject to growth. They may appear in the mind as mere sparks of light or germs of perception and craving, but as the mind dwells upon them association begins to deepen and enrich and intensify them and thus they grow into a hot spot and glowing focus that fills the whole soul with light and heat and drives the will into action. The way to control our wills is to choose our ends and multiply their associations and thereby intensify their feelings until they tip the scale of the mind into decision. When motives conflict, as they often do, throwing the field of consciousness into a state of unstable equilibrium, doubt, and perplexity, or turning it into a battle-ground of terrific strife and suffering, we have it in our power to decide the contest by choosing one side or motive and then intensifying it until it overpowers its opponents and wins the victory. This choice is not an arbitrary decision, a pitching by sheer force on one motive rather than another, but is a process and act of deliberation and consideration, weighing facts and principles, causes and consequences, ideas and ideals, deeds and duties, and thus coming to a conclusion that carries with it the will.

3. **The Freedom of the Will.**—This brings us to the age-long controversy over the freedom of the will. The question is to be settled by personal intuitional and ethical experience rather than by psychological analysis and demonstration. We are immediately aware in our consciousness of the freedom or power to control ourselves in our decisions and actions, and no argument can shake this conviction. It is the primary assumption of all our thinking and reasoning so that, without this power, our very argument over it would be vain and self-contradictory. The very fact that we discuss the question assumes the freedom we discuss. And our awareness or intuition of such freedom is stronger than any argument we can construct against it. Though we disproved all the arguments for it and proved all the arguments against it, yet we would believe in it still: for the principle of freedom is prior to the process of reasoning and gives to that process all its validity. Trying to persuade us that we are not rationally and morally free is like the attempt of the Jews to convince the man whose sight had been restored that he was still blind. " One thing I know, that, whereas I was blind, now I see." With the sun blazing in his eyes no argument, however specious and strong, could touch his experience. So in answer to all the arguments of determinism we declare, One thing we know: we control our own decisions and actions.

This insight and assurance of our intuition as to our freedom is confirmed by the fact that the denial of freedom and the doctrine of determinism uproots all responsibility and character, destroys not only ethics and religion, but psychology itself, and reduces all human character and conduct and history to physics and chemistry. The whole value and beauty and glory of our human world are swept away and only a system of mechanical cogwheels or a furnace and cinder-pile remains.

" The purely dynamic theory of the world views it as a fire, burning to an ash-heap, in which spirit is only a fine flame; as a machine, running down never to go again, in which consciousness is only a cog. This view makes short work, not only with theology, but also with ethics, psychology, and history, by reducing them to physics, and raises over the entire universe the dread spectre of fatalism and final extinction. A sure escape from this fire and ash-heap is the view that sees the world as a spiritual system in which energy is will, substance is soul, ultimate reality is personality, and God is all in all." [1]

So contradictory is the doctrine of determinism to our self-consciousness and so destructive of all human character and worth and hopes that Kant postulated the freedom of the soul, along with God and immortality, as one of the necessities of our practical belief, necessary for the very living of our life.

The freedom of the soul calls for definition and description rather than for demonstration. It does not mean an unlimited and absolute freedom. It does not escape from the natural laws of the world. By no

[1] *The World a Spiritual System: an Introduction to Metaphysics*, p. 290.

known possibility can we in this world slit the envelope of time and space and slip out of it. Gravitation cannot be coaxed or forced to relax its grip upon us. Astronomy and physics and chemistry are inexorable. All these laws bind us, and intellectual and ethical laws are not less imperious. This limitation, however, is no real bondage to our liberty, but is rather its safety and enlargement. The steel rails do not really hinder the liberty of the locomotive: on the contrary they give it all the liberty it has. It has freedom to move with speed and safety as long as it adheres to the rails; when it jumps the track it lands in the ditch and its liberty is gone. The laws of life are the necessary tracks on which we can move with safety and speed, and when we leave these tracks we lose our liberty. Law and liberty are not mutually exclusive and antagonistic, but are mutually complementary and harmonious; they do not hinder, but they help each other. Liberty is not license. The highest and fullest liberty is obedience to law.

One far-reaching limitation on our freedom is found in birth and heredity. Our century and civilization, race, language and name, and largely our physical, mental, and moral constitution, whether born as an average normal mind, or as a genius, or as an idiot, whether in a pure home, or in a den of vice, whether to be brought up in darkest Africa or in splendid America, whether as pagan or Christian,—all these and countless other things are foreordained for us by the point of our birth; and yet we have no more to do with determining this point than we have with fixing the position of a star in the sky. How great is the sovereignty of heredity over our souls.

We are also limited in various degrees by many of

the practical conditions of life. As a rule it is not
easy and sometimes not possible for us to change the
place of our residence, our home, occupation, and the
general network of our environment. Often these
things are woven about us like a mesh of steel wires.

Yet after all these and other limitations have been
allowed, there remains one field where we are free:
our consciousness, especially in our motives and decisions. Within this narrow but vivid and vital area
we can cast the deciding vote, fix the centre of our
circle, plant the seed of our harvest; and in casting
the vote we carry the election, in fixing the centre we
sweep the whole circumference of life, in planting the
seed we determine our harvest of deeds and character
and destiny. Within this narrow area of consciousness lies all the liberty we have. Our wills can never
go outside of consciousness to do anything in the external world. All we can do in the way of controlling
ourselves is to make our choice among competing ends
and motives and then multiply its associations and
thereby deepen our convictions and intensify our feelings until action results. We control and touch the
trigger in consciousness that releases links of causation
and currents of energy that leap out into the world and
effect our near or far-off purposes, possibly piercing
mountains and ultimately impinging on the frontiers
of the universe. Our freedom, then, is no unimportant
and trivial thing because of its limitations, but is decisive of all important things and has tremendous
significance and force in our character and conduct.
The pivot of a pair of scales is limited to an edge as
thin as a knife-blade, but it balances the lever that
decides which weight is the heavier. The human will
is only a knife-blade pivot, but on it trembles the

power that determines the weight of motives and decides destiny.

We have already had a glimpse into the mechanism by which we exercise our liberty. Motives are not something thrust upon us from without. They grow up within and are our own children. The opposite of freedom is force imposed upon us from the outside: no such force does or can restrain and bind our thoughts and choices. Our motives are not only born of our own nature, but they are subject to our deliberation and selection. They compete for our approval, but they do not compel it. We consider and weigh and evaluate them and choose according to our own standards. We are immediately aware of this power and act of choice; and this is a final fact in our mental and moral constitution.

And further, motives are not ready-made and fixed weights that are dropped upon our wills and determine them like weights upon a pair of scales. We not only choose, but we make our motives and determine their weight. It is in our power, as we have seen, to intensify or diminish motives by increasing or decreasing their associations so that they grow into overmastering heat and power, or cool and wither into paleness and impotency. We can feed a motive into fatness and lusty strength, or we can starve and strangle it to death; and in this power lies the very core and centre of our freedom and responsibility. The motives of the soul are the soul itself in deliberation, and its freedom is its self-activity. We are always free to choose and act according to our own nature, and this is the only real freedom.

It is true that our motives are shaped and coloured by our acquired nature or character, but this character is the product of all our past volitions and is so much deposited and crystallized will for which we are responsible. Our freedom is thus deeply rooted in our past, yet this limitation does not destroy our liberty, but only enables us to conserve and capitalize our past volitions.

It is not supposed that this psychological description of the working of our free will clears up all the difficulties and mysteries connected with it. It is still environed in difficulties and its very heart is a mystery which we may never unlock. Yet difficulties do not destroy facts, or hinder practical action, and our freedom stands in the midst of its mysteries as one of the most certain facts of our experience. The will is thus the captain of the soul and the crown of its sovereignty, pregnant with victory and glory or defeat and shame. It builds man's world, tossing mountains out of its path and creating a vast splendid civilization, carves character and determines destiny, and every man, however humble and bound in by circumstance, is, not a wind-blown bubble on the sea or atom in the storm of the world,

> But this main miracle, that thou art thou,
> With power on thine own act and on the world.
> —TENNYSON.

The three fundamental faculties of the soul, we have now seen, are intellect, sensibility, and will. This is their logical order of action, though they are interblended and simultaneous in their activities, one of them usually being dominant at a time in consciousness. The human soul is thus a three-cycle engine. Intellect acts first and produces thought; thought kindles feeling; and feeling moves the will. The action

of the will normally results and rests in a state of
satisfaction, which is the end of the particular movement. But this state or end at once suggests or stirs
another movement of the intellect, and then the process
begins all over again; and thus the mind keeps turning through its cycle and runs its endless round. The
observance of this order is of the first importance in
practical psychology and especially in the psychology
of religion, and we shall have frequent occasion to refer
to it.

II. Some General Characteristics of the Soul

There are some general characteristics of the soul
that should be noted as they have an important bearing on our subject.

1. Habit.—A habit is an acquired fixed way of acting. Anything acting in a certain way once tends to
act in the same way again. A piece of paper folded on
a line forms a crease along which it folds more easily
a second time; and all material substances are subject to this law. A new machine runs more smoothly
after it has been in use for a time, for all its parts are
adjusted to the action. A new suit of clothes grows to
fit the figure and follows all its movements and thus
becomes comfortable. Organic beings are more pli-
able than inorganic substances and quickly fall into
grooves of action. The human body is highly plastic
and subject to habits. Muscles and nerves, having
acted in one way once, tend to repeat the action, which
in time grows automatic. It is thus we learn to walk,
speak, attend to our work and carry on all the complex routine affairs of life. The skill of the performer,
such as the pianist, is a remarkable example of complex habits that are wrought into the very texture of

the nerves and muscles so that they come to act unconsciously.

These bodily habits have their origin in the soul, which is an organism highly plastic to the formation and retention of habits. The association of ideas, having linked two or more ideas together once, tends to keep them together so that the recurrence of one is apt to suggest, or to excite the neural connections of, the others, and thus they appear together habitually. Memory is a matter of habit. The oftener we revive a memory the more firmly it is fixed in the mind and the more readily it responds to our call. Judgments tend to repeat themselves and grow into fixed opinions or beliefs or prejudices. Emotions form habits. When we feel a certain way once the same feeling on a similar excitation again stirs or floods the soul, and thus emotional habits are formed. The will wears itself into grooves of action along which it slips in unconscious smoothness and ease. Moral and spiritual experiences are repeated and thus character grows. Under this law of habit the whole body and soul are ploughed and grooved into a system of habits by the automatic action of which we live. By far the greater part of all our activities, language, learning, conduct and character, work and worship, becomes cast and cooled in the mould of habit.

This fact is of tremendous importance in life. It results in the skill and often the marvellous perfection with which we do our work. The pianist strikes the instrument with rapidity the eye cannot follow and yet no finger misses a key. At first these movements are made with awkward and painful effort, and the perfection is the result of the long-continued practice by which the nerves and muscles are trained into automatic action. At the same time habits take over these acquired activities and release the attention and all the faculties of the mind and organs of the body to do other work. We thus walk without paying any attention to our steps. If we had to think about every step and calculate the problem of maintaining our balance we could not do anything else; but we hand the whole matter of walking over to habit and give our mind and eyes to other things. This is an enormous economy of our time and attention and enables us to do many things at once, while we give our conscious attention and effort to the novel situations and complex problems constantly arising which habit cannot solve. Habit thus enables us to capitalize our past actions and acquired skill in an invested fund of autonomy that carries on the general work of life. Habit keeps the world turning on its accustomed axis and is " the enormous flywheel of society, its most precious conservative agent."

This fact of course is fraught with the greatest good and evil. Good habits are steel tracks on which we drive our life with speed and safety, or they are grooves in which life slips in unconscious smoothness. They are the means of our liberty, giving to life its freest movement and its fullest joy. On the other hand, evil habits bind us in slavery. They lead us into lines of action which, however pleasant at first, at last become our bondage and bitterness from which we cannot escape with strong crying and tears. The moral and spiritual importance of habits is thus confirmed by and is grounded in their psychology.

2. Character.—Character is the system of habits we have formed; or, as John Stuart Mill expressed it, " a character is a completely fashioned will." Its original

elements are the raw materials of the inherited constitution, and these are creative and decisive in determining the general limitation and tone of character. Bodily constitution, emotional temperament, vigour of mind and energy of will are largely dependent on this native endowment, and one cannot escape this limitation any more than he can escape from the grasp of gravitation. Nevertheless, character is the form into which these elements are slowly moulded, and this process is subject to our choice and action. Every thought and emotion, choice and deed, deposits an atom of habit in the soul; bends and disposes the soul to act in that way again, and thus slowly shapes and hardens it into a system of habits that is its character and life. This law is expressed in the familiar saying: Sow a thought and reap a deed; sow a deed and reap a habit; sow a habit and reap a character; sow a character and reap a destiny.

The character, being thus once formed, is the seed-plot of the soul out of which its thoughts and actions sprout. It is the focal reflector that gathers into itself all the affinities and associations of the soul and concentrates them on its motives and ends, causing them to blaze up into vividness and to glow with heat and power. As a man thinketh in his heart, so is he. An American is an American in all his political and national ideals, and a Jew is a Jew down to the last fibre of his being. A workingman sees all things in the light of his class interest, and a professional man thinks in the terms of his profession. Every one's vision and views are coloured by his interests and prejudices and passions, or according to his party and religion. Knowing the character of a man we can predict what he will believe and do, and having his character we have the key by which we can unlock his mind and move his will.

This looks as though character constricts the freedom of the soul and finally destroys it. It does strongly commit the soul to action in accordance with its own nature. But character is itself the product of free will and is the crystallized deposit of all the volitions of the past of the soul. The soul stores up its own free action and thus gains permanence and accumulated power for its freedom. Even its evil choices were free, however they at last bind it. The soul is ever repeating and perpetuating the choices of the past and is thus eating of the fruit of its own doings. This adds immensely to the responsibility and solemnity of our choices: they are the seeds of future character and destiny. Therefore psychology says, with Goethe: " Choose well; your choice is brief, but endless."

But some freedom remains to change even the most rigid character. It is not cast in an iron mould which cannot be modified in shape or be broken up and recast. It is true that ordinarily character cannot be suddenly and completely changed by a sheer act of will, though sometimes there may be poured into it a fiery thought or molten emotion that will melt it, a powerful affection that will expel every contrary thought and feeling. But ordinarily character can be slowly modified and may in time be radically reconstructed. This leaves open the road of hope to reform and conversion.

3. Individuality.—Every soul has its own nature and acquired character. As no two leaves are cut after the same pattern, or petals dyed with the same hue, and as one star differeth from another star in glory, so much more are no two such complex and plastic organisms as human souls alike in mould and mood,

disposition and temperament. Heredity is infinitely complex, running its roots back through thousands of generations, and each of countless ancestors has poured a tiny stream of blood drops into every one's veins. Environment and training and all the myriad influences that mould the individual are never the same in any two persons and endlessly vary. As a result we have all the types and individualities of nature and character that make up our human world.

This fact has important psychological applications, especially in education and religion. In the school, ten scholars in a class may be taught to spell ten words and they may all spell them alike and correctly, and then the teacher may think that he has standardized his work and put these ten children through the same process. But what a different world of meaning each of these ten words suggests to each of these ten scholars? A word may be a meaningless sign to one scholar, and to another it may call up a cluster of associations that are good and noble, rich and inspiring, and to still another associations that are painful or evil and degrading. Each mind of the ten swarms with its own suggestions as it spells each word, and this content of meaning is the thing that counts rather than the form of the spelling. The same story may be told to the class, but it divides into as many streams of suggestion and becomes as many stories as there are children listening. The telling may seem to effect the same result in all, but any such view sees no deeper than the faces of the children, and not as deep as that, for their very faces will show the discerning teacher that they are hearing or reconstructing different tales.

Children differ endlessly in the very structure of their minds and senses. Some see things vividly,

others hear them, and others may derive their chief
impressions from sensations of touch. These children
live in different worlds and need different training.
The visualist may seem dumb when the auditory sense
is addressed, and conversely. Children are often
thought to be slow or unintelligent, when the difficulty
is in the inability of the teacher to perceive their
mental type and adapt the teaching to their needs.
These differences in individuality, thus illustrated in
children, are multiplied and magnified in adults, in
whom inherited natures and acquired characters are
thus brought out into sharper relief.

These varying types of individuality in life should be
respected. Every one has an inalienable right to his
own individuality, in so far as it is normal and not in
need of correction from abnormality and perversion.
We are strongly disposed to forget this fundamental
right in connection with the character and specially
the social customs and political and religious beliefs
and practices of others. We unconsciously, or it may
be consciously, regard ourselves as normal moulds and
authoritative models and think that others, in so far
as they differ from us, are in danger of the judgment,
at least of our censure and pity. But this is running
counter to the whole constitution of the world. When
we think that others ought to be like us we forget that
one of our kind is enough. Any suppression of diversity and constriction of people to one mould in life
would be an enormous impoverishment of the world,
obliterating its variety and picturesqueness and reducing it to a dead level of monotony and greatly impair-
ing its efficiency. We must leave room in our views of
life for all the infinite individuality with which our
human world is stamped. Such variety is the beauty

and glory of our life. " To give room for wandering is it that the world is made so wide."

4. **The Subconsciousness.**—The subconsciousness is that part of our mental life that lies below the threshold of consciousness. Our consciousness is subject to great fluctuations in its volume and level. It rises in time of excitement to surging heights and fills and over-flows all the banks of the soul, and at other times it sinks to lower levels of quietness and dulness and drowsiness and at length falls below the level of consciousness in sleep. But that all mental activity does not cease in sleep is obvious from our dreams. All kinds of mental processes go on at the lower level of subconsciousness. Problems that remain unsolved when we go to sleep sometimes appear to be worked out to their conclusion when we awake. These activities in the subconsciousness are so dim and memory of them is so frail and evanescent that we have no self-consciousness of them at the time and no memory of them afterward.

The whole life of the soul above this threshold sinks down into and is preserved in the subconsciousness. Memory has its storehouse in this deep. All our mental associations and habits are packed away in its pigeon-holes or receptacles and emerge at call from these hidden chambers. There is reason to think that this subconscious life of the soul is large compared with its conscious life. As seven-eighths of an iceberg is under the surface of the sea, so the greater part of our life is submerged in these depths. The towering skyscraper has five or six stories under the ground in which is located the machinery that lights and heats and runs the whole building; so in this underground world of the soul is located the machinery that operates all our conscious activities. This is the night life of the soul, full of shadows and ghosts and stars.

The subconsciousness plays a part of immense importance in our life. It is the storehouse into which our conscious activities are packed away so that nothing is ever lost out of our life. Up out of this huge cellar come swarming through its trapdoors and back stairways of memory and association the shadows of the past to reënforce the present. Suggestion has the power of tapping this hidden reservoir and letting it gush up in jets of thought and feeling. The most penetrating approach to and powerful control over a man are often effected through an indirect appeal to his subconsciousness, which touches him below the level of his conscious prejudices and opposition and wins and masters him before he knows it. Everything that we put into our life will sooner or later come out of our life. Long years afterward on the most unexpected occasion and in the most startling ways, " old, unhappy, far-off things, and battles long ago " will come up out of this dark chamber to strengthen and comfort us, or, like ghosts out of their graves, to trouble us. The admonition of psychology at this point is: " Keep thy heart with all diligence; for out of it are the issues of life."

> All buried life still holds a vital spark.
> The memory's mystic touch unbinds its deep
> Oblivion and starts it forth, gay with
> Its ancient revelries, or tragic with
> The blood and tears of old forgotten crimes.
> Our brains are living tombs in which are sealed
> The thoughts and deeds of generations gone;
> And these heredities still live in us
> In many a masterful or infirm trait.
> Our past is buried there; and though it seems

To sleep it will awake and plague us with
Fell retribution's gnawing tooth, or bless
Us with its resurrected strength and peace.

5. **Growth.**—The soul is a product of growth. It does not leap into being full-formed, but begins as a germ and slowly passes through many stages into maturity.

Any growing thing is a world of wonder. A seed may be microscopic in size and seem so in significance, yet that minute speck is a vast world or cosmos of order and plan and purpose in which mysterious physical, chemical, and vital elements and energies are packed in dormant latency. With the first breath of spring or other quickening influence their slumbering powers awake and the seed becomes a marvellous workshop or loom in which invisible fingers are throwing infinitesimal shuttles that carry vital threads of life and weave its wonderful web according to its preordained pattern. Embryologists peer through their microscopes into this world and describe processes so intricate and exquisite and inscrutable as to excite our utmost astonishment and make us dumbly feel how great is the marvel and mystery of life.

Once started the process of growth goes on incessantly. The tiny seed becomes the child of the universe. The earth cradles it, the soil and showers nurse it, the sun smiles upon it, and every star lends it a friendly ray. It throws out rootlets and filaments that lay hold of the globe and the whole heavens. Atom by atom it grows, gathering raw materials and transforming them by its subtle chemistry into sap and spinning them into tissue and weaving them into leaf and blossom and distilling and crystallizing them into golden wheat or rosy apple. And thus the minute seed becomes the rosebush or fruit-laden tree, a stately palm or a giant redwood that stands three hundred feet tall and was old when Cæsar was born and has defied the storms of thirty centuries. Or in the germ the life principle begins to sketch an animal, with a few swift strokes outlining spinal column and limbs, heart and brain, and in due time the same process of growth produces an insect or bird, or a man, even a Plato or a Shakespeare.

The human soul also starts as a seed or germ endowed with the same absorbent and expansive nature. It begins as a bundle of latencies, dormant faculties that lie folded up and submerged deep in the unconscious or subconscious state. Gradually they are stirred into activity by quickening influences and find their appropriate sustenance. At first the soul is an undifferentiated mass of dim feeling and only slowly does it unfold into distinct faculties of thought and sensibility and will. In its early stages of development it is wholly absorbed in its senses, drawn objectively into the outer world, and later it begins to be aware of the inner world of itself. Sight grows into insight, and consciousness into self-consciousness and conscience. It develops perception, concepts, judgment, reasoning, memory and imagination, forms habits, sees ideals and builds them into realities, makes choices, carves character and determines destiny, follows the gleam of visions and turns them into victories. And thus the babe becomes the child and man, the scholar and philosopher, the saint or the lost soul.

This process of growth has roots running back through the development and origin of the race and on backward through the process of evolution into the dim vistas of the past. The human soul has an inconceivably ancient heredity, but its real descent whether near or remote is from God, the Father of spirits. Its faculties have been fashioned, its instincts formed, and its constitution framed through a long process, and thus it has been shaped and moulded into harmony with its environment. Its whole history has been stored up in its constitution and every part of its being bears the marks of its ancient origin and the battles through which it has come And so its

> Life is not as idle ore,
>
> But iron dug from central gloom,
>   And heated hot in burning fears,
>   And dipt in baths of hissing tears,
> And batter'd by the shocks of doom
>
> To shape and use.

Growth is thus stamped upon every part of our life and is one of its most prominent and important aspects. It enters deeply into the development and training of all the faculties and processes of the soul which we have been considering and is especially important in education and religion.

Having behind us this general background of psychology, we are now prepared to follow its application in the special field of religion.

CHAPTER III

THE PSYCHOLOGY OF THE MORAL AND RELIGIOUS NATURE

THE moral and religious nature is the general constitution of the soul in its reaction towards moral and religious objects.

I. THE MORAL NATURE OF THE SOUL

The moral nature of the soul is its attitude and action towards right and wrong.

1. **Conscience.**—Conscience is the faculty that deals with the moral qualities of objects. Conscience is consciousness acting on the distinction between right and wrong. The word means the knowledge one has with himself and describes the most intimate knowledge one has of his inmost self. This distinction of right and wrong is a unique quality which is not found in material things or in organic beings below the level of personality. A stone or a star, a vegetable or one of the lower animals, has no moral nature. It cannot be or do either right or wrong: it simply is and is not subject to praise or blame. Though we do praise or blame some of the higher animals, such as a dog or a horse, yet we do not really regard them as truly moral beings subject to these judgments. It is only in the field of personality that this quality is found; and even in this field so far as acts and states are wholly instinctive and physical they are not regarded as moral; only acts which involve motives and choice are seen and felt by the conscience as right or wrong.

There are two elements in conscience so that it is a complex faculty consisting of an intellectual and an emotional factor. The intellectual factor is the perception of an act as conforming or not conforming to a law or standard of right and wrong. The feeling that attends this perception is a sense that we ought to approve and do the right and disapprove and refuse to do the wrong. The perception is an act of judgment and is subject to all the variation and error of human judgment. The feeling of obligation is a constitutional and intuitive reaction that is constant and universal in human nature. It stirs into action whenever the mind perceives the distinction between right and wrong and acts automatically. The intellectual perception is the variable and the feeling of ought or ought not is the constant element in conscience. The intellectual judgment, which determines the moral object, is the objective and the feeling is the subjective side of conscience.

A vital and endless subject of controversy in ethics is the question as to what makes a moral object right or wrong. One theory is that it is pleasure that makes an object right and pain that makes it wrong, so that pleasure and pain coincide with good and evil. This theory is contradicted by our moral intuition which does not perceive and decide that objects are right or wrong according as they give pleasure or pain; and it runs squarely against many of the facts of life. We obey duty regardless of its consequences in pleasure or pain, and the martyr or the soldier that lays down his life is certainly not impelled to this act of devotion to principle or patriotism for pleasure either for himself or for others.

Yet there is a measure of truth in this theory, as

there is in all theories that gain any currency. Pleasure does coincide with right and pain with wrong in the long run; and if pleasure is widened so as to include all satisfactions, especially the highest spiritual satisfactions of the soul, the theory approaches the truth. Yet even in this sense the theory reverses right relations, for pleasure and pain are not the cause of right and wrong, but right and wrong are the cause of pleasure and pain. Pleasure and pain are the consequences and not the causes of right and wrong. Pleasure is the music that floats off the harp of life when it is in tune and properly played. The harp produces the music, and not the music the harp. It is our business to take care of the harp and obey its laws, and then the music will come.

A second theory of the nature of virtue is the utilitarian doctrine that the right is the useful or that which promotes life, and wrong is the hurtful or that which hinders life. This theory approaches the truth much closer than the hedonistic or pleasure theory, for again, when taken in the long run, right does always promote life and wrong hinders and injures it. Even the martyr or the soldier, when his judgment is correct, promotes human life and even his own highest life by his sacrifice. But when this is granted the fact remains that the moral quality of an object is directly discerned and felt as an intuitive act and is not the result of calculating its useful results. We feel the obligation to approve and do the right when its personal consequences involve us in great loss and pain. We often feel and say that we must follow our conscience let the consequences be what they may. The results of an action often guide the judgment in applying the principle of right and wrong, but they do not constitute that principle. The intellectual factor in conscience is an act of judgment and reasoning which should use all means in coming to its conclusion, and among these means are consequences of utility; and when utility is made inclusive of all good up to the highest holiness, then utility and right always coincide.

The true object of right is worth or value, and worth is excellence of being either as a means to some higher end or as an end in itself. Conscience intuitively judges worth as right and obligatory and the absence and opposite of worth as wrong.

2. The Scale of Values.—The word right etymologically means that which is straight; a right line is a straight line. The word wrong is only another spelling of the word wrung and means that which is twisted or crooked. Both of these words thus imply a standard to which moral objects conform or fail to conform and thereby are right or wrong.

This standard or law is a scale of values on which acts are arranged according to the degree of their worth. Some acts are of higher worth and obligation than others. These objects on the scale may conflict with one another and then they compete for our approval. A moral act is always a preference and choice of one object on the scale of value in competition with another, of a higher with a lower. When we choose a lower in preference to a higher end, we do wrong, and when we choose a higher in preference to a lower we do right.

Dr. James Martineau, in his *Types of Ethical Theory,* has worked out this view at great length, and he summarizes his results as follows: " We are now prepared for an exact definition of Right and Wrong, which will assume this form: *Every action is* RIGHT *which, in presence of a lower principle, follows a higher; every action is* WRONG *which, in presence of a higher principle, follows a lower.* Thus, the act attributed to Regulus, in returning back to death at Carthage, was right, because the reverence for veracity whence it sprung is a higher principle than any fear or personal affection which might have suggested a different course, and of which we tacitly conceive as competing with the former. And the act of St. Peter in denying Christ was wrong, because the fear to which he yielded was lower than the personal affection and reverence for truth which he disobeyed. The act of the missionaries of mercy, whether of a Florence Nightingale to the stricken bodies, or of a Columban, a Boniface, a Livingstone, to the imperilled souls of men, is right, because the compassion which inspires it is nobler than any love of ease or of self-culture which would resist it. The act of the manufacturer of adulterated or falsely labelled goods is wrong, because done in compliance with an inferior incentive, the love of gain, against the protest of superiors, good faith and reverence for truth. This definition appears to me to have the advantage of simply stating what passes in all men's minds when they use words whose meaning it seeks to unfold. . . . No constant aim, no one royal faculty, no contemplated preponderance of happy effects, can really be found in all good action. More scope for variety is felt to be needed: and this is gained as soon as we quit the casuists' attempt to draw an *absolute dividing line* between good and bad, and recognize the relative and preferential conditions of every moral problem." [1]

[1] *Types of Ethical Theory*, Vol. II, pp. 270-271. For similar views of conscience, see Dr. Newman Smyth's *Christian Ethics*, pp. 23-46, Dr. Rashdall's *Is Conscience an Emotion?* and Professor G. H. Palmer's *The Nature of Goodness.*

Through a long and illuminating discussion Dr. Martineau works out a table of springs or motives of action according to their relative worth. He has thirteen degrees or groups of value on his scale. At the bottom he puts vindictiveness as purely evil and therefore below the zero point on the scale, a minus quality. Then he places in their order the organic propensities of love of ease and pleasure, the organic appetites, spontaneous activity, love of gain, the feelings of antipathy and fear, the energies of love of power and culture, wonder and admiration, the parental and social affections, including generosity and gratitude, the affection of compassion, and at the top veracity and reverence. Any table of this kind is a matter of intellectual judgment and ethical insight and is subject to all the errors of reasoning. Perhaps few philosophical moralists would agree with Dr. Martineau's table at every point, though few would dispute its broad outlines.

In the light of this table we see how men differ so widely and endlessly in their moral judgments. Even when a scale is adopted there is difficulty in fixing the point on it where any particular act falls. A moral object is rarely simple and pure, but is mixed in its nature and motives, and this involves a difference of judgment in placing it on the scale. And so men equally intelligent and moral will vary greatly in their estimate of the same action.

But a deeper difficulty lies in the fact that men have widely different scales and indeed every one has his own scale of values. The pantheist and the theist, the Buddhist and the Christian, the anarchist and the royalist, the socialist and the individualist, the laborer and the capitalist, the upright man and the criminal, have very different scales of worth in their minds.

They carry these scales as unconscious measuring rules engraven on their hearts, and in determining moral questions each applies his own standard, and so they reach divergent and even contradictory conclusions.

Another aspect of the same fact is that men are themselves developed to different stages or degrees on the scale of moral values. Some men are low in the scale, ruled mostly by instincts and selfish interests and are blind to and unconscious of its high degrees. Other men are high up on the scale and are ruled by the noblest motives. All men have the same moral sense of obligation; the coarsest conscience feels that the right ought to be approved and obeyed and that the wrong ought to be condemned and spurned. All men proclaim their allegiance to the right, but they differ in what they regard as right or in their scales of value and obligation. In fact, every man's moral nature or character is his scale by which he measures everything, or it is the lens through which he sees all things and which gives to them its colour. These intellectual and emotional and moral differences in men array them against one another and produce the confusion in ethical judgments and the dust of systems and of creeds that fill the world. Conscience is constant in its subjective feeling, but it is endlessly variable in its objective judgments.

Some paradoxical conclusions follow from this fact of differing standards. A thing may be right in one age or stage of development or condition of circumstances and wrong in another. Polygamy and slavery were regarded as right in Old Testament times, and they were relatively good in that age, for they were a higher worth as compared with the lower doom of death which was in a still earlier and lower age inflicted upon all captives. But when captives were spared their lives and kept as polygamous wives and slaves, there was an advance up the scale and these things were comparatively right, and as such were sanctioned in the Old Testament. In the New Testament, however, they are condemned as wrong because men had then moved up the scale in their moral education. Polygamy and slavery were now seen to be a lower good in comparison with the higher good of monogamy and freedom. In the light of this higher scale they were placed under the condemnation of Christian ethics and in time were banished from Christian lands. The world has made vast advances up the scale during the centuries and is still slowly progressing. Many social customs and practices, such as the use of intoxicating beverages and railway rebates and child labour in factories, that our fathers unquestioningly approved and practised, we now regard as wrong. The advance in the civilization, moralization, and Christianization of the world will take place along this line of moving upward on the scale of moral values.

3. **The Authority of Conscience.**—Conscience enjoins its obligations upon us with authority. Once we have discovered or determined its decision we are bound to obey it. This is an intuitive and final command and obligation which no other authority can set aside. The voices of self-interest and passion are hushed before it, and the decrees of kings and emperors are puny and impotent in its presence.

We must therefore follow our conscience, however wrong it may be in its judgment. It is self-evident that we ought to do what we believe we ought to do, and to do what we believe is wrong is itself wrong, though the act should turn out to be right in itself. Paul declared after his conversion, " I verily thought with myself, that I ought to do many things contrary to the name of Jesus of Nazareth," and he was right in so doing as long as his conscience told him he should. The heathen mother, casting her babe into the Ganges as a sacrifice to her god, is doing right from her point of view, dreadful as is her blindness. But her error is one of judgment and not of obedience to her conscience.

Though it is our duty always to obey conscience, yet it is also our duty to enlighten conscience, and we may be responsible for the ignorance and perversity that blind it. But how are we to enlighten and guide conscience so that it will speak with authority that we can trust? We must determine and apply the true scale of values. An act which is low on this scale is right when it does not compete and conflict with an act higher on the scale. Physical appetites and pleasures are good when they do not stand in the way of higher goods. This process runs up the scale from the bottom to the top.

One of the standards or degrees of worth on the scale is perfection of life. Whatever promotes life in its health and happiness, its individual and social wealth and worth, its fulness and richness, is right as compared with whatever hinders and injures life, physical and moral, personal and social. Life is an end and worth in itself, and therefore commands and binds conscience.

But is there not something of higher worth and more binding upon us than life itself, especially personal life? There are some ends that are absolute and ought never to be subordinated to other ends. These are truth, purity, justice, love, and reverence. Truth

is the commerce of our minds with reality, the correspondence of our thoughts with things. It is therefore
the primary virtue of the mind, the working relation
with the world, the foundation of life, the bond of
society, the intellectual bloom and beauty of life. A
lie is always so much lost soul. It puts us out of right
relations with the world, cuts the bond of fellowship,
infiltrates falseness into all the tissues of the soul, dis-
locates life at its centre and throws it out of relation
around its whole circumference. We intuitively perceive the absolute worth and claim of truth and know
that we should seek and accept and obey it. The
proverbs of many languages proclaim its supremacy
and inviolability. "Let the truth prevail though the
heavens fall." "Buy the truth and sell it not." "The
truth is always right," said Sophocles, and John Locke
wrote: "To love truth for truth's sake is the principal
part of human perfection in this world, and the seed-
plot of all other virtues."

Purity on its negative side is freedom from imperfection, especially from moral stain, and on its positive side it is the soul's self-affirmation of its righteousness. It is the essence of a being unadulterated with
inferior elements, the soul conscious of its integrity
and keeping itself unspotted. That this standard of
worth is binding upon us and cannot be outweighed
by any other end and motive is intuitively perceived
and felt.

Justice and love are the supreme altruistic virtues.
Justice accords to every one his due, and is the foundation of right social relations. It guards the soul
against selfishness and affirms the equal rights of all
souls. Love goes beyond justice and pours its favour
upon others. It is a spirit of good will which cherishes

affection for, and bestows its benefits, its sympathy, service, and its very self on, the objects of its favour. Love is the finest bloom and fragrance of the soul, its most beautiful grace, and its greatest felicity. Justice and love are not mutually exclusive, but are really complementary and harmonious. Justice, when perfectly enlightened, would do just what love would do, and love, when equally enlightened, would do just what justice would do. It must be admitted, however, that there is a larger voluntary element in love and that the claims of justice are supreme, and therefore love must find some means of satisfying justice if it would have its way.

Reverence is respect for higher worth and runs up into and culminates in worship, a word which is only another spelling of worthship and expresses our sense of the worth of God. God is the sum of all perfection, the Absolute Good, and therefore commands the highest and ultimate sovereignty over our souls. All our judgments and insights and feelings converge and climax in the inmost affirmation of our souls that " we ought to obey God rather than men." We therefore express the authority of conscience as follows: We should ever obey the voice of conscience as expressed in our sense of right and duty when enlightened and guided by perfection of life, truth, purity, justice and love, and worship.

Conscience thus sits on the throne of life and wears the crown of sovereignty over all ends and motives. It overtops and dominates all the plains of life as the Alps overshadow the hills and valleys lying around their feet. Its slopes and summits rise before the soul as majestic white visions that command our reverence and obedience. Its decisions take precedence over every other claim, and life itself must not be counted dear in its presence.   It is the battle-field on which are fought the real conflicts and issues of life, and all the outer battles of the world, Waterloo and Gettysburg, are only echoes from its inner shocks and doom. It is the real heroism and triumph of the soul, or its tragedy and shame.   It crowns man with glory and honour and makes him but little lower than God.

Stern Daughter of the Voice of God!
Stern Lawgiver! yet thou dost wear
The Godhead's most benignant grace;
Nor know we anything so fair
As is the smile upon thy face:
Flowers laugh before thee in their beds
And fragrance in thy footing treads;
Thou dost preserve the stars from wrong;
And the most ancient heavens, through Thee, are fresh and strong.
                                        —WORDSWORTH.

II. The Religious Nature of the Soul

1. **The Relation of Morality to Religion.**—In passing from the moral to the religious nature of the soul we are rising from a lower to a higher aspect and application of the same principle.   We are still within the region of value and obligation.   The moral nature deals with duty on the level of our human world.   But the human soul cannot always look down and around: it must also look up.   Man is " the upward-looking animal," and this is his highest faculty and distinction. The sense of duty in the soul implies a moral law to which it is subject, and law inevitably implies a Lawgiver.   Its scale of moral values as it runs up cannot be cut off short at the limit of our sky, but irresistibly prolongs itself through the heavens and beyond the

stars. Religion thus covers and completes morality as the sky overarches and crowns the earth.

This relation has been happily expressed by Dr. Newman Smyth as follows: "Religion opens larger prospects to duty. If ethics are regarded as the earthly science of life, then religion is the moral astronomy of it. While bent on the tasks of the former, we need the outlook and the uplift of the latter. The religious consciousness encircles and completes the moral consciousness of man around the whole horizon of his life, bending over every field of duty, as the heavens encompass and comprehend the earth. Not to have any out look of religious thought and far prospect of a boundless hope as we pursue our daily tasks, were like living on an earth without a sky. One may do his daily work with little thought indeed of the overarching heaven; but the sky is always there,—the far, pure background for all man's life on the earth,—and some enlarging and quieting sense of it will pervade our daily consciousness of toil and labour under the sun. Duty is not a task given man to be laboriously done at the bottom of a dark mine; rather it is a life to be healthfully and joyously led under the broad sky in the clear sunshine of God. In obeying duty, because it is duty, we may say in Schleiermacher's spirit, ' The religious feelings are to be as a holy music which shall accompany all the action of man; he should do all with religion, not from religion.' Though the immediate motive may be duty, religion may be its happy accompaniment always." [1] While there may be some degree of morality without religion and of religion without morality, yet the two ideas and modes of life are logically complementary: either will be starved and

[1] *Christian Ethics*, pp. 23-24.

stunted without the other, each completes and illuminates and enriches the other, and it takes both to make the full-orbed sphere of life.

2. **The Origin and Nature of Religion.**—Theories of the origin and of the nature of religion have generated endless controversy and variety of views. These two aspects of the subject involve each other, and our view of the one will affect our view of the other.

A theory once widely held was that religion had its origin in a primitive divine revelation, but there is no trace of such a revelation in the history of many nations and tribes, and the theory is now generally abandoned. Historical religions may have originated in this way, but not religion.

Another widely accepted theory is that religion is due to the fear of gods or of God. Primitive men believed, as savages still believe, that the world is thickly infested with demons that lurk in every tree and stone and natural object, waiting and watching to entrap men. This view filled the world with terror, making every forest and mountain and sea an object of dread. Men thought to propitiate these evil demons by incantations and sacrifices and other forms of worship, and thus arose the whole brood of religions.

The origin of religion has been mixed up with magic and fetishism and ancestor worship and other primitive superstitions. There has been much digging in the subsoil and slime of savagery and in the ashes of archæology, and thus religion has been connected with an ignoble origin and the impression given that it would disappear as these superstitions fade away under the light of civilization. But the true nature of a tree is better seen in its blossoms and fruit than in its gnarled roots buried in the earth; and the true nature of religion is seen in its highest and purest forms. And so far from dying out, religion grows with all the growth of man and blooms into its finest blossoms and ripens into its best fruits in the highest civilization.

Two of the greatest investigators and highest authorities in the archæology of religion are Dr. E. B. Tylor, who brings out of his researches the "minimum definition" that religion is "the belief in spiritual beings," [1] and Dr. J. G. Frazer, whose elaborate studies, extending to twelve volumes, lead him to the conclusion that religion is "a propitiation or conciliation of powers supreme to man which are believed to direct and control the course of nature and of human life." [2]

Herbert Spencer found the origin of religion in ancestor worship and resolved its irreducible and indestructible element into the sense of mystery we experience in the presence of the Unknowable Power in which we are environed and which wells up within us. This wonder gave birth to worship and must ever endure in human nature. Though he says that the subject of religion "is one which concerns us more than any other matter whatever," [3] yet he makes no provision for its cultivation and exercise in his system of philosophy and ethics, and it only falls as a passing shadow on the first pages of his *First Principles* and then disappears as a practical principle. The ambitious *Synthetic Philosophy* becomes pitifully impotent and silent when it comes to the matter "which concerns us more than any other matter whatever."

Along with Spencer's account of religion as consisting in wonder we may classify John Morley's "feeling

---

[1] *Primitive Culture,* Vol. I, p. 241.
[2] *The Golden Bough,* Third Edition, Vol. I, p. 222.
[3] *First Principles,* p. 24.

for the incommensurable things," Edward Caird's
" a man's religion is the expression of his attitude to
the universe," J. R. Seeley's " permanent and habitual
admiration," and Matthew Arnold's " morality touched
with emotion."

Schleiermacher found the essential element of religion to consist in a feeling of dependence, " the immediate consciousness of the universal existence of all
finite things in and through the Infinite, and of all
temporal things in and through the Eternal."

Professor William James, as the result of his wide
collation of " the varieties of religious experience," con-
cludes that " there is a certain uniform deliverance in
which religions all appear to meet. It consists of two
parts: 1. An uneasiness; and 2. Its solution. 1. The
uneasiness reduced to its simplest terms is a sense that
there is *something wrong about us* as we naturally
stand. 2. The solution is a sense that *we are saved
from the wrongness* by making proper connection with
the higher powers." [1]

E. S. Waterhouse sums up his study of religion in
the conclusion that, " stated in the most general manner, it would seem to be the belief in a higher order
of things into due relation with which man must
enter in order properly to adjust his life." [2]   One
more definition may be added, that of Dr. Martineau:
Religion is " belief in an Ever-living God, that is, a
Divine Mind and Will ruling the Universe and holding
Moral relations with mankind." [3]

These statements, which might be indefinitely multiplied, all lead to the general definition that religion is

[1] *Varieties of Religious Experience*, p. 508; also pp. 485-486.
[2] *Modern Theories of Religion*, p. 5.
[3] *A Study of Religion*, Vol. I, p. 1.

conscious relation to God. The God worshipped may be the evil demons of the savage, the many gods of the polytheist, the one God of the Hebrew and the Mohammedan, or the trinitarian God of Christianity. The relation is also pervaded with some degree of consciousness, for all men " live and move and have their being " in God irrespective of whether they have any religion or not. This conscious idea of some relation to a higher power or deity is the root of all religious doctrines and practices.

3. **Religion Rooted in Every Part of Our Nature.—** There is some element of truth in all of these theories from the lowest to the highest, and taken together they show that religion is deeply rooted in every part of our nature.

(*a*) It is first rooted in our intuitions and instincts, it is a constitutional and practical need of life. It appeared from the beginning universally in the world, no nation or tribe having been found that did not manifest it in some form; and it did not appear as a conscious creation or product of thought, but as an instinctive and necessary activity of the human soul. Men did not study theology and then become religious, but they lived religiously and then they studied theology. Man had a religious nature which immediately impelled him to live a religious life, just as he had a physical and a social nature which impelled him to live a physical and social life. As men lived in the sunlight ages before they studied astronomy and cultivated the soil long before they studied chemistry, so they worshipped God before they so much as thought about theology. The religious nature is just as constitutional and ineradicable in man as the mental or physical, and therefore he is necessarily and incurably religious.

It was out of human experience that belief in God arose. Men did not first construct arguments for the existence of God and then believe in him, but they first believed in him and then invented arguments to confirm this belief. God is an immediate practical necessity for man as certainly as bread, and men instinctively began to worship him. If they had not found a God waiting and seeking to meet and satisfy their spiritual needs, they would have been forced to invent one. Our belief in God is immensely older and stronger than all the reasons we can give for it. Reason did not create this belief and reason cannot destroy it. It thrives amidst opposition.

And as our belief in God thus grew up out of human experience, so did all the other elements of religious life. Faith and obedience, prayer and praise, service and sacrifice, were at first necessary expressions of human needs, the instinctive and universal aspiration of the human soul. God set eternity in the heart of man, and eternity has come out of it. Every doctrine of theology, trinity and decrees, sin and atonement, mercy and love, justice and judgment, found some affinity and analogue in human experience. These doctrines were never foreign and alien importations imposed on the human mind, but, though divinely implanted, grew up out of the human heart as their native soil.

The Bible itself is the grand illustration and proof of this principle. It was all lived before it was written and formulated in commandments and creeds. The principles contained in the Ten Commandments were not originated by or first revealed to Moses. Laws against murder and adultery and theft had been in the world from the earliest times, and ages of human experience had confirmed them as necessary conditions of life.[1] The metal of these commandments had been in use in a crude state as a means of social barter: Moses under divine inspiration minted them into current coin and put them into general and permanent circulation. The sharp die and authoritative form are his, but their substance is the raw material of universal human experience.

The same fact is true of the Sermon on the Mount. The substance of its teaching and many of its sayings are found scattered through Jewish literature [2] and can be matched even from heathen sources. This fact does not in the least detract from the divine authority of Jesus, any more than does the fact that he used human language in his preaching; rather it confirms his truth and wisdom as it shows that he made the universal experience of men the basis and substance of his ethical teaching. But he also took crude human ore and minted it into current coin and stamped it with the

[1] Detailed evidence of this obvious fact will be found in Badè's *The Old Testament in the Light of To-day*, Chapter IV. He says: "The wrong of murder, theft, false witness, and adultery required no special revelation . . . and attended the earliest manifestations of the moral instinct even in the man of the stone age" (pp. 88-89). Paul asserts the same fact in Romans 2: 14-15: "For when Gentiles that have not the law do by nature the things of the law, these, not having the law, are the law unto themselves; in that they show the work of the law written in their hearts, their conscience bearing witness therewith, and their thoughts one with another accusing or else excusing them."

[2] Abundant proof and illustration of this will be found in Edersheim's *Life and Times of Jesus the Messiah*, Vol. I, pp. 524-541. In comparing sayings in the Talmud with the Lord's Prayer he says that "it may be freely admitted that the form, and sometimes even the spirit, approached closely the words of the Lord" (p. 536). See also Geikie's *Life and Words of Christ*, Vol. II, p. 54.

image and superscription of his supreme authority and thus put it into the universal circulation of the world.[1] He gathered scattered human rays into the focus of his divine personality and shot them forth as a vivid blaze of light across all succeeding centuries. These rays had slight power and attracted little attention as they shone dimly in other teachers, but concentrated in his divine Person they made him the Light of the world. Divine revelation never reaches its goal and becomes complete until it passes into human experience. The Bible is a great body of such experience. It is not an artificial product or desiccated mummy, but it has red blood in every artery and vein, and palpitates with life in every nerve. It was all first lived before it was written, and thus illustrates and confirms the principle that religion grows out of life as fruit out of its seed.

This view, it need not be said, does not in any degree deny or disparage or impair the divine element in the Bible as an inspired revelation. God was behind and in the whole process of redemption and revelation, so that holy men spoke and wrote as they were moved by the Holy Spirit. But God had to speak to men out of their own needs and in their own language and lead them along the familiar path of their own experience to loftier visions and victories. And so he accommodated himself to human ideas and words, customs and institutions, and at every point used human experience as a

[1] Farrar, in his *Life of Christ*, Vol. I, p. 265, in speaking of "the Rabbinic parallels" to the Sermon on the Mount, quotes the following stanza from "In Memoriam":

> Though truths in manhood darkly join,
> Deep-seated in our mystic frame,
> We yield all honour to the name
> Of Him who made them current coin.

stepping-stone on which to lure and lift men to higher things, or as the necessary prepared soil out of which to grow divine harvests. In its origin and development religion is both human and divine, and neither element should be narrowed or impaired at the expense of the other.

The creeds of Christendom and all progress in theology have sprung out of the same soil of experience. Even those ancient and medieval doctrines and metaphysical distinctions that now seem to us so speculative and unrelated to practical life, if not false and abhorrent to our Christian sensibilities, over which ecclesiastics fought and even convulsed the Church and the world in blood, even those forms of faith closely fit the felt need of their times and were then living realities. And the same is true of theological creeds and changes to-day: they keep pace with and express the growing facts of experience. Whenever the Church develops a new religious experience, it soon clothes it in a new credal expression.

All this is tremendous proof that religion is, not a priestly invention or superstition or dream, but a reality rooted in the very constitution of man and expressed in the universal experience of the world. The priest and the Church did not make it, but it made the priest and the Church. The Bible did not create it, but it created the Bible. God set eternity in man's heart, and out of this original constitution religion has sprung as a normal and necessary outgrowth. Man simply cannot live a worthy life without religion, and therefore he will and must have it. His heart cries out, with Augustine: "O God, thou hast made us for thyself and we cannot rest until we rest in thee."

(b) Religion being rooted in the whole constitution

of the soul thereby has roots in every one of its fundamental faculties.

It is rooted in the feelings. The feelings are the deepest if not the oldest constituent of the soul. As life descends the scale feeling persists long after intelligence has faded out, and the heart appeared in the evolution of life long before the brain. Some psychologists try to resolve intelligence into feeling and make feeling the primal constituent of the soul that afterwards developed intelligence. In their view intelligence is anticipated or forefelt feeling. However this may be, feeling appears in the infant before intelligence and remains through life as the deepest root of the soul. Religion ramifies the feelings in six forms: fear, wonder, dependence, value, obligation, and beauty.

Fear is a constitutional emotion which is one of the safeguards of life. It is a danger signal that causes us to shrink from and avoid objects and courses of conduct that threaten us with harm. It runs up through the whole scale of life. It is dominant at the bottom of this scale, but it does not fade out at the top. While many of the lower fears are overcome or outgrown, yet higher fears are developed.

Fear leads to religion when it takes the form of dread in the presence of the higher powers that govern the world, and in the highest religion it becomes the fear of the Lord. Any God that is worthy of our respect must have such a nature and such laws of character and judgment as would excite our fear when we transgress his will. There is a base fear that grovels before mere power as of a tyrant, the fear of demons that is almost the whole of many primitive forms of religion. But however enlightened souls may lose such fear, they rise into the nobler fear of God which is the beginning of wisdom. It is not a deep and strong but a shallow and irreverent soul that has no fear of God. The agnostic poet may boast that " the menace of the years finds and shall find me unafraid," [1] but this confidence must depend on one's conscience and the course of his life. If the universe means intensely and means good and is to keep our respect it must ever utter the solemn warning, " Woe to the wicked! it shall be ill with him." Only fools mock at sin and lose all sense of fear. Fear is not a high motive, but it is a true motive that urges us into religion.

There is a large truth in Herbert Spencer's theory that wonder is the persistent root of religion. The sense of mystery we experience in the presence of the universe irresistibly hushes and awes the soul with a deep emotion of reverence. We are profoundly impressed and moved with a feeling of the transcendent greatness and awfulness of the Power that produces all these glittering constellations as the sparkling dew of its breath; and this feeling never can be explained away or outgrown, as all our growth in knowledge only makes the mystery deeper and vaster. Such wonder is akin to worship and will ever be one strand that draws and binds us to God.

A still larger element of truth is embodied in Schleiermacher's theory that religion is our sense of dependence. The babe is one of the most beautiful instances of dependence in the world. It is nourished and cared for by the mother and would quickly perish if cut off from such care. Almost its first act is to cling to anything that comes in its way. We never outgrow such dependence, but it literally grows with our growth. Life ever increases in complexity by which we

[1] W. E. Henley in " Invictus."

are brought into dependence upon a wider environment and upon a greater number of human beings until our wants are supplied by millions of toilers in all lands, farmers, manufacturers, inventors, explorers, scientists, thinkers, artists, poe⁺s, workers in every field from the lowest to the highest. We also discover that we are dependent on nature, the soil and shower and sun and all the stars. We are bound by delicate cords to every atom of the universe and are dependent upon it at an infinite number of points. This sense of dependence, whether in its lowest and feeblest development or in its highest enlightenment and widest consciousness, irresistibly leads to an ultimate point of dependence, a Power that is itself independent of all change, a Rock that is higher than we, an infinite and eternal God. We cannot rest in our dependence until we feel ourselves cradled in an everlasting Arm in final security and peace. The sense of childhood is something deep and permanent and powerful in the human heart, and it cries out as an infant crying in the night and cannot be hushed or satisfied until it finds a Father. Its great cry through all the ages is, " Show us the Father and it sufficeth us."

Our sense of value is incomplete and unsatisfied until we find a final standard and perfect embodiment of worth. We have seen that we have a scale of values ascending from lower to higher worths. Such a scale must have some absolute standard and supreme worth from which it is suspended and derives its whole value. Without this final point of suspension and ultimate standard the whole scale has no real support and value and falls to the ground. Finite and temporal worth loses its chief value if there is no absolute and eternal worth of which it is a tiny copy and on which it depends for its permanent worth and sanction. And so our sense of worth logically and irresistibly runs up into our sense of worship. The two things are so closely related that, as we have seen, the names are only slightly different spellings of the same word. Our worship is our sense of the worthship of God, and any sense of worth in the world is a stepping-stone up to the high altar of the supreme worthship or worship of God.

Our sense of the obligation of worth and right is another direct stepping-stone to the same altar. The feeling that we ought to obey the right means that we owe this obedience, and duty is that which is due. The implications of such words and relations can be explained only in personal terms. We cannot owe anything to a blind law and power, but only to a Lawgiver and Person. There is a person at one end of this ethical relation and duty, and there must equally be a Person at the other end, or this powerful chain that binds us is suspended on nothing, as though the gravitation that holds the earth in its orbit were at the other end left hanging unsupported and loose in space, instead of being rooted in the sun. Conscience is a powerful witness to a supreme Lawgiver and Lord and cries out with all its might that " we ought to obey God rather than men."

Our sense of beauty or esthetic nature is another path by which our feeling finds God. The sense of beauty within us is matched and waked into music by the beauty without us that tunes the million-stringed harp of nature, or that carves and paints the world and drenches it with beauty down to its very atoms. The eye sees and the heart feels only what corresponds with the nature of the soul, and therefore our esthetic nature finds in the world an artistic essence and nature which can be the product only of an infinite Artist. Without this ultimate source, our esthetic sensibilities are an illusion without any adequate cause and satisfaction.

Thus our feelings in their various forms feel after God if haply they may find him; and they do find that he is "not far from any one of us." As long as feeling endures as a constituent element of the human soul religion will endure and men will worship.

(c) Religion is also rooted in the intellect. There has been some reaction and even revolt in recent years against the intellect as a means of finding truth and of human guidance. Pragmatism, which puts all its eggs in the basket of practical experience, discounts and disparages the human brain as an organ of knowledge and would have us rather trust the heart. No doubt there has been some ground for this distrust of reason as a reaction against the extreme philosophical intellectualism of other days, by which every thinker spun the universe out of his own head. Pragmatism has rendered good service in emphasizing anew certain old philosophical principles, such as the place and importance of experience, of the feelings and will, and of value judgments, in our cognitive processes and practical living, but it carries its reaction against the intellect too far, almost to the length of committing intellectual suicide, and then strangely keeps on talking. It is only by using reason that pragmatists can depreciate reason and defend their pragmatism.

The intellect must ever hold its place as a fundamental faculty of knowledge and as a means and guide of our life. And so our belief in God, however deeply it may be rooted in the instincts and practical needs and feelings, is also intertwined inextricably with all the filaments of the brain. It starts as a spring of instinct and feeling, but it quickly emerges into the field of thought and must be justified at the bar of reason.

The human mind cannot stop with raw experience, but must reflect upon it, penetrate into its cause, trace its consequences and elaborate it into systematic form. Man is a thinker and cannot keep his brain from sprouting; he has an organizing instinct and will not put up with a disordered world; he is an architect and artist and seeks to build all his mental products into a symmetrical and beautiful temple of thought. Hence the raw material of every field of human experience is wrought up into a science, and so we have astronomers exploring the heavens and reducing them to order, geologists turning up and deciphering the rocky leaves of the globe, chemists and physicists feeling in among the atoms of matter, and psychologists dissecting the human soul. Religion cannot escape this process, and hence we have its pyschology and theology and philosophy.

As the instincts find God as the satisfaction of their practical needs, and the feelings find him as the appropriate object of their craving, so the intellect finds God as the result of its search. It rationalizes and illuminates and confirms all these instinctive and emotional grounds and impulses of religious faith, and then it goes on to develop arguments of its own. It studies the world as it reads a book and finds God at the end of several paths or well-known arguments for the existence and personality of God.

The cosmological or causal argument finds that the world is an object of change or a manufactured product that calls for a Maker as clearly and certainly as a web of cloth or a watch. The argument from design finds the world is intelligible in every atom and is throughout a tissue of intellectual relations and ideas. The astronomer reads the heavens, which are the real astronomy, and then copies these vast pages upon the tiny pages of his book. The geologist reads the rocky leaves of the globe, and every other scientist and thinker and poet is simply seeing the thought and beauty in nature and translating them into our language. The world is thus seen to be transparent thought and we see a Mind back of it and in it as certainly and clearly as we see the mind of the author back of and in his book. The anthropological argument applies this principle to man and finds that as he also is a product he cannot rise higher than his Maker, and therefore the supreme Cause must be a Mind and Person.

These arguments, which have been written out in many volumes [1] and are ever being enlarged and illuminated by all our increasing knowledge, have been objected to as proving only a finite cause sufficient to produce a finite world. But our sense of causation cannot rest in a finite and dependent cause and can be satisfied only as we leap back of all such dependent causes to an independent and absolute Cause, or infinite and eternal God. And this general argument still stands as the result and verdict of the human mind after all its search into the nature of this world. Unless it takes more reasoning power to construe than to construct it, the universe must ever stand as a sublime appeal of Thought to thought, of a personal infinite Mind to our finite minds.

[1] A remarkably fresh statement of these arguments in the light of modern knowledge is found in *Basic Ideas in Religion* by the late Professor R. W. Micou.

We are here getting close to deep water as to the possibility of personality in an infinite being, but modern thinkers since the day of Lotze have taken care of this difficulty, and we are only concerned with the psychological fact that our mind finds the world to be a book that tells us of its Author as plainly as any human book tells us of its writer, an older bible that rolled from the hand of the Creator and bears witness to his eternal power and Godhead.[1]

The intellect also passes upon and interprets all other evidences and forms of religion, whether in the lowest pagan cults or in the highest revealed and inspired religion. And thus the intellect reaches the same divine goal as the instincts and feelings and rests in God.

(d) The will also joins with other fundamental faculties in calling for God. We are made for action, and all our faculties of instinct and feeling and thought are so many forces pushing and guiding us into conduct and achievement. But achievement must be worthy of the powers that produce it, or life ends in failure. Men instinctively hunt for great things to do, something worth while to inspire their ambition and call out their energies and crown their visions with victory and satisfy their souls. They see larger and ever larger ends reaching farther and farther into the future; and this principle finds no worthy final end and satisfaction until it runs up into the life of God and loses itself in his service and victory. The religious nature of man expresses itself, not only in instinct and

[1] For a discussion of the question of the personality of God and other points where the psychology of religion runs into metaphysics, see the author's *The World a Spiritual System: an Introduction to Metaphysics.*

feeling and thought, but preëminently in obedience and issues in appropriate and satisfying conduct and character.

All human life thus points beyond itself for its completion and satisfaction. The human soul swarms with instincts, needs, feelings, thoughts, visions, and aspirations which look beyond the present world and cry out for the Infinite and Eternal. Life that stops at the horizon of this world and at the edge of the grave is a poor and pitiful fragment, a hopeless failure, and cruel disappointment. Instinct, feeling, thought, and will feel after and fix their filaments on God and cling to him so tight they refuse to be torn loose. The whole human soul is one great cry for God that has filled all the ages, and it will never be stilled and satisfied until his fulness

> Flows around our incompleteness,
> Round our restlessness his rest.

CHAPTER IV

THE PSYCHOLOGY OF SIN

THE natural and primal relation of man to God, we must believe, was one of harmony in which filial love and obedience blended with paternal love and care into fellowship. Historically in the beginning of the race this fellowship may have been only germinal, but it contained no seeds of discord. But something happened that broke this harmony and shattered all the music of the world. The world bears universal and abundant witness that it is out of joint, a mass of wounds and woe, a scene of discord and strife. At some point a serpent crept into its garden and poisoned its life; on some fatal day occurred

> Man's disobedience and the fruit
> Of that forbidden tree, whose mortal taste
> Brought death into the world, and all our woe.

We are concerned, however, not with the historical and theological problems, but only with the psychological nature and operations, of sin. All the way through our subject, psychology deals with religion mainly on its human and subjective side; its divine objective side falls within the field of theology.

I. THE NATURE OF SIN

1. **The Biblical Idea of Sin.**—There are three leading words used in the Old Testament and three in the New that express the Biblical idea of sin.

(a) The Hebrew words are translated sin, iniquity and transgression, and they are all found in one verse, Ex. 34:7: "keeping lovingkindness for thousands, forgiving iniquity and transgression and sin." The word translated sin, *chattath*,[1] expresses "sin as *missing one's aim*. The etymology does not suggest a person against whom the sin is committed, and does not necessarily imply intentional wrongdoing. But the use of the word is not limited by its etymology, and the sin may be against man (Gen. 40:1, I Sam. 30:1) or against God (Ex. 32:33)."[2]

The word translated iniquity, *avon*,[3] means "literally 'perversion,' 'distortion.' It is to be distinguished from *chattath*[1] as being a quality of actions rather than an act, and it thus acquires the sense of guilt. Guilt may be described as the sinner's position in regard to God which results from his sin." This Hebrew word and idea of sin is closely paralleled by our English word "wrong," which is only another spelling of the word "wrung," and represents wrong as that which is wrung out of its proper shape, or out of conformity to that which is right or straight.

The word translated transgression, *pesha*,[4] expresses "a breaking away from a law or covenant, and thus implies a law and lawgiver. It implies what *chattath*[1] does not necessarily imply, namely, the voluntariness of sin."

(b) The Greek words for sin in the New Testa-

[1] חַטָּאת.

[2] This and other quotations in this connection are taken from Hastings' *Dictionary of the Bible*, article Sin.

[3] עָוֹן. [4] פֶּשַׁע.

ment exactly parallel these Hebrew words in meaning.

The word translated sin, *hamartia*,[1] like *chattath*,[2] means missing the mark and may "mean sin as a habit, a state, a power, and also a single act of sin."

The word translated iniquity, *anomia*,[3] literally means lawlessness or anarchy. "In its strict sense it truly represents the conception of sin given in the Epistles of James and John." "Sin is lawlessness" (*anomia*). I John 3:4.

The word translated transgression, *parabasis*,[4] literally means transgressing and presupposes "the existence of a law."

These Biblical words for sin thus mean missing the mark, the mark of worth and duty that one should aim at and falling below it or going beside it to some lower or other end; twisting and perverting character and conduct into a crooked thing; and transgressing the law. These ideas all imply a standard or scale of values that should be conformed to and make sin consist in missing, perverting, and transgressing it.

These ideas also all imply and run up into the idea of God as the highest mark and ultimate standard or law that one should attain. At times this final incidence and guilt of sin is in the background of consciousness, and at other times it becomes intense as the central hot spot of consciousness, as in David's cry, "Against thee, thee only have I sinned (*chata*), and done this evil in thy sight" (Ps. 51:4), though the first incidence of his sin in this case was against a fellow-man. Any violation of the moral

---

[1] *ἁμαρτία.*   [2] חַטָּאת   [3] *ἀνομία.*   [4] *παράβασις.*

law is on its human side a wrong deed or, in the case
of the violation of civil law, a crime, but viewed in
its relation to God's law it is a sin. All crimes are
sins, but all sins are not crimes.

The Biblical idea of sin is succinctly expressed in the
definition of the Westminster Shorter Catechism: " Sin
is any want of conformity unto or transgression of the
law of God."

2. The Psychological Nature of Sin.—We have already unfolded the psychological nature of sin as a
wrong choice between a higher and a lower order of
worth and obligation on the scale of value. This scale
has as its highest point and final standard the worth
and wisdom and will of God. Any choice of a lower
in the presence of a higher good is a missing of the
mark, a perversion or twisting of the right and a transgression of that law. As God's wisdom and will run
down through the whole scale, any such act of wrong
choice is explicit or implicit rebellion against him and
is sin.

The deeper question now arises as to the essence of
sin. Wherein does its essential principle consist?
What is the tap root that sprouts into all its scarlet
blossoms and bitter fruits? The question runs into
philosophy, but it also pertains to psychology. There
are three leading theories on this subject which call for
attention.[1]

(a) The first theory is that sin is sensuousness. It
is due to our animal heredity and the survival in us of
brute instincts and passions. It is of the nature of a
physical disorder and disease. It is rooted in the blood

[1] For a full discussion of these theories, see Dr. Augustus H.
Strong's *Systematic Theology*, Vol. II, pp. 559-573, and Julius
Müller, *The Christian Doctrine of Sin*, Vol. I, pp. 25-203.

and is a bondage into which we are born and from which we cannot escape.

There is an element of truth in this theory. Many of the coarser sins of the soul, such as gluttony and intemperance, ally themselves with the flesh and express themselves in and through the body. The term "flesh" in the New Testament means the carnal or fleshly nature of the soul, or the soul as allied with and rooted in the body. The soul uses the body as the instrument of many of its sins, and leaves deposits of its sins in the tissues and habits of the body until it becomes soaked and saturated with evil.

Yet this element of truth in it being granted, the main contention of the theory as to the essential nature of sin cannot be accepted. It roots evil in a material organism and is allied to the old Manichean theory that matter is essentially evil in nature. Matter in itself is neither moral nor immoral, for it has no ethical element in its constitution.

The animal also is below the plane of personal being and has no moral character. Granting that man did derive his bodily organism through evolution, yet the animal nature in the animal was not evil or in any degree moral, and therefore could not have transmitted any evil to man. The instincts and passions of man, however they may have been derived from a lower origin, did not become perverted and evil until man made them so. And further, many sins have only the slightest connection with the body. The spiritual sins of pride, envy, malice, unbelief and enmity against God are the most heinous and the deadliest, and yet they cannot be blamed on the blood. The soul cannot point to the body, as Adam pointed to Eve, saying "She did it," and say, "The beast in me did it." Con-

science contradicts this doctrine and fastens the guilt
and essence of sin on the soul itself. If this theory is
true the soul does not need a Saviour, but only the
body needs a physician. The cure for sin is a cleansing
of the blood.

(b) A second theory of the nature of sin is that it
is due to our human finiteness. It is a necessary cor-
relative of our finite moral nature as our ignorance is
of our finite intellect. There is no escaping ignorance
because every problem solved starts a hundred others
that are not solved, and thus our ignorance, so to speak,
grows faster than our knowledge. However vast the
circle of our light, vaster still is the outlying circle of
darkness which hems the light in. So our sin is the
necessary shadow that attends our finite moral nature
and we never can outgrow it or leap away from it.
" Upon this view," says Dr. Strong, " sin is the blun-
dering of inexperience, the thoughtlessness that takes
evil for good, the ignorance that puts its finger into
the fire, the stumbling without which one cannot learn
to walk. It is a fruit which is sour and bitter simply
because it is immature. It is a means of discipline and
training for something better,—it is holiness in the
germ, good in the making." This is the view of Royce
that " Evil is discord necessary to perfect harmony ";
and of Browning:

> The evil is null, is naught, is silence implying sound;
> What was good shall be good, with, for evil, so much good more.

This view also contains an element of truth, for sin is
connected with our finiteness and could not exist in an
infinite being; and it is often turned to good in God's
grace. But the fallacy of the view is that it confuses
the imperfection of the finite with the fault and guilt

of sin. It is no sin that we cannot be omniscient or that we cannot be perfect as the Infinite is perfect. Imperfection becomes sin only when it is evil in its nature.

The radical objection to this view is that it makes sin a necessary condition and activity of the soul, and it is therefore deterministic and pantheistic. In so doing it does what all determinism and pantheism do, it reduces morality to mechanism, ethics to physics, and thereby destroys its moral nature. When freedom is gone, no moral quality remains. Human wrongdoing is as necessary and unethical as the rain or wind. Such a theory explains sin by explaining it away and cutting it up by the roots, and all conscience and judgment and history unite to deny and condemn it.

(c) A third theory of sin is that it is essentially selfishness. Selfishness is to be distinguished from that self-love which is self-respect, appreciation, and affirmation of one's own worth and dignity and even rights. Such love of self is proper and necessary, for worth in the self has the same value and rights that it has in others; and unless one appreciates, develops, and guards his own worth he has nothing with which to love others. The command to " love thy neighbour as thyself " enjoins the love of self as the prior ground and means of loving one's neighbour.

But selfishness is a perversion of self-love and consists in putting the interests and possessions, pleasures and passions of the self in the centre and on the throne as the supreme principle of life. It subordinates other persons to its service as mere means to its own end; weaves other lives as threads into its own web; makes the soul wholly absorbent, so that it is a sponge sucking up everything and creating a desert around it, instead of being a fountain flinging forth streams refreshing and fertilizing other lives.

Selfishness is the essence of sin because it always chooses a lower good on the scale of value and obligation rather than a higher and the highest good, which is the perfection of social life and the perfect life of God. In thus choosing his own will man rebels against God. And it is the essence of sin because every kind of sin is a form of selfishness. The sins of the body, such as gluttony and intemperance, are all forms of personal gratification. Falsehood and dishonesty are obviously forms of selfishness. And the more spiritual sins of avarice, ambition, envy, jealousy, pride, and vanity are equally of the same nature. The most intellectual unbelief may involve a subtle element of pride of opinion and secret reluctance to obey the truth and thereby has a core of selfishness at its heart. In all their sins men miss the true mark because they aim at a lower mark of their own choosing; they pervert the right and transgress the law of God because they are seeking their own will and pleasure. It is human selfishness, then, in all its myriad manifestations and degrees, dim-eyed and blind or keen and cunning in its purpose, feeble or enormous in its power, mild or malignant in its indulgence, that turns the world into a battle-field of strife and blood and loads it with all its crushing weight of wounds and woe.

Dr. A. H. Strong quotes Dr. Samuel Harris as follows: " Sin is essentially egoism or selfism, putting self in God's place. It has four principal characteristics or manifestations: (1) self-sufficiency, instead of faith; (2) self-will, instead of submission; (3) self-seeking, instead of benevolence; (4) self-righteousness, instead of humility and reverence." Dr. Julius Müller, in his

THE PSYCHOLOGY OF SIN   111

classic work on sin, develops this view at great length
and with searching analysis. " The idol, therefore," he
says, " which man, in his sin, puts in the place of God,
can be no other than *his own self*. The individual self,
and its gratifications, he makes the highest end of his
life. His striving, in all the different forms and directions of sin, ever has self ultimately in view; the inmost
nature of sin, the principle determining, and pervading
it, in all its forms, is *selfishness*." [1]

The effect of selfishness is to crowd God out of the
heart and life. In heathendom it has been said that
"everything was God but God himself." Heinrich
Heine declared: " I am no child. I do not want a
heavenly Father any more." " I celebrate myself,"
boasts Walt Whitman. " If I worship one thing more
than another, it shall be the spread of my own body, or
any part of it." The self is a devouring demon or monster that will be satisfied with nothing less than the
world and the universe. " Every self, once awakened, is
naturally a despot, and 'bears, like the Turk, no
brother near the throne.' " Absorbing everything into
itself it becomes " that man of sin, who opposeth and
exalteth himself above all that is called God, or that is
worshipped; so that he, as God, sitteth in the temple of
God, shewing himself that he is God " (II Thess. 2:
3-4). But at the opposite pole the greatest Character
of history, " existing in the form of God, counted not
the being on an equality with God a thing to be grasped,
but emptied himself, taking the form of a servant, being
made in the likeness of men; and being in fashion as a

[1] *The Christian Doctrine of Sin*, Vol. I, p. 136. His discussion
of sin as selfishness extends through pp. 131-203; and his discussion of sin as sensuousness and as finiteness through pp. 293-
363.

man, he humbled himself, becoming obedient even unto death, yea, the death of the cross. Wherefore also God highly exalted him, and gave unto him the name which is above every name; that in the name of Jesus every knee should bow, of things in heaven and things under the earth, and that every tongue should confess that Jesus Christ is Lord, to the glory of God the Father" (Phil. 2: 6-8).

Sin therefore is not a mere negation, the absence of good, the "silence implying sound," but a positive action of the human will and heart. It is man in the act of pulling down every throne that should rule over him and assuming and asserting his own sovereignty, as Napoleon clapped the imperial crown on his own head in Notre Dame. It is man's rebellion against every principle of right and rule of authority and usurping the very throne of God.

3. **Is Sin a State of the Soul?**—A question of great practical importance and involved in some of the deepest problems of theology is whether sin consists only in conscious volitions, or whether it also inheres in states and dispositions of the soul. There are several grounds for the view that it also resides in dispositions and states.

The disposition of the soul may be something that ought not to be, a wrong or evil in itself. It misses the mark and perverts the idea of what it should be and transgresses the law of God. It is of the nature of sin and therefore it is sin.

But it may be said that it lacks the essential element of an evil choice, the choice of a lower in the presence of a higher good. The character of the soul, however, is itself the result of choice, the accumulated deposit of countless volitions which have left each one an atom of habit in the soul and thus have slowly saturated it with evil. Character is the outgrowth of one's whole past. It is the soil that has been formed by all one's action falling into it, as the loam of the forest is formed by its own leaves. In so far as this character gives birth to our wrong choices and evil deeds, it is only giving further expression to our own free will as expressed in all these past actions. Our character is only our own free will cast and crystallized into habit and disposition, and therefore we are responsible for it.

It is the common judgment of men that the disposition may be evil in itself and a state for which men are responsible. We speak of " a bad character," and apply to the disposition all the terms of responsibility and guilt. Not only so, but we do not know how to judge one's conscious volitions and acts until we know the motives and disposition out of which they spring. If a man kills another, the moral nature of the act depends on whether he did it without malice in self-defence, or out of a murderous heart in hatred and revenge. The disposition determines the nature of the act and is as certainly guilty as the conscious act itself. In judging others we always try to go below the immediate act to the heart out of which it sprung; and an evil heart, so far from excusing, aggravates guilt. If a man were not chargeable for an evil disposition, then the worse his disposition the less blameworthy for his evil deeds would he be. On this theory the worst man would be the least guilty, and this absurdity proves the premise must be wrong. The soul makes its own disposition and must answer for it.

The deeper question whether the inherited nature is depraved and guilty belongs to theology rather than to psychology, but we may point out that human nature gives every evidence of being twisted or wrung and wrong in its constitution, and it therefore misses the mark and transgresses the law of God. It begins to show its perversity as soon as it begins to act and it calls forth the universal condemnation of men as a corrupt thing. Yet we do not regard this inherited depravity and original sin as being as heinous in its nature as sinful volitions and acquired character, and theology of various schools devises means by which undeveloped racial guilt is relieved of the consequences of sin. As a broad principle sin does not become sin for which we must answer until it receives our consent, and in the consent lies the sin.

II. A Study of Sin in Action

Having seen the psychological nature of sin, let us now look at sin in action. And at this point we cannot do better than take the record of the first temptation, as set forth in the Third Chapter of Genesis, which has never been surpassed in ethical insight and analysis and is a masterpiece of psychology.

Now the serpent was more subtle than any beast of the field which Jehovah God had made. And he said unto the woman, Yea, hath God said, Ye shall not eat of any tree of the garden? And the woman said unto the serpent, Of the fruit of the trees of the garden we may eat: but of the fruit of the tree which is in the midst of the garden, God hath said, Ye shall not eat of it, neither shall ye touch it, lest ye die. And the serpent said unto the woman, Ye shall not surely die: for God doth know that in the day ye eat thereof, then your eyes shall be opened, and ye shall be as God, knowing good and evil. And when the woman saw that the tree was good for food, and that it was a delight to the eyes, and that the tree was to be desired to make one wise, she took of the fruit thereof, and did eat; and she gave unto her husband, and he did eat (Genesis 3:1-6).

Whatever view is taken of the literary form of this narrative, its ethical truth and religious value remain the same. This temptation, while as old as the first human sin, in its essential elements is as modern as the latest sin.

This concrete instance of temptation strikingly illustrates the nature of sin as we have already discovered it. The fatal act of Eve was the choice of a lower good in the presence of a higher good. The forbidden fruit was pleasant and good in itself, but in comparison and competition with the express command or the wisdom and will of God it fell infinitely below it and thereby became an evil, or wrong, or sin. It was also an act of selfishness, for by this act Eve put her own will above the will of God and her selfish gratification above the supreme good of the race.

1. Temptation Tipped with Doubt.—The temptation begins in a doubt suggested by Satan to the mind of Eve. The tempter approached her with the question, ' Yea, hath God said, Ye shall not eat of any tree of the garden?" The question seems reasonable and innocent, and yet it cunningly conceals a poisoned suggestion; for it as much as says, " Is it possible that God would be so unjust and unkind, hard-hearted and cruel as to forbid you this innocent and good thing?" The woman unsuspectingly answered that they were permitted to eat of the fruit of the trees of the garden, but that of this particular tree God had said, " Ye shall not eat of it, neither shall ye touch it, lest ye die." Then Satan made his master stroke. He gave the lie

direct to God, declaring to the woman, " Ye shall not surely die," and went on to accuse God of denying them this tree because he knew it would make them wise, even as God himself. Eve made the fatal mistake of parleying with the tempter and listening to this evil suggestion until it got rooted in her mind and she began to have a doubt as to God's wisdom and right in forbidding her to eat of the tree. Thus the entering edge of this sin, the poisoned tip of this arrow of temptation, was doubt of God. When her faith in the absolute goodness and wisdom of God faltered ever so little she was losing her balance and was ready to slip and fall. And this is still often a first step in temptation.

Doubt sometimes has a legitimate place in our intellectual and religious life, as we shall see later, but it is also often a guilty thing and is then the first step towards a fall. A man hardly ever does a wrong thing until he at least momentarily doubts that it is wrong and persuades himself that it is right. He first doubts truth and duty, righteousness and goodness, and then he can easily see wrong things in the coloured light of his own desires. If we doubt in our hearts the fundamental verities and sanctities of life, especially if we doubt God and goodness, we have weakened our faith and courage and will in our stand against temptation and are ready to slip and slide into a lower life, if not into the ditch. " As a man thinketh in his heart, so is he." The first word of psychology against temptation is, " Keep thy heart with all diligence ; for out of it are the issues of life " ; especially does it bid us have deep roots of fundamental convictions that are never shaken with doubt and can stand against every storm of temptation.

2. **Entrance of Temptation Through Sense Percep-**

tion.—" And when the woman saw that the tree was good for food." The suggestion of the first temptation, which was distrust of God, entered through the ear-gate, and this second suggestion entered through the eye-gate. All our senses are so many gates which are being assailed by a constant series of assaults; for as a temptation may be a good thing in competition with a higher good, all the countless sounds, sights, and other sensations that are ceaselessly pouring in upon us are possible temptations.

The human body is a marvellous mechanism of nerves, a harp of a million strings, and it is played upon by all the impacts upon the senses that set it vibrating in sensation. These sensations kindle in the soul ideas and feelings, desires and passions, and may set it aflame with pleasure or consume it in agony. And thus a sight or a sound, perhaps incidentally and accidentally caught on the wing, a mere flake of sensation that lights on us as we pass along, a face at a window, a whiff of odour or a strain of music floating out of an open door, a gleam of gold in a purse or the flash of a jewel on a hand, a mere word heard in a crowd, any sensation, however trivial and insignificant it may seem, may start a suggestion that tempts us, be the spark that kindles the evil nature in our hearts. And as our sensations are our most vivid and vital forms of knowledge, they cut into the very quick of the soul and draw blood, they sway us at times with sovereign power as tornadoes sweep their way through forest and city. The man with a craving for strong drink is in the grip of his appetite, the odour of the saloon as he passes by is a match to the tinder of his desire, and he is almost irresistibly taken captive by his sense of smell and becomes its pitiful victim.

And the senses are inlets, not only to temptations of sensual gratification, but also to the more refined and spiritual temptations of the soul. Ambition and pride were kindled in Eve by the suggestion of the fruit that could make her wise, and the world in all its million-fold aspects of wealth and power, position and influence, is appealing to our ambition and vanity and selfishness and dropping sparks of spiritual temptation into our hearts. Our souls are highly sensitive and absorbent to these things to which we are constantly exposed. Like men carrying packages of powder through a burning building we are loaded with explosive materials in our natures while we walk through a flaming world showering sparks upon us from every side. That the world should be so constituted may seem to us a terrible mystery and tragedy, but this is its stern reality.

3. Association Intensifies Temptation.—We next see how the first suggestion of temptation is intensified by association. The woman's mind immediately began to multiply associations around the forbidden fruit and to enhance its attractiveness. She " saw that the tree was good for food, and that it was a delight to the eyes, and that the tree was to be desired to make one wise ": three powerful suggestions giving accumulated charm and force to the temptation. " Good for food,"—sin always presents itself as good, clothes itself as an angel of light, and hardly ever does one deliberately do a wrong until he has found some justification for it and persuaded himself it is right and good.

And it was " a delight to the eyes,"—it was not only good but also beautiful, an appeal to her esthetic nature. Sin is not always coarse but may be something fine. The artistic nature in us is a fine-stringed harp

capable of exquisite music, one of the great joys of
the world, but it is also a source of danger and may be
full of discord and tragedy, as all the history of art and
artists shows.

And " to be desired to make one wise,"—this is something higher and finer still. It is an appeal to the intellectual and moral nature, to the thirst for knowledge
that has driven the human mind to such high endeavours and grand achievements, and to the very
search for wisdom that leads the soul deepest into the
meaning of life and closest to the will of God.

Thus the mind and imagination of Eve played around
and brooded over this forbidden thing. It multiplied in
her mind rich and alluring associations and kindled
ever stronger desires, hushed all the voices of duty and
danger and fear, lulled into a deeper sleep her sense of
obligation to God, laid an ever more fascinating and
fatal spell on her senses, until it obsessed her whole
soul and she was ready for the decisive deed. This is
the psychology of all deliberate sin. It is a growth.
It begins with a sense perception or with an idea which
attracts to itself all the kindred associations of the
mind that enrich and strengthen it; it weaves around
itself a web of witchery, it crowds its guilt and fatal
consequences into the background and hides all its
repulsive features in a halo of light, it roots itself in
the whole heart, and thus it decides and moves the will.
The devil is a master psychologist and knows how to
play on all the complex strings and keys of the human
heart.

And this suggests the way to resist temptation. The
inhibitory ideas and associations must be aroused and
rushed to the rescue. Lying around on the margin of
the mind in a more or less dim and dormant state are

various ideas and feelings that are opposed to the central idea that is the temptation. Just at this point lies our chief power and responsibility. We can turn our attention to these marginal ideas and intensify them so that they will take the centre of consciousness and crowd out the evil thought. If Eve had fixed her mind on the duty of loyalty to God and of trusting his wisdom and will, however strange and even unkind and cruel it seemed; if she had considered the danger that lurked in that forbidden fruit so that she would have seen that its rosy glow was as the hectic flush of a deadly fever or the gleaming fires of hell; if she had pictured the possible consequences of disobedience and seen the flaming sword shutting her from the garden, she would, like Jesus in the wilderness, have resisted the devil until he would have fled into the darkness whence he came.

The tempted soul can always arouse and marshal opposing ideas, fears of consequences and feelings of loyalty and right and duty, and thus check the insurgent temptation and drive it from the centre of attention and out of the field of consciousness. Association is just as strong a power for good as it is for evil. It can weave webs of fascination and paint pictures that will make good look attractive and evil repulsive. And when association has deep roots of faith and the fruitage of a rich mind and good life to draw from, it can marshal such forces of character and resolution as will conquer spiritual hosts of wickedness, " casting down imaginations, and every high thing that is exalted against the knowledge of God, and bringing every thought into captivity to the obedience of Christ." This is the victory that overcomes the world.

4. **The Act of Sin.**—This brings us to the decisive

act and deed of sin. " She took of the fruit thereof, and did eat." *She* did this deed. Satan did not do it for her, and the tree did not do it, the garden did not do it, her environment and circumstances did not do it, and God did not do it. And it was not her heredity that led her to do this deed, and it was not even the pleasant associations that enriched the fruit with goodness and beauty and charm that did it, but "*she* took thereof, and did eat." This deed was her own personal, individual, wilful, responsible act, and the blame of it must rest on her forever.

And so is it with every sinner and every sin. Whatever conditions of heredity and birth, training and opportunity, whatever means and motives entered into it, whatever the depraved disposition out of which it sprung, every sin is the sinner's own personal responsible act, and he cannot roll the blame of it on anybody or anything else. Of course heredity and disposition and training and circumstances do enter into and modify the degree of guilt. No two men are any more alike in their inner nature than in their outer circumstances, in their sin than in their saintliness; yet every soul commits its own sin and must bear the burden of its own guilt. ", So then each of us shall give account of himself to God."

The tendency is strong in our day to tone down the guilt of sin and resolve it into heredity and environment, or to roll it upon the social order. Bad heredity is supposed to foreordain a man to a criminal career, and the social order is held responsible for all human sins. If we were only all born of pure blood and especially if we were only placed in a just and good and beautiful social order in which we would all have comfortable homes and fine clothes and plenty to eat and little to do, we would all be good. But the history of this first sin does not bear out this rosy view. There was nothing wrong with the heredity of Eve, and the pleasant garden did not save her from falling into sin: rather it was the very occasion and temptation of her sin. All human history shows that increase of wealth is not in itself a safeguard of virtue, but is often a rank soil out which grow scarlet sins of the vilest rottenness and deepest guilt. A bad social order aggravates human ill and evil and every effort should be made to correct it, but it is not the real root and cause of human sin. Bad environment does not make evil souls so much as evil souls make bad environment. The soul is not the slave of its circumstances, but is rather their master and sits upon its own throne.

We are here face to face with the fact of the sovereignty of the human soul over its ethical life. As we have already seen, the contents of consciousness, its sense perceptions, ideas, memories, feelings, associations, are not an ungovernable flood on which the will floats rudderless and helpless, but the soul has its own rudder and engine by which it can steer and drive its boat to its own destination. It can throw its attention upon any point in its consciousness, as a searchlight can be thrown around the horizon, and wherever it falls and is fixed the idea under its light blazes up into vividness and glowing heat and power and becomes the controlling centre of the mind and life. Eve chose to magnify the attractive associations of the forbidden fruit, instead of choosing to intensify its hidden sting and poison and to emphasize and deepen her sense of the goodness and beauty and blessedness of obedience to God; and essentially the same psychological process takes place in every sinner in the act of sin. The soul

has various competitive objects in its field of consciousness, some of which it knows are of higher worth and
obligation than others; it always has the power of making its choice and fixing its attention upon one rather
than upon another, and then of multiplying and en-
hancing its associations and motives until they carry
the will as with a flood into decision and action. This
is the inescapable point of human responsibility. Psychology is severely orthodox at this point and fixes the
guilt of sin on the sinner himself.

5. The Sense of Sin.—The act of sin in an unseared
conscience is followed by the sense of sin. Immediately
after the first sin " the eyes of them both were opened,"
and they were aware of their physical and moral nakedness. A sense of guilt filled them with fear and they
hid in the garden of the Lord from the Lord of the
garden.

Sin seizes the soul with a sense of its guilt and vileness and degradation. The purer the soul the deeper
and keener this sense of the wrong and bitterness of
sin. Often the act of sin is instantly followed with an
awful sense of guilt and remorse. The soul may ago-
nize and cry out in despair. But this sense of guilt
becomes hardened through repeated acts of sin until
conscience is seared and hardened and guilt almost
ceases to be felt.

The sense of sin varies as widely in its forms and
feelings as individual souls differ in their constitution
and temperament and in all the circumstances of their
temptation and fall. Professor E. D. Starbuck made
an inductive study of " preconversion " experience by
sending out a list of questions to about two hundred
persons asking for personal details in the matter and
then tabulating the answers. He summarizes the re-

sult as follows: " There are many shades of experience in the preconversion state. An attempt at classification of them gave these not very distinct groups:—Conviction of sin proper; struggle after the new life; prayer, calling on God; doubts and questionings; tendency to resist conviction; depression and sadness; restlessness, anxiety and uncertainty; helplessness and humility; earnestness and seriousness; and the various bodily affections. The result of an analysis of these different shades of experience coincides with the common designation of this preconversion state in making the *central fact in it all the sense of sin, while the other conditions are various manifestations of this, as determined, first, by differences in temperament, and, second, by whether the ideal life or the sinful life is vivid in consciousness*. . . . The cases arrange themselves pretty naturally in two series. In the first place, they form a series as determined by temperament. There are those at one end of the line, who are thrown back on themselves, and who remain helpless, depressed and estranged from God. At the other extreme are those who reach out in the direction of the new life, who strive toward it, and pray toward it, or, if the forces which awaken the impulse toward the higher life have dawned unawares and in spite of themselves, they wilfully oppose the new influences. Between these two extremes are those who are eminently conscious of sin, but remain poised in a state of restlessness and anxiety, or who vacillate between activity and passivity. This temperamental series, that is, ranges all the way from persons, on the one hand, who are passive, to those, on the other, who are active and positive." [1]

The various experiences of sin may also be viewed or

[1] *The Psychology of Religion*, pp. 58-59.

classified with reference to the dominant object on which the sense of it fastens itself. This object may be the sinner's self as he is conscious of having violated his own sense of right and dignity and self-respect, of having polluted his own purity and marred his own worth. He is conscious of having lost his own soul, and this sting may go deep and inflict great suffering. Or the sense of sin may fasten on the fellow-man whom the sinner has wronged. The offender is then conscious of having invaded and violated the rights of another and of having wronged him in his person or property or reputation, or of having stained and corrupted his soul, and this fills him with regret and remorse.

The sense of sin, however, when it follows out its logical implications and incidences, runs up against God as the first and the final object of its transgression and wrong. The soul is conscious of having violated his law of truth and right and of having offended his justice and goodness and grace. This sense of sin against God ranges in directness and degree from a faint conception and feeling of " uneasiness in the presence of the higher powers," to revert to Professor James's phrase, to the intense consciousness that the offence against God swallows up all other aspects and consequences of sin, and the penitent soul cries out, " Against thee, thee only, have I sinned, and done evil in thy sight."

The sense of sin may also predominately fasten itself on some special idea or aspect of it. It may be conscious chiefly of its pollution, its wrong, its guilt, its remorse, or its retribution. Its pollution is the stain with which sin spoils the purity and beauty of the soul and corrupts it with its vileness. Its wrong is the fact that the soul fell below its own sense of value and obligation and chose a lower in the presence of a higher good. Its guilt is the sense of having violated the law and justice of God so as to be responsible to him. The remorse of sin is its "biting" the soul, as the word means, gnawing at its very vitals with distress and intolerable pain. The retribution of sin is the penalty paid back by it to justice as its due return. The enlightened soul may have a deep sense that its sin violates the justice of God and owes to it the satisfaction of its own penalty and pain.

This aspect of sin runs into the question of why punishment for sin is inflicted and endured, a point that goes deep into government both human and divine and may determine our doctrine of the atonement. One theory is that punishment is inflicted only as a reforming and deterrent instrument in its influence on the offender and on others. Of course punishment does have this effect, and this is one of its incidental objects; but it is not its direct and main end. The direct ground of punishment is the ill desert of sin and its direct object is the satisfaction of the justice it has violated. This is intuitively perceived and felt by the conscience as the ultimate fact in the nature of law and justice. To punish a man to deter him or others from wrong acts not yet committed is itself an act of injustice. It is doing wrong in the hope that right may result, evil that good may come, and this is a self-contradictory principle that never can be justified. Punishment is just only when it is inflicted as the due desert of sin, and then it may act as a reforming and deterring influence on the individual and in society as its indirect result and aim.

Instances are not infrequent of men that have committed sin, which was covered up and forgotten, and

that afterwards led lives of respectability and success.
But the hidden sin kept burrowing and gnawing deep
in their souls, burning them as a pent-up fire and tor-
menting them as flames of hell. A sense of their guilt
and just desert of retribution gave them no rest, until
at length they unbosomed themselves in public confession and not only exposed their guilt but asked and
demanded punishment as their just retribution and
satisfaction to human and divine justice. The human
heart is tremendously orthodox at this point and often
insists on paying the price and penalty of sin, however
bitter it may be.

Literature bears abundant witness to this solemn
fact. Victor Hugo gives a memorable instance of it in
Jean Valjean, Greek tragedy voices its inexorability, fiction and poetry, drama and painting portray it in
powerful forms and vivid colours, and from a cross on
Calvary floats a voice declaring, in the agony of death,
"And we indeed justly; for we receive the due reward
of our deeds." Retributive justice is an essential element in the divine nature, a foundation stone of the
throne of the universe. " Be not deceived; God is not
mocked: for whatsoever a man soweth, that shall he
also reap."

6. The Enslavement and Contagion of Sin.—Sin follows the law of habit. A wrong choice tends to repeat
itself. An evil deed leaves a network of associations in
the mind, and on the next occasion of temptation this
network revives its tendency and power and lures or
drags the soul back into the same deed. Repetition
grows into a habit, and one habit associates itself with
others and grows into a system of habits or character.
Evil acts and habits also react on the nature of the
soul, leaving a deposit of evil in the heart, and this

process goes on until the whole soul is stained and saturated with evil and hardened into an evil disposition. Conscience slowly loses its sensitiveness and becomes seared and can in time consent to the wickedest or vilest deeds without compunction. Men thus become "wise to do evil," "hardened sinners," and "dead in trespasses and sins."

As every one sees the world through his own soul so that he sees things not only as they are but also as he is, when one is soaked and corrupted with any form of evil, such as avarice or lust, everything stirs this evil nature in him, and finally he sees the whole glorious universe, which to the good and beautiful soul is only a scene of divine purity and splendour, as a hideous mass of corruption.

The soul is thus enslaved in bondage that may be more binding and bitter than prison bars or slave-driver's lash. The worst master any one can have over him is an evil disposition within him. A spirit of consuming egoism and selfishness, or of irritability and evil temper, or of suspicion and jealousy and hatred and malice, blinds and binds the soul as in a prison cell. Evil habits become the most galling chains that strong crying and tears cannot break. No slavery is so dreadful as that of a nature saturated with sin and bound with evil habit. Many a man beats against the prison bars of his own soul and cries out in his despair, "O wretched man that I am! who shall deliver me from the body of this death?" And yet this terrible imprisonment does not excuse him from responsibility for his condition, for it is the outgrowth and fruitage of his repeated acts of free choice, and he is simply eating of the fruit of his own doings.

While sin is enslaving to the self it is also contagious

to others. The woman " gave also unto her husband,
and he did eat." And Adam, having caught the infection, immediately showed the working of sin in himself.
He became adept at excusing himself and blaming
somebody else. " And the man said, The woman whom
thou gavest to be with me, she gave me of the tree, and
I did eat." He took fifteen words to tell what the
woman had done and only three words to tell what he
had done. The self-deception of sin at once began to
blind the soul, and the art of blaming others was born
full-grown and expert into the world. Thus the contagion of sin infected the race at the fountain head
and started its virus coursing down the veins of all
succeeding generations.

   That sin is catching is one of the most obvious facts
of the world. The human soul is intensely social and
absorbent and readily gives and receives both good and
evil. An evil state in one heart begets a like evil state
in another heart by a process of induction or suggestion. Language is a living stream of communication
which transmits thoughts, feelings, states and deeds
and habits from one person to another; and all actions,
gestures, tones of the voice, play of the features and
glances of the eye are subtle channels of transmission
from one soul to another. The whole contents of the
soul may thus pour in a flood into another soul and
fill it with its good or evil. A word, a touch, an expression of the face or eye may be the infection by
which one soul poisons and pollutes another. All social
institutions and means of instruction recognize this
contagion of evil, and many precepts and proverbs in
all languages warn against it. " Evil communications
corrupt good manners." We warn our children against
evil companions and try to guard them against all evil

infection. Particular kinds of evil may run in families, or communities, or races, and some families, such as the " Jukes " family, have become notorious for the bad character transmitted and bred from generation to generation. Evil gravitates to and generates in the slums of cities, and particular places become breeding grounds and plague spots of sin and crime. Saloons and dens of vice are pests that spread their evil contagion abroad and poison whole neighbourhoods and infect the very air.

Thus sin is a terrible power that enslaves the sinner and a highly contagious disease that spreads through society and has infected the whole of humanity. The prophet Isaiah's diagnosis of his own nation applies to all the world: " Ah, sinful nation, a people laden with iniquity, a seed of evil-doers, children that are corrupters! . . . From the sole of the foot even unto the head there is no soundness in it; but wounds, and bruises, and putrifying sores " (Isaiah 1: 4, 6).

III. Is the Sense of Sin Declining?

This question is usually answered in the affirmative. The pulpit proclaims the fact of such decline, religious newspapers and magazines publish it, and people generally affirm and feel it. What can be said as to this evident change?

1. **Abatement of the General Sense of Fear.**—There has been an abatement of the general sense of fear. In ancient times it was believed that the world swarmed with evil demons that lurked in every object, waiting and watching to seize their human victims. They infested every forest, hovered over every path and hid behind or within every stone, and were the cause of dis-

ease and of every disaster, such as fire and flood, and of every individual misfortune. This is still the prevailing belief among primitive people, such as savages, and in some heathen countries, such as China, and it fills the world with fears and makes life a constant terror. Science has swept these demons out of the world and made it a safe place. It has also removed or relieved many other fears, such as witches and ghosts, and has cleared up the apparent confusion and caprice of nature into law and order. All this has greatly abated fear and increased the sense of security and life has lost much of its mystery and dread.

This decline of fear in general has had some effect in abating the fear of sin. Men have connected religious fear with these fears that have vanished and think that it may be only another false alarm and not so serious after all. They may feel that it is a childish weakness to fear sin and declare that they refuse to be caught and cowed by this religious ghost.

> Beyond this place of wrath and tears
> Looms but the Horror of the shade,
> And yet the menace of the years
> Finds and shall find me unafraid.

Yet on what meat have men been feeding that they have grown so great as to outgrow fear? Do they not still fear fire and flood and disease and is not fear a fundamental fact and safeguard of our life at a thousand points? And if we experience and are governed by fear on the lower levels of life, why not on the higher? If human justice is a true ground of fear to evil-doers, is there not an infinitely greater ground to fear the justice and judgment of Almighty God? There is much to justify the general abatement of fear and this has relieved our life of much terror and has blessed it, but we go too far and rebound to an opposite extreme and will surely run into ruin if we eliminate the fear of sin and treat it as a light thing. " The fear of the Lord is the beginning of wisdom."

2. Reaction Against Extreme Views of Hell.—There has been a decided reaction against extreme views of hell. The old view of hell was that it was a literal lake or furnace of fire in which the lost forever burned and raved in physical agony. The horrible scenes portrayed in Dante's *Inferno* expressed the literal belief of the Middle Ages, and the terrible illustrations supplied to the poem by Doré have given further expression to the same view. This doctrine has passed out of our theology and preaching. It is not supported by a true understanding of Scripture and is intolerable to our views of God. Reaction against one extreme nearly always swings to another, and this has taken place at this point. The flames of hell have almost died out in the pulpit. Only sensational evangelists now preach them in lurid rhetoric, and even they are not taken seriously by the audiences that listen to them with scarcely concealed incredulity and with lightness of mind that in the midst of such discourses is ready to ripple into a smile or break into laughter.

This change in the form in which the doctrine of future punishment is held and preached has undoubtedly abated the sense of sin. Men do not fear spiritual retribution as they did literal flames. The modern hell is sometimes represented as a quite tolerable if not a comfortable and respectable place, and men are not inclined to take it seriously. In passing from one form of a doctrine to another there is always danger of losing something in the transition, and it takes time to realize that a spiritual hell may be as terrible as a lake of fire.

3. **Changed Views of the Character of God.**— Changed views of the character of God have also affected our sense of sin. The old theology and modes of preaching painted God in terrible colours. In his famous sermon on " Sinners in the Hands of an Angry God," Jonathan Edwards addresses sinners in the following language: " The God that holds you over the pit of hell much as one holds a spider or some loathsome insect over the fire, abhors you, and is dreadfully provoked; His wrath towards you burns like fire; He looks upon you as worthy of nothing else but to be cast into the fire; He is of purer eyes than to bear you in His sight; you are ten thousand times as abominable in His eyes, as the most hateful and venomous serpent is in ours." Jonathan Edwards believed in the literal reality of this dreadful picture and his audience believed in it, and this fact gave the sermon its terrible power. People cried out and fell down upon the floor under its awful judgments. But such a sermon would not be preached in any enlightened Christian pulpit to-day. It is a libel on God. A change of climate has come over our views of God and we think of him as the Father of our spirits and a God of mercy and love.

The modern view is nearer Scripture teaching and is truer to the God and Father of our Lord Jesus Christ, but like other reactions against extremes it is in danger of going too far and giving us a soft and indulgent Father who will not deal with sin severely. According to this conception, God is too kind and courteous to hurt us, too polite to punish us. Some hold that " God is too good to punish sinners and sinners are too good to be punished," and any such view will greatly weaken the sense of sin. Huxley revolted against the soft sentiment which " represents Providence under the guise of a paternal philanthropist " and thought the old theologians were " vastly nearer the truth than the ' liberal ' popular illusions " because they " recognize the realities of things." [1]

4. **Changed Views of Sin Itself.**—Sin itself has received some explanations that explain it away. One such theory denies the fact of sin outright, and declares that it is wholly a delusion of the mind and that the simple way to get rid of it is to forget it. This theory goes to pieces on the sharp and terrible rocks of reality. Any pantheistic or deterministic theory of the world cuts up sin by the roots and reduces it to pure mechanism and necessity so that it is no more a guilty choice and act than the growth of grass or the fall of a stone, and such views have been popularized in much of our literature. Socialism is predominately materialistic and deterministic in its underlying philosophy and it is being widely diffused. Many have also largely resolved sin into heredity and environment and a wrong social order. Man is doomed to be bad by his bad birth. Society soaks his soul in the slums, and how, then, can it expect him to be good? Unjust poverty and the dire necessity of hunger drive men to lie and steal and thereby render virtue a physical impossibility. Adam blamed his sin on Eve, Eve blamed it on the serpent, and thus was started this theory of rolling sin off on the environment and the social order. Sin thus becomes a misfortune and not a fault, and the sinner is a victim and not an offender. He has not done wrong, but wrong has been done to him. He does not owe

[1] See *The World a Spiritual System,* p. 277.

penitence to God, but God owes him an apology. As
Omar Kháyyám expresses it:

> O Thou, who Man of Baser Earth didst make,
> And even with Paradise devise a Snake,
>   For all the Sin wherewith the Face of Man
> Is blackened—Man's forgiveness give—and take!

Or as poor James Thomson in his " City of Dreadful
Night " expresses it more boldly if not blasphemously:

> Who is most wretched in this dolorous place?
>   I think myself; yet I would rather be
>   My miserable self than He, than He
> Who formed such creatures to His own disgrace.

These pantheistic and deterministic views have per-
colated deeply and widely through our literature and
life, and more than any other cause they have weakened
our sense of sin.

The counteractive to this error is the appeal to and
affirmation of our intuitional conscience in our immediate and ineradicable sense of free agency and responsibility and guilt in connection with our sin, a responsibility that is affirmed in all the laws and is
reflected in all the literature of the world and that
rolls its solemn voice through all the ages.

5. **Our Modern Life Less Subjective and More Objective.**—There has been in our day a marked change in
the nature of our life. In former days life was more
introspective and subjective. People were more conscious of themselves and grew meditative and morbid.
They looked within and worked much with their in-
wards. They indulged much in self-examination. They
held fast days when they shut out the world, reduced
their bodily life to its lowest limits, and intensified

their consciousness of their souls. Sin was a dominant fact in this introspection, the burning centre of their self-consciousness. They deepened and darkened their sense of guilt and agonized over their sin. Religious literature was largely devotional and meditative, and such books as Bunyan's *Pilgrim's Progress,* Jeremy Taylor's *Holy Living* and his *Holy Dying,* Baxter's *Saints' Everlasting Rest,* and Doddridge's *Rise and Progress of Religion in the Soul* were the popular religious books of their day. The preaching partook of the same character and turned the gaze of the hearers inward upon their own spiritual condition.

Our life has become predominantly objective. We live in a unified world which has become a vast amphitheatre where the drama of humanity is being played before our eyes. We all hold reserved seats in this theatre and see all that is going on. Book and daily newspaper and illustrated magazine, telephone and telegraph and wireless communication, have brought the ends of the earth together, and everything of any importance and countless things of no importance happening anywhere are thrown on the screen before us in a moving-picture show that is giving a continuous performance. As a result we are absorbed in our senses. The heavens are full of shooting stars and, while looking at one wonder, we are distracted by another. We have little time and disposition to look within because of the great, chaotic, noisy, booming world without. We live in a riot of the senses and are too excited to think. Our literature is emotional and sensational, and our newspapers scream at us in red-letter headlines from two to four inches deep. Even the pulpit in many instances turns itself into a platform on which some kind of a performance is going on to draw and hold an audience, and travelling evangelists take to extemporized tents and tabernacles in which the wildest sensationalism is often the chief attraction.

Meditation is thus becoming a lost art. People are always craving a crowd and itching for a new thrill. They seek excitement in society and shun solitude. They have meagre inner resources and little comfort and contentment in themselves. We are losing acquaintance with ourselves and may become such strangers to our own souls that we would hardly recognize them on the street. In such a world, to which we are not yet adjusted, we are losing much that is valuable and fine out of our inner life, and our sense of sin is being submerged and swept away in this flood of external excitement.

There is much that is good in this objective life, but we are swinging to a dangerous extreme and need to return to and restore the inner life. The inner must balance the outer, or life will lack depth and proportion and poise, and be one-sided and shallow, feverish and fretful. There must be inner roots of conviction deepened by self-examination and meditation in order that there may be a strong and fruitful outer life. The Delphic oracle was wise enough to enjoin upon the seeker after the secret of life, " Know thyself," and we are in special need of the same admonition and practice in our day. Such self-knowledge will bring us face to face with our sin and convince and convict us of our guilt and drive the sense of sin deep into our souls.

6. Increased Emphasis on the Positive Side of Life. —Increased emphasis is now being placed on the positive side of life. There are two ways of controlling ourselves and moving men to action: the negative way of checks and fears, and the positive way of active im-

pulses and hopes. The one intensifies inhibitory ideas and motives, and the other stresses positive motives and ends. The one cries out, " Woe to the wicked; it shall be ill with him "; and the other proclaims, " Say ye to the righteous, that it shall be well with him." The one holds back, and the other draws forward. The one emphasizes retribution, and the other holds up reward. The one points to hell, and the other to heaven. Both of these means and motives are proper and should be used in their due proportion.

Now in former days the chief stress was put on restraint and fear, but in our day it has shifted to action and hope. Men are now more aroused and governed by hope than by fear, by reward than by retribution. They want to be energized to do something positive and not simply checked and held back. They are lured and inspired by great visions that can be turned into victories and have small concern simply in avoiding danger and disaster, even the traps of Satan and the pit of hell.

The preaching of to-day reflects this changed attitude. Its dominant emphasis is put upon positive doctrine and deeds rather than upon negative restraints. It preaches the great things of the gospel, the personality and character of God, the Saviourhood of Christ, the greatness of the kingdom of God, the worth of life, the blessedness of service and sacrifice, and the crown of life that fadeth not away. Of course the guilt and ruin and bitter fruits of sin are also preached, as they ought to be, but the purity and peace and power of righteousness are preached more. Salvation is made to overshadow sin, and good to crowd out evil. Men can be interested more in doing right than in not doing wrong. They are urged to gird themselves up as strong men to

run a race, not to escape enemies, but to win a prize.
This is good psychology, for the way to get evil out of
the soul is to crowd good in, but this change has had
the effect in some degree of drawing our consciousness
off from sin and concentrating it on righteousness.

7. **A Broader and Finer Ethical Sense.**—The picture
on which we have been looking is growing less dark and
increasingly taking on brighter colours. In the midst
of these ominous conditions and changes we are developing a broader and finer ethical sense. While some
things that in former days were regarded as deep sins,
such as dancing, cards, and the theatre, are losing their
darker aspects and are fading out into general toler-
ance if not acceptance among Christian people, other
things that former generations did not consider wrong
are now pressing on our conscience as grave social sins.
Slavery, once thought right and even defended as a
divine institution, is now branded as " the sum of all
villainies." Gambling, once a gentleman's game, is
now banished from most respectable circles. Intemperance, once indulged in without social or religious
disapproval, is now a grave sin and scandal.

Significant also is the growth of conscience in the
political, business and industrial worlds. Politics is
undoubtedly subject to higher ethical standards than
in former days and is growing cleaner and more hon-
ourable. Public opinion appears to be growing purer
and more powerful. Business and industrial legislation is making constant progress along ethical lines.
Railroad rebates, given or extorted only a generation
ago without any one questioning them, are now pro-
hibited by law as social crimes. Monopolies and trusts
are also now regarded as unjust and are forbidden by
law. A great body of legislation is growing up regu-

lating child labour, the labour of women, the hours of labour, protection from dangerous machinery and unsanitary conditions, compensation for injuries and related matters, all of which mark and measure progress in social conscience. While individual conscience at some points is growing less tender, social conscience is growing more sensitive and imperative.

The sense of truth is growing finer and more exacting. We feel more the obligation to reach reality at any cost and not be governed by tradition or public opinion or partisan or personal interest. The church is being held to stricter account for the character and conduct of its members, and there is an increasing insistence that Christian profession be matched with practice. The scientific spirit of truth-seeking is pervading the intellectual realm and the Christian spirit of brotherhood is being diffused through social life from top to bottom.

Broader and more hopeful still, there is developing a world consciousness and a world conscience. The world, once broken into dissevered and constantly warring fragments, has grown into unity and is forming a court of world morality in which its ethical sense is steadily moving up the scale of worth and obligation. Humanity is beginning to realize its brotherhood and to speak on international questions with a majestic voice. And this is true in the face of the present world war, which is giving a mighty impulse to the growing world consciousness and conscience, and which may be one of the last dreadful convulsions of the whole insanity of war. At any rate, there is a growing conscience against war which was scarcely felt five centuries or even one century ago, and the world appears to be moving towards the long dreamed-of " parliament

of man and federation of the world." And thus conscience is developing a broader and finer sense, and
this immensely hopeful fact is to be placed to the credit
side of this account.

8. The Terrible Fact of Sin Remains.—The final fact
on this subject is that notwithstanding the sense of sin
has declined at some points and in some ways, the terrible reality of sin remains. Some of these conditions
that have dulled the sense of sin are reactions against
the extremes of other days, and the pendulum is bound
to swing back and rest nearer to the normal middle
position; others are less serious than they seem, and
still others are a positive gain. But in and through
them all the fact of sin has not been removed or shaken.
The soul is aware of its own transgression and guilt
and all the multitudinous seas cannot wash out this
stain. No self-deception can permanently blind the
soul to its guilt, no false theory can explain it away.
Conscience cries out against itself, and its voice cannot be hushed. Sin is still a frightful fact in the
world. It writes its ruin in vice and crime, in individual murder and in the colossal convulsions of war,
in all human selfishness and cruelty, trials and tears,
sufferings and sorrows, broken hearts and lost souls.
It is the awful tragedy of the universe. Only fools
mock at it. Angels weep over it, and the Son of God
gave himself as a sacrifice to atone for its guilt. Its
retribution cannot be escaped. Hell cannot be dug
out of the universe or its fires be put out. God's justice never slumbers or sleeps. He cannot overlook sin
and be a respectable God. The integrity of the universe
will not tolerate it. God will not let it mock him, and
it is still an eternal law of life that the wages of sin is
death.

We should not, then, let our sense of sin be lulled into indifference and dulness and drowsiness, but we should arouse it and keep it alive and alert, and the prophets and preachers of the age should cry aloud and spare not.

CHAPTER V

THE PSYCHOLOGY OF CONVERSION

THE shadows of sin have swathed the world in gloom and doom, but there is light that can break through this cloud and at length roll it away from the individual soul and, in an increasing degree, from the world. Sin is terrible bondage and bitterness, but its power can be broken. Conversion is the human side of regeneration, as regeneration is the divine side of conversion. Theology studies regeneration, which is prior to and conditions conversion, and psychology studies conversion only as a human experience.

I. The Nature of Conversion

Conversion is a turning from one state to another, as the word means. The soul has a general capacity for such change. However it may be predisposed by native disposition and determined by choice and crystallized in character and hardened in conduct by habit, its state is never fixed and final, but it may be, slowly or suddenly, changed and modified, revolutionized and reconstructed, melted down and recast into a new disposition and life. In this plasticity of the soul lie the hope and power of conversion.

We commonly think of conversion as a purely religious change, but it may also take place at other levels of thought and feeling or in other fields of life.

143

Every one has changing moods from grave to gay, from deep depression and pessimism to exultant hope and jubilant optimism, or one's life may encounter a crisis and ever after flow in a different channel, and such changes are of the nature of conversion.

1. Conversion in the Non-Religious Field.—Literature affords notable instances of non-religious conversions that throw some light on our subject.

(a) An interesting case occurred in the life of Carlyle. He was a man of violent moods and fits and experienced many changes of emotional level. When he had finished the second volume of *The French Revolution*, he lent the manuscript to John Stuart Mill, who in turn lent it to another friend. This friend, after reading the absorbing story far into the night, left the manuscript on his study table, and the housemaid the next morning, hunting around for something to start the fire with, found the loose heap of paper, and so it went up in the flames, like the French Revolution itself. When the fatal news was told to Carlyle he was staggered by the heavy blow and sat disconsolate in his despair for many days. One morning, while sitting by his open window brooding over his misfortune, he happened to see, across acres of London roofs, a man working on a brick wall. Patiently the workman laid brick after brick, affectionately tapping each one with his trowel and all the while singing blithe as a lark. "And in my spleen," says Carlyle, "I said within myself, 'Poor fool, how canst thou be so merry under such a bile-spotted atmosphere as this, and everything rushing into the region of the inane.' And then I bethought me and said, 'Poor fool, thou, rather, that sittest here by the window whining and complaining!'" And he arose and washed his face and "felt his head anointed " and went to work, and presently *The French Revolution* was finished again.

The incident is a fine instance of the contagion of unconscious influence, for that humble bricklayer unwittingly infected Carlyle with his happy spirit of toil and lifted him out of his despondency and helped to write that literary masterpiece. But the profound change that Carlyle experienced illustrates the nature of conversion. The expulsive power of a new interest excited by a contagious personality entered his life and made him a new man.

(b) A similar but somewhat deeper change occurred in the life of John Stuart Mill himself. Mill had been brought up by an agnostic father protected against religious influences. When he was twenty years old he fell into deep despondency of which he gives an account in the wonderfully interesting chapter in his *Autobiography* entitled " A Crisis in My Mental History." " I was in," he says, " a dull state of nerves, such as everybody is occasionally liable to; unsusceptible to enjoyment or pleasurable excitement; one of those moods when what is pleasure at other times becomes insipid or indifferent; the state, I should think, in which converts to Methodism are when smitten by their first ' conviction of sin.' In this frame of mind it occurred to me to put a question directly to myself: ' Suppose that all your objects in life were realized; that all changes in institutions and opinions which you are looking forward to could be completely effected at this very instant: would this be a great joy and happiness to you?' And an irrepressible self-consciousness distinctly answered, ' No!' At this my heart sank within me: the whole foundation on which my life was constructed fell down. All my happiness was to have been found in the continual pursuit of this end. The end had ceased to charm, and how could there ever again be any interest in the means? I seemed to have nothing left to live for. . . . I frequently asked myself, if I could, or if I was bound to go on living, when life must be passed in this manner. I generally answered to myself, that I did not think I could possibly bear it beyond a year. When, however, not more than half of that duration of time had elapsed, a small ray of light broke in upon my gloom. I was reading, accidentally, Marmontel's *Memoires,* and came to the passage which relates his father's death, the distressed position of the family, and the sudden inspiration by which he, then a mere boy, felt and made them feel that he could be everything to them—would supply the place of all they had lost. A vivid conception of the scene and its feelings came over me, and I was moved to tears. From this moment my burden grew lighter. The oppression of the thought that all feeling was dead within me was gone. I was no longer hopeless: I was not a stock or a stone. I had still, it seemed, some of the material out of which all worth of character, and all capacity for happiness, are made."   A little later he read Wordsworth for the first time and " I found," he says, " that he too had had similar experience to mine; that he also had felt that the first freshness of youthful enjoyment of life was not lasting; but that he had sought for compensation, and found it, in the way in which he was now teaching me to find it. The result was that I gradually, but completely, emerged from my habitual depression, and was never again subject to it." [1]

This experience also illustrates conversion. The en-

---

[1] *Autobiography,* Chapter V.

trance into Mill's depressed soul of a new interest caught from other personalities profoundly changed the level and course of his life.

(c) Reference may be made in this connection to those abnormal changes known as alternating and multiple personalities. Many instances are on record of persons that were subject to a sudden change of consciousness in which they were virtually different persons from their former state. Professor James in his *Psychology* relates a number of these cases and gives an account of a notable instance that came under his own study. On January 17, 1887, Rev. Ansel Bourne, of Greene, R. I., drew some money from a bank in Providence and boarded a street car, and was then entirely lost to his friends for two months. Two weeks after his disappearance a man calling himself A. B. Brown opened a small stationery and fruit store in Norristown, Pa., which he conducted six weeks, when he woke up one morning in a fright and called the people of the house to tell him where he was. He gave his name as Ansel Bourne and knew nothing of his store-keeping, his memory going back to his drawing money from the Providence bank. He had lived as an entirely different person during these two months, having no knowledge of his former life and exciting among the people with whom he lived and dealt no suspicion that there was anything abnormal about him.

In some cases three or four of these multiple persons are lying dormant in the same consciousness, and they alternate from one to another. Professor James supposes that there are different and independent sets of association paths in the brain and that a change of personality is caused by switching from one of these to another, a theory that leaves unexplained the great

difficulty of how the brain, having developed one set
of association paths, could suddenly flash into another.
The whole subject of these abnormal states and changes
is full of puzzles and of mystery.[1] But they illustrate
the possibility of profound changes that go down to
the roots of personality, and throw a vivid light on the
saying of the prophet Samuel to Saul, "Thou shalt be
turned into another man" (I Samuel 10:6).

2. **Conversions in the Religious Field.**—Religious
conversions are so common that only several striking
cases need be cited.

(*a*) Tolstoy underwent a profound change from the
life of a man of wealth and the world to that of a
deeply if somewhat morbidly pious man. His story as
told in *My Confession* is one of the marvels of religious
literature. At fifty years of age he found himself in
the midst of a happy family with his wife and children surrounded with all the comfort and luxury of
wealth and at the height of literary fame. Yet the
feeling crept into his heart that all was vanity and
vexation of spirit. " I was like a man," he says, " lost
in a forest, and who, terrified by the thought that he is
lost, rushes about trying to find a way out, and, though
he knows each step leads him still farther astray, cannot help rushing about. It was this that was terrible.
And to get free from this horror, I was ready to kill myself." For months the great soul groped around in this
darkness until there broke through it a single gleam of
light in the thought that God exists. " ' He is,' I said to
myself. I had only to admit that for an instant to feel
that life re-arose in me, to feel the possibility of existing
and the joy of it. Then, again, from the conviction of
the existence of God, I passed to the consideration of

[1] See James's *Psychology*, Vol. I, pp. 373-401.

our relation toward Him, and again I had before me the triune God, our Creator, who sent His Son, the Redeemer. Again, this God, apart from me and from the world, melted before my eyes as ice melts; again there was nothing to do but to kill myself, while, worst of all, I felt also that I should never do it." But when he would relapse from his faith the thought " There is no God " became intolerable to him, until he rested in his final faith. " God is life," he said. " Live to seek God, and life will not be without God. And stronger than ever rose up life within and around me, and the light that then shone never left me again. . . . When and how this change in me took place I could not say. As gradually, imperceptibly as life decayed in me, till I reached the impossibility of living, till life stood still, and I longed to kill myself, so gradually and imperceptibly I felt the glow and strength of life return to me." [1]

Thus a life that was thoroughly saturated and crystallized in worldliness underwent a profound reconstruction; yet the process took place gradually; and back underneath it all was the early orthodox training of Tolstoy that furnished the subconscious soil out of which this change grew.

(b) One of the most remarkable books in the literature of conversion is Harold Begbie's *Twice-Born Men*. It contains accounts of nine conversions which occurred in the slums of London by which men of the lowest and vilest degradation were thoroughly converted into the cleanness and liberty of the Christian life. In his Preface the author says: "Here in this little book, which tells the story of a few humble and quite commonplace human beings, is such astonishing psychology

[1] *My Confession,* pp. 18-19, 56-58.

as must surely bewilder the metaphysician, the social reformer, the criminologist, the theologian, and the philosopher; and it is unearthed, and brought to the surface of observation, this incredible psychology, from a single quarter of the city, from a few shabby streets huddled together on the western edge of the metropolis, forming a locality of their own, calling themselves by a particular name, and living almost as entirely aloof from the rest of London as Cranford from Drumble." Every one of the cases recorded in this book is such a profound change in a human personality that it shows that no human being can be so degraded and soaked in sin that he cannot be converted and restored to newness of life.

A single one of these cases is here condensed from several paragraphs of the story. A Salvation Army adjutant " had seen many of the lowest and most depraved people in London, but until she saw Old Born Drunk never had she realized the hideousness and repulsive abomination to which vice can degrade the human body. This man, the child of frightfully drunken parents, had been born in drink, and was almost certainly, as his name declared, actually born drunk. He had been taught to drink and had acquired an insatiable appetite for drink in earliest childhood. He was now, at the age of five- or six-and-forty, habitually drunk. The vileness of his clothing and the unhealthy appearance of his flesh did not strike the adjutant till afterwards. Her whole attention was held in a kind of horror by the aspect of the man's eyes. They were terrible with soullessness. She racks her brain in vain to find words to describe them. She returns again and again to the word *stupefied*. That is the word that least fails to misrepresent what no lan-

guage can describe. Stupefied! Not weakness, not
feebleness; not cunning, not depravity; but stupor.
They were the eyes of a man neither living nor dead;
they were the eyes of nothing that had ever lived or
could ever die—the eyes of eternal stillborn stupor.
These eyes were hardly discernible, for the flaccid lids
hung over the pupils, and the bagged flesh of the swol-
len white face pressed upon them from below. There
was just a disk of glazed luminosity showing in each
dwindled socket—a disk of veiling existence, perishing
life, of stupor. For the rest he was a true Miserable,
lower than anything to be found among barbarous nations, debased almost out of humanity. He was short,
thick-set, misshapen, vile; clothed in rags which suf-
focated those who blundered near to him—a creature
whom ragged children mocked with scorn as he passed
down the street."

In a Salvation Army meeting he came forward and
cried out, " Oh, I want to be like Joe!"—one of the
men who had testified. Afterwards he gave this account
of what happened at that meeting: " While I was
listening to Joe, thinking of what he's been, and seeing
what he's become, all of a sudden it took me that I'd
find God and get Him to make me like Joe. It took me
like that. I just felt, all of a sudden, *determined* to
find God. *Determined!*" he repeated, with energy astonishing in this broken and hopeless creature of
alcoholism. " And while I was kneeling, while I was
praying, I felt the spirit of God come upon me. I said,
' Oh, God, make me like Joe!' and while I prayed, I
felt the Spirit come upon me. I *knew* I could become
like Joe. I know I'm saved."

A life tested by fierce temptations cunningly devised
by his old companions proved the reality and perma-

nence of this conversion. "This once ruined creature was now happy and whole. His conversion appeared so extraordinary to the people in the neighbourhood, extraordinary in its lastingness as well as in its effects, that he became a power for righteousness without exerting any missionary zeal. People looked at him in the streets. Vicious and degraded men at street corners, or at doors of public-houses, regarded the old man, born again and living in respectability and happiness, with something of the same stirring in their brains as once had made him exclaim, ' I want to be like Joe.' He advertised salvation." [1]

In this conversion we see illustrated the degradation of sin, the hope kindled by a new ideal and the power of determination in the human will.

(c) The most remarkable conversion in the history of Christianity is that of Paul. He was a Jewish lawyer and Roman citizen, educated in Greek and Hebrew learning, and a man of powerful intellect, fiery emotions, and indomitable will. His whole nature was fused in the burning focus of his consciousness and flowed forth in a molten stream. He was a Hebrew of the Hebrews, an intense zealot in the religion of Moses. At the appearance of Christianity he violently opposed it and went about trying to suppress it by the slaughter of its followers. In his view Jesus was a false prophet and the greatest heretic and most dangerous man that ever lived. If ever a man was set in his way, unified and compacted and fused in his whole nature and life, that man was Saul of Tarsus. Yet suddenly, while on the way to Damascus to persecute Christians, under a noonday sky a flash of light blinded him and he heard the voice of Jesus and was instantly con-

[1] *Twice-Born Men*, Chapter IV.

verted from the bloody persecutor to the apostle of faith who turned the world upside down.

There may have been a deep psychological preparation for this sudden change. Saul knew something of the life and teachings of Jesus, and he was present at the stoning of Stephen and the wonderful bearing of that martyr may have left some impression in his subconscious mind. We cannot know and perhaps he did not know what secret preparation had been going on in his soul. The long ride across Syrian sands afforded leisure and solitude for meditation, which may have ripened these slumbering seeds in his subconsciousness and prepared them for their sudden sprouting. The Spirit works in ways that are hidden from us.

The extraordinary and startling feature in Saul's conversion was the midday vision above the brightness of the sun in which the risen Lord Jesus was manifested to him. The supernatural element in the background of every conversion flashed into the foreground in his experience and changed his whole attitude in a moment. "I was not disobedient unto the heavenly vision," was Paul's own explanation of the reversal of his will. From that hour through the silent years of his meditation and preparation and the thirty years of his missionary activity he poured out his soul in a stream of service and sacrifice that has never been paralleled in the history of Christianity. More than any other personality, except Christ himself, he has shaped the doctrine and life of Christianity and dug the channel in which the Christian centuries have flowed.

These three instances of conversion illustrate widely varying types, but they all have the essential elements of this change. Tolstoy, the man of the world, "Old

Born Drunk," at the bottom of human degradation, and Paul, the powerful thinker and fiery zealot, were all turned from sin unto God by the entrance of a new idea and ideal which they followed in faith and obedience.

II. The Means of Conversion

Let us now look more in detail at the means of or steps in conversion.

1. Conversion Primarily an Act of Mind.—Conversion, being a turning of the soul from sin to God, is primarily an act of the mind and will. This fact is clearly expressed in the Greek word *metanoia*.[1] This word is translated "repentance" in both the Authorized and the Revised Versions of the New Testament, but this translation is misleading. The word "repentance" emphasizes a change of feeling in penitence or pain for sin. But *metanoia* means a change of mind. In his book entitled *The Great Meaning of Metanoia,* Treadwell Walden brings out this meaning. "*Nous,*" he says, "is the precise equivalent of 'mind.' *Meta* is a preposition which, when compounded with *nous,* means *after*. Metanoia is the after-mind: perception, knowledge, thought, feeling, disposition, will, *afterwards*. The mind has entered upon a new stage, upon something beyond." He quotes a correspondent as follows: "The root of *meta* is the English 'mid,' and *meta* is at bottom the English 'amid.' From this idea (one of situation) it progresses to another idea of *direction;* and in this use it has the sense of 'going right against,' in the sense of 'striking fair and square,' or 'right in the middle.' Thus it gets the meaning of 'oppositeness

[1] μετάνοια.

of direction,' and its force in 'metanoia' is to show
that the action of the mind is now precisely in the opposite direction to what was before the case." De
Quincey had grasped this meaning and is quoted as saying: "I understand by metanoia a revolution of
thought—a great intellectual change—in accepting a
new centre for all moral truth from Christ; which
centre it was that subsequently caused all the offence
of Christianity to the Roman people." Matthew Arnold is also quoted as saying: "Of 'metanoia,' as Jesus
used the word, the lamenting one's sins was a small
part; the main part was something far more active
and fruitful, the setting up an immense new inward
movement for obtaining the rule of life. And 'metanoia,' acordingly, is a change of the inner man."

Rev. Mr. Walden says on the meaning of the word:
"That spiritual perception of the right and the true
which grows within and around a mind that is being
gradually educated up to the divine standard; the nature wide open in front, not only looking behind, and
receiving the whole counsel of God, not a part of it;
every faculty enlightened, every feeling inspired; the
entire man engaged; conviction, not excitement; earnestness, not impulse; habitude, not paroxysm; the
heart tempered by the understanding, the understanding warmed by the Leart; this, the consummate and yet
attainable condition. . . . This is not conveyed in
the 'Repent ye!' of our gospels, nor does it come within
the range of much of the teaching which falls on the
world's ear. The all-encompassing grandeur of an
announcement which takes in the whole life, and calls
upon man to enlarge his consciousness with the eternal
and the spiritual, to live on the scale of another life,
to let his character grow under this great knowledge, to

let his conduct fall into the lines of the revealed divine will—all this is lost."[1]

When John the Baptist began his ministry, saying, "Repent ye: for the kingdom of heaven is at hand"; when Jesus began preaching, "Repent ye, and believe the gospel"; and when Peter climaxed and closed his great sermon on the day of Pentecost with the call, "Repent, and be baptized every one of you in the name of Jesus Christ," each of these preachers called out to his hearers, "Change your minds." Change your mind! this is the cry that rings through the New Testament from beginning to end; and it is to this day the initial word and call of the gospel. Conversion is an act and movement of the whole mind and soul out of sin into righteousness.

This change is not a sheer or blind act of the will, but a rational process. The general means by which conversion is brought about is the creation of a new interest, a changed view and vision of life, the introduction into the mind and heart of a more powerful motive, or, in Dr. Chalmers' famous phrase, "the expulsive power of a new affection."

"A great and priceless thing," says Mark Twain in one of the fine serious passages scattered through his books, "is a new interest! How it takes possession of a man! how it clings to him, how it rides him! I strode onward from Schwarenbach hostelry a changed man, a reorganized personality. I walked in a new world, I saw with new eyes. I had been looking aloft at the giant snow-peaks only as things to be worshipped for their grandeur and magnitude, and their unspeakable grace of form; I looked up at them now,

[1] *The Great Meaning of Metanoia*, by Treadwell Walden, pp. 23-24.

as also things to be conquered and climbed. My sense of their grandeur and their noble beauty was neither lost nor impaired; I had gained a new interest in the mountains without losing the old ones. I followed the steep lines up, inch by inch, and noted the possibility or impossibility of following them with my feet. When I saw a shining helmet of ice projecting from the clouds, I tried to imagine I saw files of black specks toiling up it roped together with a gossamer thread." [1]

Such is the effect of a new interest upon us. It wakes up our dormant powers, renews our fatigued faculties, enlivens our satiated senses, dispels any gloom and discouragement and pessimism that have been hanging around our spirits, reorganizes our whole personality and lifts life to a new level. Many a life that has been worn out and lost all hope has blazed up into an intense fire of energy and enthusiasm when touched with the torch of a new interest. Then some mountain that has long stood in sight and become a familiar and commonplace thing suddenly takes on new meaning and power, and the soul views it with searching gaze from base to summit and is absorbed in its wonders and resolves to conquer its heights.

Conversion is such a change. The soul can be lured from sin only as it is drawn by some more powerful attraction. Sin can be driven out of the heart only as it is crowded out by some stronger good. A heart that is simply swept empty of evil will presently be visited and occupied by seven devils more vicious than the one expelled, and its last state will be worse than the first. We can persuade men to leave the old life only as we offer them something better. This was strikingly illustrated in the three conversions described in

[1] *A Tramp Abroad*, Vol. II, p. 73.

the preceding section. " God is," was the thought that let the first light into Tolstoy's groping soul. " I want to be like Joe," was the pitiful cry of " Old Born Drunk." " I was not disobedient unto the heavenly vision," was the testimony of Paul.

Conversion, then, being an act of the mind, does not begin with the emotions, fears, or hopes. The way to win converts is not first to stir up their feelings into a frenzy of excitement, but to present to them some great and worthy new interest that will lead them to change their minds and turn from sin unto righteousness and God. Christianity is ever a rational religion, and its great instrument is preaching the truth. It appeals to the minds and motives of men. It reasons, as did Paul before Felix when " he reasoned of righteousness, temperance, and judgment to come." And so preaching is not ranting: it is reasoning; and conversion is brought about by reasoning along three lines.

2. **Three Steps in Conversion.**—These three lines of reasoning and steps in conversion are repentance, faith, and obedience.

(a) Conversion is, first, a change of mind on the subject of sin. Every normal person has some sense of sin, however sodden his soul and dull his conscience. Whether savage or civilized, illiterate or learned, vulgar or refined, agnostic or Christian, sinner or saint, every one's own heart condemns him; and if we say we have no sin John says we do lie and the truth is not in us. But this sense of sin varies in degree and depth from indifference and almost total insensibility to a keen consciousness of guilt and agonizing remorse. Various conditions and influences lull this sense of sin into sleep or deaden it into insensibility, and others wake it into life and power. A sermon, a gospel song, a revival meeting, the timely sympathetic word or warning of a parent, teacher or friend, some truth or circumstance leads the soul to consider its state and quickens its conscience into a lively sense of its guilt, and then the mind sees sin in its true light as human guilt and folly and disobedience against God; and it considers the consequences of sin in increasing guilt and evil habit and finally in degradation and bondage and bitterness. Seeing its sin in its true light the soul then experiences penitence or the pain of guilt, and its sin, that possibly had long been forgotten and thought dead, grows keenly alive or flames up in burning power. The mind's perception of the true nature of sin lets loose the emotions of penitence, and these flow upon the will and turn the soul from sin. The man thus changes his whole mind towards sin in thought, feeling, and will.

(b) Conversion is first an act of repentance in turning from sin, and second it is an act of faith in turning towards God and Christ. Faith is a kind of knowledge: knowledge that rests on relation to a person as contrasted with knowledge that rests on sense perception or on logical demonstration. It is not a less trustworthy kind of persuasion than sense perception or logical proof and may be just as solid and sure. Vastly the greater part of our knowledge rests on trust in others and by faith we live every day and hour. It is by an act of faith that we read and depend on books and newspapers and on the whole world of communication with others. Conversation is a continual exercise of faith, and without such trust in one another we would all quickly perish. Our knowledge of the world and of nature largely consists of faith. We may not have seen London or Pekin, and

yet we are not only sure of their existence but may
even practically know as much about them as we do
of the city or town in which we live; and such knowledge is pure faith. And our knowledge of science
outside of our personal observation is of the same
nature. Our belief that the sun is ninety-three millions of miles distant from the earth, in so far as we
derive this knowledge from others, rests on faith;
and so is it with the whole range of our scientific
knowledge except that part or field of science in which
we have first-hand knowledge. Not only so, but scientific men themselves are dependent on faith for most
of their knowledge, for they must trust experts outside of their own fields. And so faith is the common
ground under all our feet on which we walk, it is the
very air of life which we consciously or unconsciously
breathe. Faith is not, then, an illegitimate or uncertain and untrustworthy or even weaker kind of knowledge, but may be as certain and solid ground as we
ever find under our feet.

The same principle of trust which runs through our
human life and by which we necessarily live runs on
up into our relations with God. It is just as reasonable and natural and necessary that we should trust
in him as that we should trust in one another; and
faith in him is fraught with a greater burden of blessing than is our faith in one another by as much as he
is greater than man. Religious faith does not differ
in principle from the faith of our common secular life.
It is not an invention of the priest or church. It is
not a secret or a mystery peculiar to religion. Faith
in religion is just what it is in science, or in industry
and trade, or in society and friendship. Christian
faith has sometimes been analyzed and explained until

its very simplicity has become a puzzle and a mystery, and, instead of setting it afloat in the air, we need to keep it down upon the ground of our common life.

Religious faith is belief in God and Christian faith is belief in Christ as the Son of God and our Saviour. The grounds of such faith are all the historic facts and Scripture teachings and personal experiences that lead to and demand such belief; and these grounds justify Christian faith as certainly as nature and society justify our faith in science and in one another. In conversion faith lays hold of God as a God of righteousness and justice and also of mercy and forgiveness; and it lays hold of Christ as the Son of God who is mighty to save and will hear our cry and cleanse us from all unrighteousness. Faith casts its burden of guilt and bondage on Christ and receives his atoning grace by which its guilt is propitiated in the sight of God's justice and its bondage is unloosed and the penitent soul is set free in the glorious liberty of the sons of God.

Faith as belief releases the feeling of trust. This is the characteristic emotional element in faith. All belief involves some feeling of trust, such as confidence in our own faculties and in the constitution and regularity of the course of nature. But in faith the factor of feeling rises to a fuller volume and may reach a flood tide. We trust in a person with a feeling of confidence and affection such as we do not experience in other forms of knowledge. Faith in God is filled with this feeling, which may be the main constituent so that it may submerge the intellectual element of belief, though of course thought is always present in consciousness, however deeply it may be immersed in the feelings. Faith in Christ is still fuller and livelier in its feeling element, because Christ comes nearer to us in his humanity. God as the infinite and eternal Spirit seems far off and shadowy, but in Christ " the Word was made flesh and dwelt among us (and we beheld his glory, glory as of the only begotten from the Father), full of grace and truth." Christ is God come down to us so that we can see him. He is the sunrise and sunburst of God, whose immediate splendour fills our eyes. His humanity brings him close to our side and lets us into his experience, and thus we can feel a trust in him and a personal affection for him such as we cannot so vividly exercise towards the infinite and eternal God. One purpose of the incarnation is to bridge the wide barrier of space that seems to separate us from God and bring God to us and us to God so that we can have vital and fruitful personal faith in and fellowship with him.

Faith brings us into saving relations with Christ. Faith in any person commits and binds us to him so that we are made one with him and all that he is becomes available for us. When we commit ourselves in faith to a physician all his knowledge and skill is put at our service and is more efficient for our healing than if we had it in our own minds. The soldier trusting his general shares in and is guided by all the superior knowledge and training of the officer. A nation is as wise as its statesmen and as strong as its army. The scholar has at his service all the knowledge of the teacher; and, most beautiful of all illustrations, the child by its faith in its father and mother shares in and is guided and trained and strengthened by all that they are and have. Faith thus so identifies us with the person on whom our faith rests that we are one

with him in all that he is. A fundamental law of life
is: ' Have faith in your mother and you will be saved
in childhood; Have faith in your teacher and you will
be taught; Have faith in your physician and you will
be healed.' In the most literal sense we walk by faith,
we live by faith, and by faith are we saved.

In the same way faith commits and binds us to
Christ so that we are united with him in a union that
makes all his saving power available for our salvation. His atonement covers the guilt of our sin as
effectually as though we had rendered this atonement
ourselves. His grace is communicated to us through
his Word and Spirit so that we are fashioned into his
likeness, and thus more and more we " become par-
takers of the divine nature." " Being therefore justified by faith, we have peace with God through our
Lord Jesus Christ; through whom also we have had
access by faith into this grace wherein we stand; and
we rejoice in hope of the glory of God " (Romans 5:
1-2). All this is in accordance with the psychology of
faith in all spheres. It is not by magic or mystery
that faith saves us, but by its natural working. Christ
saves us, as the physician heals us, through our faith.
Faith puts us in saving relations with him and becomes the vital artery through which he can pour his
grace into us. Faith is the hand by which we grasp
the hand of Christ, and then he lifts us out of our sin
into newness of life.

(c) The third step in conversion is obedience by
which faith completes itself in fact. Obedience is predominantly an act of the will, and the will has already
been active in repentance and faith, each of which
involves thought, feeling, and will. Obedience to truth
and duty and to God and Christ in all the duties and

graces and service of the Christian life is the necessary fulfilment of faith, as the fruit is the necessary
outgrowth and completion of the root. Obedience fixes
and deepens faith in the mind, intensifies its feeling,
and thus causes faith to grow into clearer vision and
greater vigour and final victory.

The relation of faith and obedience is clearly stated
by James: "What doth it profit, my brothers, if a
man say he hath faith, but have not works? can that
faith save him? If a brother or sister be naked and in
lack of daily food, and one of you say unto them, Go
in peace, be ye warmed and filled; and yet ye give
them not the things needful to the body; what doth it
profit? Even so faith, if it have not works, is dead in
itself. Yea, a man will say, Thou hast faith, and I
have works: show me thy faith apart from thy works,
and I by my works will show thee my faith" (James 2:
14-18). There is thus no contradiction or antagonism
between faith and obedience, but they are two aspects
of the same thing: one is subjective and the other objective; one is the root and the other is the fruit. Both
are equally necessary, and all the three steps of repentance, faith, and obedience are necessary to complete the one act by which the sinner changes his
whole mind from sin unto salvation and life.

Conversion thus runs the three-cycle round of
thought, feeling, and will in its complex act of repentance, faith, and obedience. The soul in conversion
perceives the truth as to sin and turns from it; faith
believes in God and in Christ and commits the soul to
him; then it feels and may be flooded with a sense of
its guilt and of trust in Christ; and this stream of
feeling pours upon the will and moves it to action in
obedience. This cycle of psychology is fundamental

in conversion and in all our Christian living and preaching, and a clear understanding of it is of the first importance in our Christian experience and work.

The way to move the will to obedience is to stir up the appropriate feelings, and the way to stir the feelings is to create and intensify the proper thought, and the way to create the thought is to present some efficient object that operates by the expulsive power of a new interest. In general, this new interest in religion is the stronger attraction of a better life in fellowship and service with Jesus Christ. The righteousness and the reward, the duty and beauty and blessedness of likeness with Christ and service in his kingdom, are to be held up and enriched and intensified by associations into a powerful magnet to draw men out of their sin to the Saviour. Conversion is thus at bottom the impact and contagion of one personality on another. This personal contact and contagion may at first be that of a parent, teacher, pastor or friend, but at last it is the impact and power of the person of Jesus Christ on the soul, the entrance of his Spirit into the conscience and heart so as to capture the soul and bind it to him in faith and fellowship and service; and this is salvation.

3. **Conversion and the Subconsciousness.**—Thus far we have been considering conversion as taking place in the field of consciousness. But we have seen that the soul has a subconscious life or region in which are stored away all its past experiences, thoughts, feelings and deeds, and these constitute a reservoir which is tapped by every idea that comes into the mind and which then sends forth a stream of associations to enrich and intensify it.

This subconsciousness plays an important part in

conversion. The truth that is pressed upon the mind
in conversion, the ideas of sin and faith and obedience,
penetrate this reservoir and draw forth the accumulated associations of the past to reënforce the truth and
give it converting power. These revived associations
are usually connected with the early home life and
teaching and experiences of the hearer. The old home,
a father's pious example, the prayers that were learned
at a mother's knees, the lessons of the Sunday school,
some memory of a revival sermon or song, some remarkable happening, many are the memories of the past
that may spring up out of the subconsciousness as a
flood and pour their energizing power on the truth
that is being preached. Most conversions that take
place in mature life are caused by this uprush out of
the past to reënforce and decide the duty of the moment. Revival preaching always plays upon these
subconscious strings in the heart and wakes into life
their old music. Once get a man back into the dear
scenes and precious memories of his childhood home
and life and these old, forgotten, far-off things come
back upon him with strange power and lay their spell
upon him, he grows tender and susceptible, the fountain of his tears is opened and he is carried off on their
flood into action. On entering a mission hall in one
of our great cities where nightly gathers a motley
crowd of men, most of them down-and-outs, the first
thing that one sees staring him in the face is the question, painted in large letters on the wall, " How long
is it since you wrote to your mother? " There is
psychology in that question. It appeals to the past
and taps the subconscious life of every one of those
wandering men, and in many cases must start a flood
of memories and penitent thoughts and good resolu-

tions that moves many a tramp and drunkard to turn around in conversion.

In preaching and teaching we must learn to touch these deep-hidden strings of the heart and wake their tender music. In addressing a hearer we are appealing to more than his conscious mind: we are slipping suggestions beneath his consciousness into his subconsciousness and waking up the whole man and making deeper and more powerful appeals than the man himself knows. This appeal to the hidden life should not be made too often or too obtrusively, or it will wear out or even stir up opposition. It may be done in such a way that men will resent it and arm themselves against it. It should be done rather by way of indirection and allusion than by a frontal bold attack. Suggestion by the very meaning of the word goes under the conscious thoughts into the subconscious; instead of knocking at the front door and publicly announcing its intentions, it stealthily steals in through the back door and catches a man before he knows it. It throws a man off his guard and takes him unawares. Many a man has gone to a religious meeting in a state of indifference or of hostility, even as a scoffer, but the truth slipped under his unconcern and antagonism and tapped deeper depths and took him captive, he knew not how, and he may have been as much surprised as anybody at the result. Such indirection calls for delicate tact and skill, quick insight and sympathy and the ability instantly to adapt the means used to the situation or case in hand, and then it has wonderful subtlety and power in penetrating the great deeps of human souls and moving them to action.

4. **Conversion and Revivals.**—A familiar fact that is confirmed and elucidated by psychology is that re-

vival is a powerful means of conversion. This grows
out of the fact that the human soul is intensely social
and absorbent, a veritable sponge that sucks up all
around it. The psychology of the crowd has been
closely studied by the psychologists with fruitful results.[1] Every one has experienced the contagion of a
crowd and knows how common thoughts and feelings
seize and sway it, suppressing or overriding all individual differences and mastering and moving it as a
storm sways a forest. The principle of a mob is that
one overpowering idea inhibits all antagonistic ideas
and unbinds the passions and sweeps all before it.
The contagion of a crowd works largely through the
subconscious nature, tapping the deep primal instincts
and passions and letting them loose in an overwhelm-
ing flood of power. There may thus be a violent explosion of human nature, suddenly unloosing long pent-
up passions and as suddenly subsiding.

There is no fixed dead level anywhere in the world;
all things are subject to fluctuations. The atmosphere
has its changes of temperature, the sea its tides, the
earth its seasons, and the sun its periodicity in its
spots. Life is especially subject to this law. Agricultural life is more active in summer and quiescent in
winter. Business is usually livelier in the fall and
winter and spring and stagnant in the hot season. Intellectual life at times rises into a glow of interest and
then cools into indifference and sinks into dulness.
Political life is especially subject to violent fluctuations, rising into intense excitement in a campaign and
then subsiding into inactivity.

Religion is subject to the same law. It cannot main-

[1] *Social Psychology*, by Edward A. Ross, is an illuminating
book on the subject.

tain itself at a level, especially at a high pitch of intensity, but rises and falls. It is intensely infectious and contagious. Religious interest in a church or community is kindled by some spark and begins to spread and blaze and may grow into a conflagration. Christianity started off under the powerful impulse of the greatest revival in its history on the day of Pentecost. A fire was kindled on that day that has lighted all succeeding ages. Revival has been a marked feature and force in Christianity ever since. The Crusades were powerful outbreaks of crowd contagion, and the Reformation was a tremendous revival. Great historic revivals attended the preaching of the Wesleys, Whitefield, Jonathan Edwards, Finney, and Moody, and revivalism under evangelists is one of the most prominent facts in Christianity to-day.

A revival follows all the laws of social psychology. It spreads largely through the power of suggestion in reaching the subconscious nature. Revival preaching never deals in new theology but in old theology, the primary facts of sin and salvation; and it especially penetrates the subconscious life of the hearers by touching on their childhood teaching and memories. These associations are greatly quickened and strengthened by the contagion of the crowd, and once they get started they spread like fire and begin to burn and blaze and may melt the most obdurate hearts. It is always easier to do what others are doing, especially when others of our kind are doing what chimes in with our own deepest nature and needs. Conversion is thus catching and may run through a whole church and community, or city and country.

A revival renews religious interest and life in all Christians, and it is a harvest season when many souls are brought to decision and action. Many of these converts have been reared in Christian homes and are believers in Christ, but they need the impulse of common interest to push them into public confession; and others have wandered far from early teaching into worldliness and sin, and the revival brings them back to their early faith and leads them to turn it into fact. Revivals are often attended with instances of conversion out of utter unbelief or worldliness or deep wickedness into faith and confession as wonderful as anything recorded in Scripture, except the conversion of Paul which was extraordinary and unique, or in *Twice-Born Men.* The grace of God has lost none of its saving virtue and is ever able to make souls willing in the day of his power.

Good and blessed as revivals are, yet they have their dangers, as many pastors and churches know to their sorrow. Chief among these dangers are the excesses that may attend them. Great historic revivals have sometimes been disfigured by abnormal and dangerous features. The great revival under Edwards led to physical manifestations against which he protested, and of the Kentucky revival of 1799-1800 we read: " The heart swelled, the nerves gave way, the hands and feet grew cold, and, motionless and speechless, they fell headlong to the ground. In a moment crowds gathered about them to pray and shout. Some lay still as death. Some passed through frightful twitchings of face and limb. At Cabin Creek so many fell that, lest the multitude should tread on them, they were carried to the meeting-house and laid in rows on the floor. At Cane Ridge the number was three thousand. The excitement surpassed anything that had been known. Men who came to scoff remained to preach. All day and all night the crowd swarmed to and fro from preacher to preacher, singing, shouting, laughing, now rushing off to listen to some new exhorter who had climbed upon a stump, now gathering around some unfortunate who, in their peculiar language, was 'spiritually slain.' Soon men and women fell in such numbers that it became impossible to move without trampling them, and they were hurried to the meeting-house. At no time was the floor less than half covered. Some lay quiet, unable to move or speak. Some talked, but could not move. Some beat the floor with their heels. Some, shrieking in agony, bounded about, it is said, like a live fish out of water. Many lay down and rolled over and over for hours at a time. Others rushed wildly over the stumps and benches, and then plunged, shouting Lost! Lost! into the forest." [1]

Such excesses unleash the bonds of self-control and easily run into relaxed morals and even gross immorality. Mind and matter lie close together and sometimes it is only a slip from spirituality into sensuality. The flesh steadily pulls against the spirit and is watching its chance to get the better of it, and appetite and sense must be held in with a tight rein, or they may bound away with us. As it is only a step from the sublime to the ridiculous, so in the midst of such revival excitement and excess there is danger of a fall from the spirit into the flesh.

Undue emotionalism is one of the dangers of a revival even when it does not unhinge the reason and rise into hysteria. When it floods the soul so as to submerge the judgment it may rush the will into unconsidered action from which there will be a reaction. This is a common result of revivals. They often sweep through a church

[1] *Social Psychology,* by Edward A. Ross, pp. 50-52.

and community in a flood tide that carries many into the church, but they quickly subside and leave their wreckage in the form of deeper indifference and lapsed members strewn along their banks for years. It is literally true that after some revivals the last state is worse than the first. For this reason some pastors are slow to enter upon revival movements and some churches discourage them altogether. But the abuse of revivals can be avoided without abandoning their use; that they are a legitimate and powerful means of religious conversion and life is proved by all the history of the Christian church, and they are not an abnormal and irrational means of promoting quickened interest, as is shown by the fact that the same principle is freely used and is effective in other fields.

The pastor that knows how to use this agency sanely and wisely has a Scriptural and efficient means of promoting spiritual life in his church and winning converts. The best kind of a revival, as a general rule, is one that the pastor conducts in his own church. In many churches the pastor holds special evangelistic meetings at regular intervals several times a year and secures the assistance of a brother pastor of an evangelistic type to do the preaching during a week or more, while he works among his people. Such seasons, when properly prepared for and efficiently conducted, result in a healthful revival, free from the danger of excesses, and yielding a harvest of quickened religious life and converted souls.

The chief danger in revivals results from the failure to observe and use the three-cycle movement of the soul from thought to feeling and from feeling to will in their due order and proportion; but often an immediate effort is made and every means is used to stir up

the feelings into excitement which may reach the pitch
of frenzy. Sermon and song and prayer and all the
accessories of the meeting are made to converge in the
focus of the feelings so as to fuse them into white
heat. Sometimes means are used that pass into ex-
travagance and border on burlesque and blasphemy.
Gesticulation and gymnastics, contortions of the face
and figure, dishevelled and flying hair, coarse speech,
slang out of the gutter and all the lingo of sport, carica-
ture of Scripture scenes, lurid pictures of the flames of
the pit, stories and jokes that excite loud laughter,
familiarity with sacred things and with God, irreverence that approaches blasphemy,—many are the arts
used by some evangelists, even by men of ability and
genius, by which they draw crowds and count their
converts by the thousand. Much of this work is painful
and pitiful and does immense harm. Yet these abuses
and excesses do not inhere in revivalism, and revivals
can be and mostly are conducted in accordance with
Scripture and psychology, sanity and sense. The
preaching and all the influences used in revival should
be primarily addressed to the reason and conscience so
as to lead men to change their minds, and then the
feelings will take care of themselves, and the will will
follow with the appropriate action. It is not meant
that no appeal should be made directly to the feelings
and the will, but the primary appeal should be to the
mind and conscience. " Change your mind," is the first
call of the gospel, and when this order is reversed the
mind is thrown out of gear and balance and then it
works badly. Conversion is a rational process and
should always take place along this line. When revivals follow this law they are legitimate in their
methods and have then always proved the power of

God unto salvation, winning hundreds and thousands of converts, quickening congregations, shaking great cities and leaving their impress upon countries and upon centuries.

5. The Power of the Will in Conversion.—There arises once more at this point a very important psychological and ethical question in connection with conversion: Being an act of the mind and judgment, a question of truth and duty, is not conversion subject to fact and reason, to evidence and logic, and hence can it be a mere act of choice and will? How can we urge a man to believe on Jesus Christ when the evidence does not convince him of the Saviourhood of Christ? How can a man believe in God when his logic drives him into agnosticism? Ought not a man to be loyal to his sense of truth above everything else, whatever it may cost him?

The first answer to this question is that a man ought first and above all to be loyal to his sense of truth. Truth is the primary virtue and duty of the mind, the fundamental basis of all character and conduct, the highest obligation of the human soul. And our preaching should always recognize and respect and emphasize this primary virtue and duty. Never should we give the impression that men are to believe the gospel or receive a creed irrespective of its truth as an arbitrary choice of the will, or as a traditional and partisan attitude and act. " I adjure thee, that thou say nothing but the truth to me," said an ancient king to a Hebrew prophet (II Chronicles 18: 15), and the Christian minister, disciple of him who said, " I am the truth," should obey the same injunction to-day. Let us know and obey the truth though the heavens fall. And the preacher should ever be a sincere truth-seeker, open minded, frank and fair, candid and charitable in all his endeavours to persuade men.

However, when we have emphasized this attitude towards truth we have not said all that is to be said on this point. It is not a mere act of will by which the sinner turns from sin to righteousness in conversion, but a change of mind involving all his faculties, his reason and motives and feelings as the ground of the decision and action of his will. The sinner ought not to be converted or yield to conversion against his reason, but he should yield only in accordance with the full play of his reason and his whole mind.

And further, the matter of believing truth is not as clear and simple as at first it may seem. Truth is not an object that stands over against the mind in such lucidity and certainty that all we have to do is just to look at it and then we cannot miss it. " No bell in us tolls," says Professor James, " to let us know for certain when truth is in our grasp." On the contrary, truth, especially moral and religious truth, is something for which we select the materials and then put them together in form and meaning: that is, ethical truth is something we make.

We have already seen that it is in our power to control the process of attention by which we throw it from one object to another and by which we select the associations that gather around the chosen object and intensify it until it persuades the mind as truth and then moves the will. This selective power of attention and association is itself a control that goes far towards choosing and creating our ethical beliefs. And, further, our moral disposition, our prevailing instincts and impulses, aims and ambitions, ideas and ideals, subtly but powerfully infect and form, colour and

mould our beliefs and determinations. Every one
knows how his own attitude and action, mood and temper, disposition and habits, and especially how his
interests and desires and passions tend to sway and
shape his belief and choice. Our own souls are the
soil out of which our beliefs grow. And we are responsible for the whole state of the soul and for its
processes, for we have formed and cultivated this soil
by constantly dropping into it our own free acts, as
the forest by shedding its leaves has formed its own
loam.

In a still deeper sense we create our own ethical
ideals and beliefs. In many instances an ethical truth
is true only as we make it true. Our faith is a fact in
process of its realization. An ideal of character is
obviously realized only as we believe in it and commit
ourselves to it in obedience. We make our own moral
life, and our faith in such a life precedes and conditions and creates it. The same principle extends to
other lives: we can make their lives good only as we
believe in goodness and as we have faith in them. And,
extending the same principle, we can make a good
world for ourselves in so far as we believe in the possibility of such a world and commit ourselves to it in
conviction and courage, service and sacrifice. It is our
right and it is within our power to vote for a rational
universe and good world, and our faith will turn this
belief for us into a fact. Ethical objects are not what
they are independently of us, but in a large degree we
make them what they are for us; and herein lies a large
part of our responsibility.

Professor William James, in his book entitled *The
Will to Believe,* has worked this view out into completeness, stating it with all its limitations and guard-

ing it from misunderstanding and misapplication, and the following quotations will indicate his line of thought: "There are, then, cases where a fact cannot come at all unless a preliminary faith exists in its coming. *And where faith in a fact can help create the fact,* that would be an insane logic which should say that faith running ahead of scientific evidence is the 'lowest kind of immorality' into which a thinking being can fall. Yet such is the logic by which our scientific absolutists pretend to regulate our lives! . . . The freedom to believe can only cover living options which the intellect cannot by itself resolve; and living options never seem absurdities to him who has them to consider. When I look at the religious question as it really puts itself to concrete men, and when I think of all the possibilities which both practically and theoretically it involves, then this command that we shall put a stopper on our heart, instincts, and courage, and *wait*—acting of course meanwhile more or less as if religion were *not* true—till doomsday, or till such a time as our intellect and senses working together may have raked in evidence enough,—this command, I say, seems to me the queerest idol ever manufactured in the philosophic cave. . . . Often enough our faith beforehand in an uncertified result *is the only thing that makes the result come true.* . . . If your heart does not *want* a world of moral reality, your head will assuredly never make you believe in one. . . . This life *is* worth living, we can say, *since it is what we make it, from the moral point of view.* . . . I confess that I do not see why the very existence of an invisible world may not in part depend on the personal response which any one of us may make to the religious appeal. God himself, in short, may draw vital strength and increase of being from our fidelity. For my own part, I do not know what the sweat and blood and tragedy of this life mean, if they mean anything short of this. If this life be not a real fight, in which something is eternally gained for the universe by success, it is no better than a game of private theatricals from which one may withdraw at will. But it *feels* like a real fight,—as if there were something really wild in the universe which we, with all our idealities and faithfulnesses, are needed to redeem; and first of all to redeem our own hearts from atheisms and fears." [1]

Browning teaches the same truth in "Bishop Blougram's Apology":

> Once own the use of faith, I'll find you faith.
>
> . . . . . .
>
> You criticize the soul? it reared this tree—
> This broad life and whatever fruit it bears!
>
> . . . .
>
> Like you this Christianity or not?
> It may be false, but will you wish it true?
> Has it your vote to be so if it can?
> Trust you an instinct silenced long ago
> That will break silence and enjoin you love
> What mortified philosophy is hoarse,
> And all in vain, with bidding you despise?
> If you desire faith—then you've faith enough.

But who taught this principle of psychology long before philosopher and poet expressed it? He who said, "If any man willeth to do his will, he shall know of the teaching, whether it is of God, or whether I speak from myself" (John 7:17). This truth is frequently expressed in the Bible. "The meek will he guide in justice; the meek will he teach his way." "The friend-

---

[1] *The Will to Believe*, pp. 23 to 61.

ship of Jehovah is with them that fear him; and he
will shew them his covenant " (Psalm 25 : 9, 14).

The principle of this method is that "obedience is
the organ of spiritual knowledge," to use the title of
Frederick W. Robertson's famous sermon on the subject. When we enter upon a line of obedience to a
truth it unfolds before us in clearness and certainty,
opening before us as a road out of a forest. Experience proves it step by step, and then shadows and
clouds are swept from its path as morning mist before
the sun. It is thus we learn any science and art. We
really know these things only as we do them. We cannot start out with a complete knowledge of any subject: we gain only a glimpse of it, and this grows into
clearness as we follow it up in obedience. It is thus
the chemist masters his science or the musician acquires skill in his art.

And just so is it in the field of religion. We cannot
know much spiritual truth until we obey it, and obedience ever opens the way from partial knowledge or belief into fuller understanding and surer faith. The
sinner at the moment of his conversion is not required
or asked to believe everything in the creed or in the
Bible. He need only have a sense of his sin and a desire
for a better life. God may be a dim conception to him
and his knowledge of Christ very fragmentary and
defective and even erroneous. There may be great
and grave gaps in his creed. The restored blind man
did not know whether Jesus was a sinner or not: that
surely was a serious defect in his knowledge. But he
could affirm, "One thing I know," and that one thing
followed out in obedience led him on until he exclaimed,
"Lord, I believe. And he worshipped him." The sinner at conversion may have equally serious defects in

his faith; but if he follows the light he has it will lead him into clearer knowledge of and a fuller faith in Christ. In the hour of conversion the sinner should not be urged or asked to believe everything or to believe too much; more than he can honestly accept and obey. One may try to believe too much, more than he can digest, as he can put too much food in his stomach, or too much fuel on a fire. But when he obeys what he does know he shall find the truth and the truth will set him free.

Conversion, then, is not an arbitrary act and does not violate the supreme law of truth and duty; but it is an act of the whole mind in which the will can select its object and fix its attention upon it until it grows into power, and it makes the object of its ethical faith and life by casting its own deciding vote for it and by obedience turning faith into fact; and on these grounds we can appeal to the sinner to exercise this liberty and responsibility and power in believing religious truth and turning from sin unto God.

III. The Age of Conversion

Psychology confirms and elucidates the familiar fact that the favourable age for conversion falls in the early years of youth.

1. **The Facts as to Early Conversion.**—Professor Starbuck has made an inductive study of conversion and has plotted the cases of 235 males and 254 females, resulting in the curve shown on the opposite page. He also plotted 276 conversions from the Drew Theological Seminary Alumni record, and the resulting curve is closely the same. A similar study, based on 272 male conversions and published by the American Sunday School Union, gives a practically identical curve.

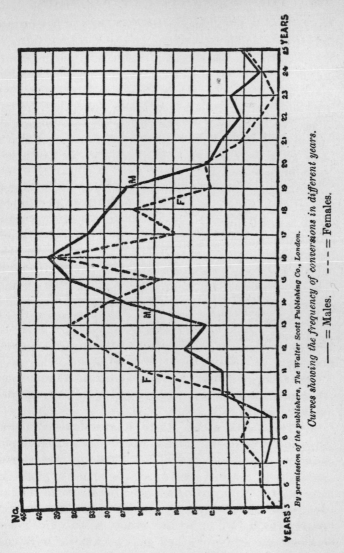

By permission of the publishers, The Walter Scott Publishing Co., London.

Curves showing the frequency of conversions in different years.

——— = Males.   – – – – = Females.

These several inductions with the same result are a scientific confirmation of the well-known fact of early conversion.

Commenting on the facts Professor Starbuck says: " Conversion does not occur with the same frequency at all periods of life. It belongs almost exclusively to the years between 10 and 25. The number of instances outside that range appear few and scattered. That is, *conversion is a distinctively adolescent phenomenon.* It is a singular fact also that within this period the conversions do not distribute themselves equally among the years. In the rough, we may say they begin to occur at 7 or 8 years, and increase in number gradually to 10 or 11, and then rapidly to 16; rapidly decline to 20, and gradually fall away after that, and become rare after 30. One may say that if conversion has not occurred before 20, the chances are small that it will ever be experienced.

But our reading is too rough. With adolescence it appears that such awakenings are much more likely to take place at some years than at others, and that the preference of years varies greatly with sex. The event comes earlier in general among the females than among the males, most frequently at 13 and 16. Among the males it occurs most often at 17, and immediately before or after that year." [1]

2. The Explanation of the Facts.—The explanation of these facts lies on the surface. Early youth is the period when all the plastic powers of the mind and body are rounding into form and taking their set for life. Professor Starbuck, in looking for the psychological reason for early conversion, says: " The years at which conversions really begin (9 or 10 for boys and

[1] *The Psychology of Religion,* Chapter III.

11 for girls) coincide fairly with the years at which Dr. Hancock [1] in his experimental tests found a sudden increment in children's ability to reason. After this the reasoning power develops rapidly but intermittently into the teens. Mr. J. W. Davids [2] reports, as the result of experiments on the contents of children's minds, an increment in the mental life at about 11. Although the same mental processes are not involved in reasoning and in religious awakenings, Dr. Hancock's tests probably indicate a mental capacity which is a necessary condition for attaining spiritual insight. The point with which we are here concerned is that they, together with some other tests which we shall notice, help to mark off a somewhat natural prior limit of conversions." [3]

Another cause of early conversions is found in the physiological changes that occur at puberty. A curve showing the increase of height and weight of average American boys and girls for each year of youth presents striking similarity approaching identity with the curve of age in conversion. Yet the climaxes in the curve of height and weight do not fall exactly on the points of climax in the conversion curve, but slightly earlier. The conclusion drawn by Professor Starbuck is that *" conversion and puberty tend to supplement each other in time rather than to coincide; but they may, nevertheless, be mutually conditioned."*

The fact of this coincidence of conversion with puberty may be pressed too far, and some have connected religion closely with the sex instinct and even

---

[1] John Hancock, " Children's Ability to Reason," *Educational Review,* October, 1896.

[2] *Interna. Cong. für Psychologie,* Munich, 1896, p. 449 *et seq.*

[3] *The Psychology of Religion,* p. 35.

gone so far as to allege that it is a form of sex degeneration. Such a view is too absurd to be considered. The true explanation is that early youth is the springtime of life when all its seeds burst into bud and bloom. "The voice changes," says Starbuck, "the beard sprouts, the proportions of the head are altered, the volume of the heart increases, that of the arteries diminishes, the blood pressure is heightened, and central among the changes are those of the reproductive system, which makes the child into the man or woman. The amount of carbonic acid in the breath is greatly increased at this period, showing the increment in the processes which tear down and build up the system." Concomitantly with these physiological changes the development of the lower mental processes, such as the senses and memory, slows down and may even come to a standstill, and the higher mental operations of discrimination and judgment and imagination leap forward. Sight passes into insight, and consciousness into conscience. It is to be expected, then, that the still higher mental and spiritual powers would awaken in this general springtime, or be caught up on this rising flood and carried to high tide. The soul is a unit, the whole personality of soul and body, shares in a common life, and all its faculties spring out of one seedplot and bloom together.

Psychology thus confirms and emphasizes the teaching of Scripture and experience that early youth is the time to seek the Lord. All powers are then plastic and easily moulded into religious faith and life. The flood of capacity and susceptibility is then rising and, being seized, surely leads on to spiritual fortune. But the plastic powers soon cool and harden into habits which in after years strong crying and tears may not break.

The flood of youthful susceptibility being " omitted, all the voyage of their life is bound in shallows and in miseries."

Scripture is emphatic and insistent on this point. " Those that seek me early shall find me." " Remember now thy Creator in the days of thy youth, while the evil days come not, nor the years draw nigh, when thou shalt say, I have no pleasure in them." The great Teacher, who understood psychology at every point, knew this principle: " Suffer the little children to come unto me, and forbid them not; for of such is the kingdom of heaven." And the psychologist, rising from his investigations and writing in the cold dry light of his science, says: " One may say that if conversion has not occurred before 20, the chances are small that it will ever be experienced."

This point, then, should be pressed upon the young with all earnestness and solemnity. That rapidly descending curve after 20 is an ominous prospect and prophecy for the young. They should be led to see in its descent their lessening chances and be urged to act on the admonition, " Now is the accepted time; now is the day of salvation." And yet this truth should not be so presented and pressed as to exclude from hope or discourage those who have passed early youth and have not accepted salvation. Many are converted in the later years of life, perhaps more than we know. Some, who passed through a conversion experience in youth, in after life find that they were only superficially and temporarily converted, and they experience a deeper change of conviction that is a real and permanent conversion, and such cases are not always reported among conversions. The door of this duty and hope should never be closed in this world. One thief was saved on the cross: but apparently only one, a fact that contains both hope and warning.

IV. Types of Conversion

Conversion is subject to all the variations of individuality, and therefore manifests different forms or types. These may be classified in various ways, and any such classification is more or less arbitrary. The following will serve to mark the chief types.

1. **Childhood and Adult Conversions.**—Childhood conversions usually take place as the result of the atmosphere and training of a Christian home and may unfold by a process of contagion and education. Regeneration may be effected at any period of childhood and even before birth, as appears to have been the case with John the Baptist (Luke 1:41). There is such solidarity between parents and children that the method of both nature and grace is that the life of parents should flow into children and mould them from earliest infancy. Under this process the children of Christian parents should grow up in the Christian life and know no other. This is the ideal type of conversion.

The Scriptures teach and frequently illustrate this type. " Train up a child in the way he should go; and when he is old, he will not depart from it." " Bring them up in the nurture and admonition of the Lord." " He hath blessed thy children with thee," " for the promise is to you and to your children." This sense of continuity and heredity in the religious life was very strong in the Hebrew home and race, and the divine blessing upon the chosen people from the beginning was promised " unto thee, and to thy seed after thee." The child Samuel was a beautiful instance of one who

was dedicated to the Lord from before his birth and
grew up in the knowledge of the Lord, and Paul dated
Timothy's Christian life from his grandmother, when
in writing to him he called to his remembrance " the
unfeigned faith that is in thee, which dwelt first in thy
grandmother Lois, and thy mother Eunice." And the
great example is Jesus himself, who was perfect in his
childhood as in his manhood, and from his infancy " increased in wisdom and stature, and in favour with God
and man," and in his boyhood was about his " Father's
business." The expectation of the Hebrew prophets
was that the time would come when this type of conversion would become universal and normal. Isaiah
declared, " All thy children shall be taught of the Lord ;
and great shall be the peace of thy children " ; and
Jeremiah prophesied, " They shall all know me from
the least of them unto the greatest of them, saith the
Lord." These prophecies will be fulfilled as Christianity becomes universal and the Christian home realizes
its ideal.

This view of childhood conversion was wrought out
with illuminating power by Horace Bushnell in his
book on *Christian Nurture*. The proposition of the
book is " That the child is to grow up a Christian, and
never know himself as being otherwise." Some quotations gathered from its pages will show his teaching.
" Never is it too early for good to be communicated.
Infancy and childhood are the ages most pliant to
good. And who can think it necessary that the plastic
nature of childhood must first be hardened into stone,
and stiffened into enmity towards God and all duty,
before it can become a candidate for Christian character ! There could not be a more unnecessary mistake,
and it is as unnatural and pernicious, I fear, as it is

unnecessary. There are many who assume the radical
goodness of human nature, and the work of Christian
education is, in their view, only to educate or educe
the good that is in us. Let no one be disturbed by
suspicion of a coincidence between what I have said
and such a theory. The natural pravity of man is
plainly asserted in the Scriptures, and, if it were not,
the familiar laws of physiology would require us to
believe, what amounts to the same thing." "It is not
designed to assert a power in the parent to renew
the child, or that a child can be renewed by any agency
of the Spirit less immediate, than that which renews
the parent himself." [1]

"The most important age of Christian nurture is
the first; that which we have called the age of impressions, just that age, in which the duties and cares
of a really Christian nurture are so commonly post-
poned, or assumed to have not yet arrived. I have no
scales to measure quantities of effect in this matter of
early training, but I may be allowed to express my
solemn conviction, that more, as a general fact, is done,
or lost by neglect of doing, on a child's immortality, in
the first three years of his life, than in all his years
of discipline afterwards." "Parents, therefore, in the
religious teaching of their children, are not to have it
as a point of fidelity to press them into some crisis of
high experience, called conversion. Their teaching is
to be that which feeds a growth, not that which stirs a
revolution. It is to be nurture, presuming on a grace
already and always given, and, just for that reason,
jealously careful to raise no thought of some high
climax to be passed. For precisely here is the special
advantage of a true sacramental nurture in the prom-

[1] *Christian Nurture,* pp. 22 and 31.

ise, that it does not put the child on passing a crisis, where he is thrown out of balance not unlikely, and becomes artificially conscious of himself, but it leaves him to be always increasing in faith, and reaching forward, in the simplest and most dutiful manner, to become what God is helping him to be." [1] Yet Dr. Bushnell also says, " I do not affirm that every child may, in fact and without exception, be so trained that he certainly will grow up a Christian."

So common has the expectation of a crisis in conversion come to be entertained that parents are sometimes anxiously concerned when their children do not experience it and seem simply to grow up in the Christian life; and Christians are sometimes concerned when they do not have this experience themselves. This was the case with Baxter as he explains in his autobiography: " My next doubt was lest education and fear had done all that was ever done upon my soul, and regeneration and love were yet to seek; because I had found convictions from my childhood, and found more fear than love in all my duties and restraints. But I afterwards perceived that education is God's ordinary way for the conveyance of grace, and ought no more to be set in opposition to the Spirit than the preaching of the Word; and that it was the great mercy of God to begin with me so soon, and to prevent such sins as else might have been my shame and sorrow while I lived; and that repentance is good, but prevention and innocence is better: which though we cannot attain unto perfection, yet the more the better." [2]

Early conversions partake of the nature of childhood. Young converts usually exhibit entire confi-

[1] *Ibid.*, pp. 248 and 381.
[2] *The Life of the Reverend Mr. Richard Baxter*, pp. 6-7.

dence of faith, tenderness of feeling, and exuberance of zeal. They are naïve in their inexperience, are little aware of doubts and difficulties, and have little foresight or foreboding of coming trials. God is very real to them and is often conceived of in anthropomorphic terms, and the Bible is taken literally and is all equally important. The church and its ordinances are so vital in their thought that they become identified with religion itself, so that their religion is predominantly ceremonial and external. Young converts are moulded by their environment and reflect the teaching of the home and church. They are great conformists and show little originality or tendency to depart from traditional teaching and forms. They are strongly conservative and orthodox.

Starbuck found from his answers to questions that child converts are marked by credulity. "Children, for the most part, accept in an unquestioning way the ideas taught in church, Sunday school and home, and unconsciously conform to them." And he further found that "religion is distinctively external to the child rather than something which possesses inner significance."

Young converts early become settled in their faith and habits in the Christian life. Of course many of them fall away in mature years, but a large percentage of them remain steadfast through life, and on the whole they form the most stable and fruitful Christians. Adult converts, being more reflective in their decisions and experiences, usually exhibit characteristics somewhat different from those of child converts, and these will appear in the types that follow.

2. **Gradual and Comfortable, and Sudden and Violent, Conversions.**—When conversion takes place in

mature years it often occurs as the result of religious training which gradually ripens into conviction of duty and results in action under some favouring circumstance or influence. A typical instance of this kind of conversion is that of Lydia under the preaching of Paul at Philippi: " And on the sabbath we went out of the city by a river side, where prayer was wont to be made; and we sat down, and spake unto the women which resorted thither. And a certain woman named Lydia, a seller of purple, of the city of Thyatira, which worshipped God, heard us: whose heart the Lord opened, that she attended unto the things which were spoken of Paul. And when she was baptized, and her household, she besought us, saying, If ye have judged me to be faithful to the Lord, come into my house, and abide there. And she constrained us " (Acts 16: 13-15).

This is a beautiful instance of a gradual and comfortable conversion, unattended with any excitement or special personal distress. Lydia went to the place of accustomed prayer where she worshipped God according to her light and heard the gospel. At this point a divine link is inserted in the process as the Lord opened her heart. The human steps are then resumed and she gave attention to the truth and yielded to it in baptism and at once proceeded to enter upon active Christian service. These steps mark deliberation and gradual progress in enlightenment and obedience. There are many such conversions in every church and Christian community. The truth as to sin and salvation through Christ is presented in the ordinary places and ways, and as it is heard attention is given to it until it stirs the feelings and moves the will. No special sense of sin and guilt is experienced but only a quiet conviction of these things, and no ecstatic joy accompanies the act of decision and confession, but gradually as the night melts into the morning or as a bud unfolds into its blossom the soul passes from darkness to light or opens into the flower and ripens into the fruit of the Christian life.

On the other hand, there are sudden and violent conversions. Nature ordinarily works through quiet gentle influences, sunshine and growth and imperceptible noiseless agents and activities. But occasionally her calm order is interrupted with a tremendous upheaval, as when a tornado sweeps a path of destruction through forest and village, or a storm at sea lashes it into foam and fury, or an earthquake shakes and cracks the rocky ribs of the earth, splitting mountains and destroying cities and causing an awful cataclysm. Such events are not wanting in the spiritual world. Our mental life is subject to profound shocks and crises, and our religious experience at times culminates in an explosion. There were sudden and violent conversions on the day of Pentecost, as great modern revivals witness them by the hundred and thousand, and Paul had a notable and extreme experience of this type. The quiet and orderly conversion of Lydia was quickly followed by the earthquake conversion of the Philippian jailer. In such instances the soul comes to a crisis and climax, though it may have been long preparing for and approaching it. The truth has been slumbering in the subconsciousness, secretly nursing its vitality, like seeds lying dormant in the soil waiting for the coming summer.

The nature of this crisis varies endlessly. Starbuck has gathered instances of many forms, some of which are the following: " This is the first aspect of conversion: the person emerges from a smaller, limited world of existence into a larger world of being. His life becomes swallowed up in a larger whole." In another aspect, " conversion is the surrender of the personal will to be guided by the larger forces of which it is a part." " The individual learns to transfer himself from a centre of self-activity into an organ of revelation of universal being, and to live a life of affection for and oneness with the larger life outside." Another form of this crisis is the sudden disruption of life into antagonistic forces. " There are forces in human life and its surroundings which tend to break the unity and harmony of consciousness; and its unity once destroyed, the contrast between what is, and what might be, gives birth to ideals and sets of two selves in sharp opposition to each other." These " two selves " struggled in fierce combat in Paul (Romans, chapter VII), and they often disrupt a man at the time of conversion so that he cries out, " And ah for a man to arise in me, that the man I am may cease to be."

The conditions of such crises also vary. They may arise as the result of some peculiar happening in the personal life, or in connection with revival excitement and contagion, or as the consequence of some word or sermon or song that drops into the subconsciousness and taps the deep early training and accumulated experiences or even explodes it as a spark of fire explodes a powder magazine. The most trivial happening may suddenly take by surprise and conquer a soul that thinks it is intrenched and secure against religious invasion and capture.

> Just when we are safest, there's a sunset touch,
> A fancy from a flower-bell, some one's death,
> A chorus-ending from Euripides,—

And that's enough for fifty hopes and fears
As old and new at once as nature's self,
To rap and knock and enter in our soul,

and then conversion takes place. When conversion thus precipitates a crisis in the soul, it breaks its unity and peace and sets up a conflict that may be fierce as a battle; and peace may come slowly as the result of a long process of adjustment of these conflicting elements, or quickly as the result of a sudden total surrender of the will to a sense of duty and to the grace of God.

Some souls thus have an easy and comfortable conversion and are born the second time almost as unconsciously as the first time; and others have a sharp and even a terrible experience and are converted almost in a convulsion.

3. **Intellectual and Emotional Conversions.**—Some conversions are predominantly intellectual in their processes and others emotional, although of course both of these elements are always involved in this change. The intellectual man acts on reasons seen and considered by which he is persuaded of truth and duty. And appeal to mere tradition or authority and much less an appeal to mere feeling does not tend to convince him: on the contrary it is likely to excite his opposition and even resentment. His mind follows logical processes and with him fact and evidence and proof are the first and main consideration. His faith must be rationalized and only as he is convinced can he be converted.

This is a legitimate process and demand. The Scriptures recognize it throughout. It is not the method of any prophet or apostle, much less of Jesus himself, to override reason and carry the soul off by sheer authority or on a flood of feeling. " Come now, and let us reason together," is the appeal of Jehovah himself. " Come and see," was the invitation to Nathanael. To John the Baptist in his doubt Jesus did not send a dogmatic answer, but gave him more facts and told him in effect to reason the question out for himself. Paul, with a mind of logic all compact, forging every argument into logical links of steel, " reasoned of righteousness, temperance, and judgment to come." We are constantly urged in the Scriptures to see for ourselves and use our own judgment and to " let every man be fully persuaded in his own mind." God did not give us reason and then stultify it by refusing to let us use it or by giving it nothing to do. He honours the reason he gave us and requires us to use it, and wants us to serve him on rational grounds.

The intellectual man, then, has a right to be given facts and reasons that will appeal to his mind and convince him that Jesus Christ is Lord and able to save unto the uttermost. The intellectual convert may be slow in arriving at truth and duty and action, but he usually has deep roots and is established in the truth and rooted and grounded in Christ. He is not easily shaken in his matured convictions and stands strong and fruitful, like an oak in a storm, when superficial emotional converts have cooled off, or when their shallow roots have withered away.

Our preaching and teaching should respect this right and demand of the human mind. Preaching should deal honestly with the reason. It should present facts and all the facts as they are, evade no difficulty, indulge in no illogical and unfair arguments, be perfectly candid, and seek first and foremost to know and declare only the truth. Many an unconverted hearer in the pew sits in indifference or in secret opposition and rebellion under the ill-informed or ignorant, dogmatic, illogical, fallacious, and unfair reasoning in the pulpit. We must meet such men on the ground of reason and seek to persuade them of the truth, and the truth will set them free.

On the other hand, the emotions have their place and right in human action and especially in conversion. We have great instinctive feelings that well up within us and carry us into action as a practical need and necessity. Religious truth awakens these emotions and this is a legitimate and normal process. But some souls are sensitive and vibrate more easily and deeply than others in their emotional nature, and in them the intellectual factor may be slight and the feeling factor predominates. A mere touch agitates them violently, a spark sets them on fire or explodes them. Different emotions may prevail in different persons or in the same person at different times. Fear is one of the first as it is the lowest emotion, and it drives many through the gate of conversion into the kingdom of God. At the opposite pole of feeling is the emotion of love, and this fine and noble feeling woos and wins many to the Saviour. The emotions of reverence and worship, the esthetic sense of the beautiful, regard for parents and friends, the contagious excitement and feeling of a revival season,—many are the forms and degrees of feeling that move the will in conversion. It is right to present and press such truth and arguments as will appeal to and stir up the feelings. Men never move, the coldest intellects never act, until they feel the emotions that pour as a stream on the will and push it into decision and action.

It is right and necessary, then, to preach and teach so as to touch and fire the feelings. But this process needs to be guarded against a mere appeal to feeling and against such excessive emotion as will submerge the reason and carry the soul off in an ungovernable flood. This is one of the dangers and abuses of revivals. Converts that are swept off in conversion in this unreasoning way are likely to be shallow and short-lived. The fire of straw quickly burns itself out and leaves only a heap of ashes. The mushroom that grew up in a night has no depth of earth and withers under the sun of the next day. Almost every exciting revival leaves burnt-out converts scattered as cinders along its track. Zeal without knowledge is dangerous in every field of life and especially so in religion. Emotion is good and necessary, but the emotional convert needs to be rooted and grounded in the truth that he may have roots that will endure and feed his life through all changes of spiritual weather and vicissitudes of temptation and trial. Emotional Christians are a vital element in our churches. They give warmth and zeal and liveliness to our church life. Feeling is one path to God and to Christ. But it is the truth that more deeply and permanently converts us and sets us free.

St. John saw the holy city lying foursquare with three gates on each side, open day and night. These gates symbolize the various types of conversion and modes of entrance into the kingdom of God. One convert enters through the gate of childhood in the early morning on the east side, and another late in the evening time far down the western slope of life. One enters gradually and comfortably without any serious distress or disturbance, as the dawn melts into the day,

and another through a storm of doubt and perplexity
or through a sudden convulsion of violence and agony.
One enters through the door of the mind, persuaded by
fact and reason of the truth and duty of the Christian
life, and another through the door of the heart, impelled
by feeling. One is driven in through the gate of fear,
and another is coaxed and wooed in through the gate
of love. One is attracted by one truth in the teaching
of Jesus or grace in his character or call to his service,
and another by another element that enlists his interest. One is charmed by his meekness, and another is
inspired by his manliness. One sits with Mary in
passive meditation at his feet, and another like Peter
follows Christ the busy worker and must always be
doing something. " Thus one man learns best to love
God through the thought of the Incarnation, another
through the thought of the vicarious sufferings of a
Saviour. One is practical and builds up his faith on
the Sermon on the Mount, and loves Christ as the great
Social Leader; another is speculative, and gets at his
Lord through far-reaching ideas; while still another
is mystical, believing he enters into the most intimate
personal communion with God, spirit to spirit. Yet it
is the whole Personality of Christ in its infinite riches
that is given us, and it is fellowship with Him as He
in actuality is that saves us." [1]

All of these and other types of conversion are to
be expected and respected as right and good, each in
its own way. And let not him that is converted in one
way envy or disparage or despise him that has some
other type of experience. We are all disposed to think
that other people ought to conform to our type, and we

[1] *The Psychology of the Christian Soul,* by George Steven, p.
184.

may try to compress them into our mould. Parents are
especially in danger of this anxiety and effort, as they
think their children should follow them in their conversion, and even the mother of Jesus was perplexed
and pained at his unfolding spiritual life. But God
has given us gifts differing and he fulfils himself in
many ways. He has opened twelve gates to let all
kinds of people through all types of conversion into
his kingdom, and we should not try or think to close
one of them. " The wind bloweth where it listeth: so
is every one that is born of the spirit."

CHAPTER VI

THE PSYCHOLOGY OF THE CHRISTIAN LIFE

THE Christian life, having had its divine principle breathed into the soul in regeneration and its human activity initiated in conversion, is now to be studied in the means and methods of its growth and fruitage.

I. GROWTH

1. **The Christian Life a Growth.**—The Christian life is a growth. We have seen, in Chapter II, that the soul is a growth and have looked into this wonderful process. The religious life follows the same law. The moral and spiritual nature is at first germinal and plastic and gradually unfolds into ethical sensibility and spiritual maturity and fruitfulness. The religious instincts of dependence and yearning and practical needs stir and assert themselves, religious beliefs and habits are formed, the soul turns from sin and lives in conscious relation with God a life of faith and prayer and obedience, and Christian character is developed and bears its fruitage. Thus the babe in Christ becomes the full-grown and victorious Christian.

2. **Pedagogical Applications of the Principle of Growth.**—Being a growth, teaching and training, doctrine and duty should be adapted to the Christian life in its early stages. Knowledge and experience and service that may be demanded of it in later years should

not be expected of it in the beginning. Truth and duty
should not be crowded on it too fast. Patience and
charity should be exercised in dealing with it. Babes
in Christ should be fed on milk, and strong men on
meat. Parents therefore should not urge their children
forward and endeavour to bring them up under en-
forced hot-house growth in the Christian life, and they
should not grow unduly anxious if their children unfold slowly in this life. Some children grow much
slower than others, and they should be given time.
Precocity is not to be stimulated in the Christian life,
any more than it is in intellectual growth. Anything
that may encourage children to become self-conscious
and push forward and make themselves conspicuous so
as to attract attention and excite remark in their religious experience and life is to be avoided, and any
such spirit is unhealthy and is to be discouraged.
When Jesus at twelve years of age was " found in the
temple, sitting in the midst of the doctors, both hearing
them, and asking them questions," he was not, as is
sometimes supposed, instructing the rabbis and showing off his superior wisdom and smartness, but he was
sitting at their feet receiving instruction in all humility; he was not teacher but scholar. And our children
should be taught to sit in the same reverent and teachable spirit.

The pedagogical principle goes deep into the history
and psychology of the Bible. God dealt with the
Hebrews in their early days as children and accommodated his teaching to their immature condition and
permitted them to hold beliefs and follow practices
which afterwards were outgrown and left behind, while
under prophets and apostles they went on to perfection. The teaching in the Old Testament was also

illuminated and interpreted by the picture language of symbols in sacrifices and all the gorgeous ceremonies of the tabernacle and temple, while in the New Testament these ceremonies were superseded by spiritual worship in which men come directly to God and worship him in spirit and in truth.

Our teaching and preaching should follow the same principle. We should accommodate our teaching in the Sunday school to the minds of the scholars, grading it from beginners to adults. And within the same class the teacher should endeavour to adapt the instruction to the individuality of each scholar so that it will meet and match his type of mind and degree of development. Preaching should observe the same principle so far as possible. It encounters the difficulty that its audience is not composed of the same general class or grade, but contains hearers of all ages and conditions of mind and education, and this mixed audience is one of the preacher's problems. How to shape and shoot arrows of truth so as to hit the general mind and not go over the heads of the young or under the feet of the more highly educated hearers is a difficult art and one that the preacher should constantly study and practise. It is possible, however, to present truth in such varied and picturesque forms that it will appeal to young and old, illiterate and learned alike. The sermon should not all run on the same level, but should be diversified and wind around and up and down, and thus at different points specially interest different classes of hearers and yet in some degree carry them all along its course. Some ministers meet this point by preaching a " children's sermon " before the principal discourse, and this plan often works well. But the main sermon should be level to the understanding of all classes, unless it be the very small children. The preaching of Jesus was so simple and varied and picturesque that all the people, including many children, heard him gladly.

II. Environment

Life is always a frail and delicate thing and must have its proper environment, or it easily perishes. A seed cast upon a bare rock cannot sprout and bloom, and a baby tossed into a snowbank would not long survive. The Christian life must be protected and nourished, or its spark will expire.

Life depends first on the harmony of its inner processes with its outer conditions. Seeds must find their appropriate soil and showers and sunshine, and few plants or animals can stand a violent change of climate or habitat. The Christian life thrives best in a Christian environment, and a sudden or violent change into unfavourable circumstances and associations may chill or kill it; and, conversely, a change to more congenial spiritual conditions, a warmer religious air, may cause it to thrive and bear fruit. The religious life is very sensitive to its environment and absorbent of the atmosphere in which it is immersed. Consciously or unconsciously it drinks in the teachings, example, and subtle influences in the midst of which it lives and assimilates them into its own life. Religion, as we have seen, is intensely contagious. Hence the immense importance of the Christian home and school and community, of pure and wholesome associations and companionships.

The home is the first mould in which young fluid life is cast and in a large degree fixed for life. The pervasive influence of parental example and spirit infuses itself into the whole atmosphere of the home and shapes and colours the character of the children. Many a home is so deeply imbued with the Christian spirit that the children grow up in it as Christians and never know any other life. But a home filled with an irreligious spirit, the constant drip of worldly conversation at the table, the daily talk about money-making and fashion and pleasure, occasional sneers or scoffs at religion, an irritable temper and selfish spirit, will inevitably mould the children into the same life.

It is also important that the school and college and university should be at least friendly to religious life. While the introduction of positive Christian teaching is generally inexpedient in such institutions, we have a right to insist in our Christian civilization that they be not hostile to religion. A worldly teacher in the day school and an agnostic and sneering professor in a college or university can chill and blight the religious life of the young and plant in their minds seeds of scepticism that will be hard to dislodge and may bear bitter fruit. But a teacher who is sincerely Christian in spirit and conduct will silently impart the same spirit to the scholars and students. An American teacher was once employed in a secular school in Japan under a contract which bound him not to say a word on the subject of Christianity. The obligation was scrupulously kept, but it could not obscure the unconscious influence of a Christian spirit which wrought in him a daily transfiguration. He was steadily watched as the unconscious virtue went out of him like a divine halo about his life, and the young men under his teaching began to seek the source of that speechless but all-conquering form of life. Forty of them, unknown to him, met in a grove and signed a covenant to abandon idolatry. Twenty-five of them entered the Kioto Christian training school, and some of them became ministers of the gospel. Not a word was spoken on the subject of religion by this Christian teacher to his students. He simply lived the Christian life before them: unconscious influence did the work. If the teachers and professors in our schools and colleges were of this spirit they would leaven these institutions with Christianity so that they would be a congenial and inspiring environment in which Christian life would grow.

The whole community, broadening out into the nation and the world, is the field in which our Christian life must be lived. It is vital, then, that this field be as favourable as possible to this growth. City slums, saloons, and dens of vice degrade the environment into a poisonous soil and atmosphere. Unhealthy and tainted amusements and social diversions infect it. The suggestive and sometimes vile pictures on the billboards of the theatre are flaming patches on the streets that enter into the education of children and colour the thought of the community or city. While on the way to the day school or the Sunday school a boy or girl may see an unclean sight that all the good instruction and influence of the school cannot obliterate or counteract. An unprincipled press and impure literature poison social morality, and corrupt politics pollute it. The whole domestic, sanitary, industrial, educational, moral, and civic life of the community is the environment in which our Christian life must grow, and hence it should be cleansed and uplifted throughout. Sanitation promotes sanctification. Pure politics are a part of piety. Clean streets, clean homes, clean sights, clean amusements, clean government,—all should be maintained as a wholesome atmosphere in which Christian life can flourish. The child should be set in the midst of the community and city and state and the whole environment built around it to protect and promote its life.

A mature Christian life is also sensitive to its surroundings and should guard itself against evil associations and keep itself immersed in Christian influences. No one can expect to grow in the Christian life who thrusts and soaks his soul in the muddy and foul stream of the world and exposes it to the contagion of the devil. That evil communications corrupt good manners, that like begets like, that both good and evil are infectious, is a law of psychology as well as of Scripture, and the Christian life can grow only in accordance with this condition. " Wherefore come out from among them, and be ye separate, saith the Lord, and touch not the unclean thing; and I will receive you."

III. TRUTH

The second broad means of the Christian life is truth. Every living thing must have its appropriate food, and truth is the food of the mind.

1. **The Nature and Function of Truth.**—Deep psychological and philosophical questions and difficulties start up at the mention of truth, and we may well regret that when Pilate asked the great Teacher, " What is truth? " he hurried off without waiting for the answer. But psychologically truth is the agreement of our ideas with reality, the correspondence of our thoughts with things. Truth is harmony with God. The fundamental importance of truth consists in the fact that it is the basis of our relation with the world, with one another, and with God. When we know the

truth our minds match reality and are in working relations with it as cogwheels fit into each other and work together; and when we are in error our minds are out of gear with reality and then the machinery of life works badly or stops altogether. Untruth of any kind is misleading and deceptive, puts us in false relations with things and works confusion, cuts away the common ground on which we stand to do business with others and dissolves all the bonds of human intercourse and fellowship. And most deeply and fatally of all, untruth throws us out of right relations with God and thereby cuts us off from the centre and source of all life.

Truth is the food of the mind in that it is the stimulus and sustenance of the mental faculties that wakes them into action and causes them to grow and enables them to seize and masticate and assimilate all facts and relations. The human mind when fed on truth develops an enormous appetite and digestive capacity and will eat up all history and science and literature, the world and sun and stars. It leaps to the frontiers of the universe and leaves no space or spirit unvisited.

Religious truth is the food of the religious life, awakening the soul to its sense of God, to its own condition in sin, to its need of atonement and pardon, and enlightening and strengthening it in all its religious duties and blessings. Truth is thus the primary foundation of the Christian life, or the root out of which its fruit and beauty and blessedness must grow. Hence the immense importance and emphasis laid on the truth in the Bible and especially in the teaching of Jesus. " I am the truth." " And this is life eternal, that they might know thee the only true God, and Jesus Christ, whom thou hast sent." "Sanctify them through thy truth: thy word is truth."

2. The Bible a Storehouse of Religious Truth.—We have already seen [1] that the Bible is a mass of religious experience embalming, as ancient insect life in amber, the beliefs and fears and doubts, the trials and tragedies and tears, the growing visions and victories of the chosen Hebrew people of God, as the light of revelation fell upon them ever more clearly until it culminated in the rising of the Sun of Righteousness and Sunburst of God in Jesus. "Now all these things happened unto them by way of example; and they were written for our admonition, upon whom the ends of the ages are come." "For whatsoever things were written aforetime were written for our learning, that through patience and through comfort of the scriptures we might have hope." "But these are written, that ye may believe that Jesus is the Christ, the Son of God; and that believing ye may have life in his name." The Bible is thus not simply a treasury of ancient and obsolete thought and life, a storehouse of curious lore of interest only to the antiquarian or archæologist, but it is fresh bread for our souls and a perennial fountain to reinvigorate and vitalize our life.

We may now look more closely into the psychology of this process. Jesus said, "The words that I have spoken unto you are spirit, and are life." How can this be?

3. The Psychology of Words.—A word is a wonderful thing. Though it is the very oldest human invention and one that has lost its wonder through having become so familiar and apparently simple and commonplace, yet a word is still the most marvellous of all

[1] Pp. 23-24, and also 90-93.

human achievements and is incomparably the most powerful instrument of our life. A word is a sound or a printed sign: this is its outer form or shell; but its inner meaning goes as deep as the human soul and is as mysterious as life itself. A word is a symbol of thought. It is a bridge that connects one mind with another, or a window through which one mind looks into another. It is the telegraphic or telephonic conductor that discharges the contents of one mind into another. It leaps from the lip to the ear, or from the printed page to the eye, and closes the circuit so that thought flashes from mind to mind. A word is a winged idea that flies from one mind and lights in another and there unloads its burden of meaning. A thought is crystallized into a word in one mind, and the crystal is transported, it may be, across continents or centuries, and dropped into another mind, and then dissolves back into its original idea, so that the two minds are saturated with the same thought, or they think as one. Words are a universal sea of life rolling around us and sending their waves up on the shore line of each individual mind.

And thus words are the means of all human intelligence, communication, action, progress, and power. We cannot think, except in the most rudimentary degree, without words. "To think," Max Müller says, "is to speak low, and to speak is to think aloud." The enormous chasm between the savage and the civilized man is measured by the three or four hundred words of the Patagonian compared with the three or four hundred thousand words of the Englishman. Words transact all the business of life for us. They furnish the journalist with his record for the history of a day, the lawyer with his brief, the physician with his prescription, the minister with his sermon, the scientist with the instrument for his investigations, the metaphysician with the terms of his subtle distinctions, the statesman with his laws and constitutions, the orator with the music and majesty of his eloquence, the novelist with the colours for his pictures of life, and the poet with the airy drapery for his dreams. They carry on our conversation and weave the whole web of our social life. They buy and sell our goods, administer our government, unite us at the marriage altar, bury our dead, conduct our worship, roll aloft our psalms and prayers, and " fleet beyond this iron world to him who made it."

A drop of ink falling on a thought multiplies it a millionfold and makes the whole world think. Printed words embalm all the centuries and transmit to us the thoughts and deeds of the innumerable dead and resurrect all the pageantry of the past. Words are fossilized history and life. Libraries are the fossilized brains of thinkers that are gone. The thoughts that soared in Shakespeare's imagination spread their wings in our minds, and the ideas that glowed in Plato's intellect burn again in our brains, as the light of suns that shone millions of years ago glows in our coal fires. The pomp of Assyria is lying latent in our words, and all " the glory that was Greece and the grandeur that was Rome." " A dead language is the graveyard of the people who spoke it and is full of their monuments. Their swords and shields are in it; their faces are pictured on its walls; and their very voices ring through its corridors."

Words reflect all the hues of our many-coloured spirit world. They are transparent with clear thought, or misty and muddy with obscurity. They are clean-cut, like sharply minted coins, with precision and firmness, or mutilated and muffled with vagueness and uncertainty. They gleam and sparkle with cheerfulness and wit, or are heavy and dull with stupidity. They are icy cold with haughtiness, or warm with sympathy. They shoot to their mark as poison-tipped arrows, hissing with hate, or they breathe tender and ardent love. They speak poniards and every syllable is a stab, or they drop dew and honey. They are pliant and plastic, many-tinted and iridescent, to express all the shapes and shades of thought and feeling. They can forge ponderous anchor chains of thought, or spin the most delicate silken threads of sentiment. They can reproduce the myriad aspects and activities of nature, recreating the dawn and the sunset and all the glory of the constellations, or they can reconstruct the more wonderful inner world of the human mind. They can gather up all the energies of the soul and strike them in one terrific blow. In his reply to Hayne, Webster simply pointed his finger and launched a single sentence at his opponent, and the miserable man bowed his head and doubled up in his seat as though he had been struck by a cannon ball. Words have in them the potency of all life. They are big with the issues of time and eternity. They have kindled wars and slain empires, and they have been the white-winged messengers of peace. A single word has saved a soul, or broken a heart. When God communicated with the world of his lost children he sent the glorious Word, splendid with the radiance of his infinite and eternal purity and beauty, in whom we see the express image of his person and the brightness of his glory, and through whom he most fully reveals himself to us and we hold fellowship with him.

We have drawn out at some length this psychology of words because it enables us to understand how the words of Jesus and all the words of Scripture " are spirit and are life." These words spoken by prophets and apostles and by Jesus himself bring to us their very thoughts and recreate them in our minds so as to beget in us the same spiritual states and experiences they had. The laws of Moses and the Psalms of David, his penitence and tears, aspiration and attainment, the splendid visions of Isaiah and the lamentations of Jeremiah, the proverbial wisdom of Solomon and the sublime poetry of Job are dropped as crystals into our minds and hearts and melt back into substantially the same states in us, and thus we are not only taught by their precepts but are also in a degree filled with their life.

The whole Old Testament is thus dissolved in us and absorbed into our spiritual blood, and the New Testament passes through the same process. The life of Jesus is lived over again for us from his birth through to his death and resurrection and ascension. Again we witness his mighty works and hear his very words. We are present at Pentecost and on Mars' hill, and we hear Peter and Paul preach. We are spectators of a momentous conflict and epochal victory as Christianity struggles free from the swaddling bands of Judaism and steps out into the Gentile world and lands on the shore of Europe. We go with Paul to Corinth and Rome, and we look over his shoulder and read his letters as he writes profound theological epistles or drops a brief note to a friend. Paul's very thoughts are recreated in our minds, and our hearts glow with his emotions. John infuses his mystic gospel into our spirits and unrolls his grand apocalyptic pictures before our imagination.

Words thus carry us back into the scenes and sayings of the Bible and reproduce it all in our minds, dissolve it in our souls. It makes us live over again the lives and experiences of the prophets and apostles and fashions us into their likeness. It pours their blood into our veins. It crowds our minds back into their consciousness, even into the human consciousness of Jesus. We need often to recall his saying, " The words that I have spoken you are spirit, and are life." Absorbing and assimilating these words we live and yet not we, but Christ liveth in us.

This is how the truth contained in the Bible feeds us and causes us to grow in the Christian life. This is the reason such constant and strenuous emphasis is put on the Bible by the church and by the Bible itself. This is why we should ever read, mark, and meditate upon it and thus dissolve it in our spiritual blood that it may reappear in the strength and fruitfulness, the beauty and blessedness of our Christian life.

4. The Comprehensive and Progressive Nature of Religious Truth.—All truth is religious. Every truth comes from God, as every ray of daylight and of gaslight and electric light shoots from the sun, either straight from its blazing surface, or indirectly through reflection and diffusion or through ancient coal beds. And therefore every fact and truth, whether of science or philosophy, history, literature or art, tells us something about God and will enlarge and enrich our religious life. " For all things are yours; whether Paul, or Apollos, or Cephas, or the world, or death, or things present, or things to come; all are yours." And we may add, whether of Newton or Darwin, or astronomy or

geology, or evolution or higher criticism: all the truth
discovered by these thinkers or found in these fields
belongs to us as Christian believers. We should therefore be on our guard against narrowness and illiberal-
ity in our attitude towards human knowledge, but
should keep the windows of our minds open to every
breeze that blows, welcome all showers of truth, gather
harvests from all fields, and feed on all knowledge: for
whatever widens and deepens our knowledge by so
much enlarges and enriches our Christian life. Of
course we should also be on our guard against error,
against " profane babblings and oppositions of knowledge falsely so called," for error throws life out of adjustment and may poison and blight it. We are to " believe not every spirit, but prove the spirits, whether
they be of God," for many false prophets are still gone
out into the world. We should ever endeavour to cultivate and exercise the truth-loving and truth-seeking
spirit that will enable us to distinguish the true from
the false.

Religious truth is progressive because it is ever studying and gaining a deeper appreciation and fuller ap-
propriation of the Bible, and because it is ever gathering into itself the increasing volume of progressive
human knowledge. It would be incredible that theological and religious knowledge should stand still and
stagnate amidst the onward rush and broadening
stream of secular knowledge, and such a fact would be
fatal to religious faith. But Jesus himself had a far
different outlook and promised us some better thing
than such stagnation. " I have yet many things to say
unto you, but ye cannot bear them now. Howbeit when
he, the Spirit of truth, is come, he shall guide you into
all truth: for he shall not speak from himself; but

what things soever he shall hear, *these* shall he speak: and he shall declare unto you the things that are to come. He shall glorify me: for he shall take of mine, and shall declare it unto you" (John 16:12-14).

This splendid promise has been in course of progressive fulfilment through all the Christian centuries and is still unfolding its treasures. Such a work as Fairbairn's *The Place of Christ in Modern Theology* shows with magnificent sweep of vision and wonderful wealth of learning how Christianity as it has marched down through the centuries has appropriated and assimilated successively Greek philosophy and Roman law and medieval scholasticism and Reformation theology and modern criticism, and thus, like a rolling snowball, has accumulated the mighty mass and meaning of its faith. Our Christian knowledge should follow the same process with the same result. We should not be afraid of any new truth, scientific or philosophical, historical or literary, but take it up into our thought and life. Every stone that the scientist or critic quarries and cuts should be taken by us and fitted and built into the temple of Christian faith. President James McCosh, of Princeton University, did this when he early adopted the doctrine of evolution and built it into theism, and ex-President Francis L. Patton, of the same institution, has done similar useful work in his popular lectures on "Christianity and the Modern Man" in the light of modern knowledge. Our Christian faith will thus not be in constant antagonism with our growing knowledge, irritating and alienating educated and cultured believers in or sympathizers with the Christian religion, and it will not grow obsolete and be left behind, but it will ever keep abreast of the age and appeal to and hold the most sincere and thoughtful minds.

Our faith must ever grow out of the past and in this sense it is ever old, but it should also embody and express itself in terms of the present and in this sense it should be ever new. Jesus urged us to bring out of our treasures things old and new. Old and new are not antagonistic or mutually exclusive, but are complementary and harmonious. It is the old sun that shines upon us, but its light is new every morning. The clouds are very old, but their silver nets and golden fringes are ever resplendently new. The old bushes remain, but their roses are fresh every June. We still wear clothes as our fathers did, but we cut them after our own fashion; we eat food, but the dishes differ. And so we believe in the old faith in its fundamental facts and principles, but its form and expression should be our own. Theology is not a dead and desiccated science, but it is still full of new blood and fresh life and ever develops into larger growth and fuller vitality and finer fruit. Its divine principles are eternal, but its human expression should ever be adapted to the present time and needs, and its voice should be a living voice. We should not cling to the old simply because it is old, or reject or fear or suspect the new simply because it is new; neither should we disparage the old or rush to the new as such; but we should welcome and hold to both only because and in so far as they are true. We shall thus ever have religious knowledge that is both conservative and progressive, taxing all the world in its interest and keeping pace with all our progress, so that it will ever express living realities, fitting the facts of life and appealing vitally and vividly to and satisfying our religious needs.

5. The Formation of Beliefs and Creeds.—The re-

ception of religious truth into the mind and heart leads
to the formation of religious beliefs and creeds. The
whole state of mind of the Christian convert involves
belief in the religious realities of God and Christ, sin
and salvation, prayer and obedience and righteousness.
These beliefs at first are traditional and nascent and
vague, amorphous and unorganized. They may be the
jelly-like mental protoplasm which is to be developed
into definite beliefs and the bones of an articulated
creed. The mind inevitably begins this process of defining and fixing its beliefs and arranging them in a
systematic order. Its organizing instinct cannot put
up with a disordered world in the field of religious
thought and experience any more than it can in the
field of scientific knowledge. As the mind gathers truth
from study and experience it brings the new materials
into relation with the old, and the two forms of truth
necessarily modify each other and may struggle together and thus grow into harmony. Thought grows
wider and deeper as it attracts to itself and absorbs
into itself all its associations. The dim vague beliefs
with which the mind starts evolve into clearer forms
with deeper roots and wider branches and more intense
convictions. The traditional faith of the child becomes
the reasoned belief of mature life. Individual religious
beliefs thus grow through the years as they are fed
and exercised, and they may also wither through starva-
tion and adverse influences.

These individual religious beliefs in time get organized into creeds. A creed is an official and social statement of religious faith as contrasted with personal
beliefs. It is the organizing instinct going beyond the
individual mind into the social mind. A creed is necessary as the common ground on which men agree to

stand as the basis of religious faith and action and thus corresponds with agreements in friendship, contracts in business, platforms in politics, constitutions in states, and treaties in international relations. A creed is secreted out of the common consciousness of a church or religious body and forms the bones and skeleton that give shape and unity and efficiency to the organization. It is the psychological foundation and framework of the building that houses the thought and life of the church. Every church of necessity has a creed, whether or not it has been formally written and adopted, and the closeness with which the creed fits the consciousness of the church, or the sincerity and intensity with which it is believed and experienced, will determine its efficiency and fruitfulness. For this reason most churches find it necessary from time to time to revise their creeds in order to make them fit more snugly and work more efficiently.

6. Doctrinal Preaching.—This leads to the subject of doctrinal preaching. Should we preach doctrines? Of course we should and must. Doctrine is the necessary foundation on which duty and deed are built, or the root out of which they spring as flower and fruit. Every rational deed issues from a thought, thought when it becomes critical and constructive shapes itself into a doctrine, and doctrine builds a system of truth. Thus every one is a psychologist and theologian and philosopher, though he may not know it and, like the Frenchman in the play who was surprised to find that he had been speaking prose all his life, he may be surprised to find it out. Christian preaching and practice must root itself in doctrine and cannot be clearer and stronger than the doctrine out of which it grows. Yet "doctrinal preaching" is not a popular programme

and is supposed to be somewhat repellent. There is no avoiding it, however; the very denial of doctrine is itself a doctrine, and the rankest sensationalist, loudly denouncing doctrine, is yet himself preaching it, though it may be of a very poor kind.

One danger with our doctrines is that they may fall out of touch with our day, if not in substance and spirit, then in form and expression. They necessarily change with the intellectual, social, and spiritual climate of their age, a change that may be slow and unperceived in a short time, but is sure and obvious in the long run. When one reads a sermon fifty or a hundred years old he is at once aware of a style and tone different from the preaching of to-day. Such change is evidence of the continuous growth and adaptability of Christian truth to varying and advancing human needs; a sign, not of decay, but of vigorous and fruitful life. Christianity is permanent in its essential nature, but its interpretation and application are progressive. Yet this doctrinal expression may change too slowly and thus lag behind the times and grow obsolete. If doctrines are preached in the phrases of former times they will strike the present generation as strange and unattractive; whereas if they are set forth in the life and language of to-day they may find a welcome reception.

Doctrine should also be presented, not as a dry and rattling skeleton, but clothed in flesh and blood and pulsing warm with life. Bones are useful members of the anatomy, but in the higher animals they are buried in the flesh. Doctrine should appeal directly to experience. It should be woven of the same threads as the general web of human life, and illustrations of it should be drawn direct from daily happenings. This will relieve it of its foreign and uninteresting air and bring it home to every one's business and bosom. The gospel of Christ fills a deep and permanent want in the universal human heart, and when its doctrines are thus presented they prove attractive and popular, satisfying and successful, and the people still hear it, as they did when it fell from the lips of Jesus himself, gladly.[1]

7. **The Place of Doubt in Religious Belief.**—Doubt is uncertain belief. It is the borderland between knowledge and ignorance, the twilight between light and darkness. It is therefore a mixed state of mind and varies in degree from almost certain knowledge to the faintest belief or hope. It may be the morning twilight in which an uncertain truth or hope or speculation is growing into positive knowledge, or the evening twilight in which an accepted truth or theory is withering away.

Doubt attends all our knowledge and is inherent in the constitution of the human intellect. It is due to our finite faculties, and we can no more escape it than we can slip out of our own skin or elude the laws of our own mind. However much we may know and however positive and final may be our knowledge, at the point or margin where what we do know begins to impinge on its boundary and fade out into the twilight of what we do not know, there doubt necessarily begins. Only an omniscient mind can be free from doubt, or else a mind that does not think at all. The thinker can no more escape from his doubts than he can run away from his own shadow, and the more he thinks the more he will doubt; for the more he knows the more he will see that he does not know. The wider

[1] See the author's *The Basal Beliefs of Christianity*, Preface.

is our circle of light the vaster is the surrounding circle of darkness, and our ignorance is ever outrunning our knowledge. Doubt is thus a permanent element in our life and grows with our growth.

And yet doubt does not interfere with our practical living. All of our knowledge is more or less infected or margined with doubt, and yet we often do not hesitate to act on an imperfect and even doubtful belief. We cannot be absolutely sure of anything we are about to do, and yet we act. We do business with others without knowing much about them, and we start on a journey without knowing whether or not we shall reach our destination. If we demanded certain knowledge before we acted, we could not do a single thing, not even take a step or draw a breath. Probability is the guide of life, the necessary foundation on which we build all our conduct in society, business, science, and religion.

Not only is doubt not a hindrance to our living, but it is a highly useful factor in our knowledge and life. Doubt is the great destroyer of error, the scythe that mows down the weeds of baleful beliefs, the scavenger that removes the corpses of false hopes and dead faiths. Doubt of demons and ghosts has cleared our world of terror and has given us a sense of security and peace. When doubt attacked the Ptolemaic astronomy it tore down the low-roofed hut of heavens that cabined and confined the human race, dwarfing all its thought, and thereby cleared the way for the grand heavens that have given us an infinitely larger universe and enormously expanded our vision and all our views.

Doubt is not only a great destructionist, but is also a great constructionist. Its negative work prepares the way for positive advance. The withering of a great error through doubt is often at the same time the budding of a great truth. While the old heavens were coming down the new heavens were going up on an infinitely larger scale. Doubt is a pioneer that goes beyond our certain knowledge to explore the land of our ignorance and open up new worlds. Like Columbus, it sets out on an unknown sea and its " purpose holds to sail beyond the sunset, and the baths of all the western stars." A theory is a searchlight of the mind thrown forward into the twilight and night of our ignorance; it is the mind feeling into the unknown. Our scientific investigation is largely an effort to clear up our doubts and reach greater lucidity and certainty. Much of our mental activity in study, business, politics, and social life is solving doubts. So doubt is a root of our mental growth and the advance agent of our intellectual expansion and power, the evening of error and the dawn of new truth.

The question of the moral quality of doubt now confronts us. It is often thought of as a guilty thing. Doubt has been closely connected with damnation, the first slip and step down the broad road. But the moral quality of doubt depends on its motive and end. In the scientific field doubt may be purely intellectual and almost devoid of any moral quality, although doubt can hardly ever be wholly free from some slight tincture of such spirit. But in fields involving our personal interests and desires and duties, such as business and politics, profit and pleasure, character and conduct, these factors are a strong and perhaps a dominant influence in determining our doubts. If a man wants to carry through a dishonest business transaction for the sake of its profit, it is easy for him to doubt whether it is dishonest and then to believe it is right. His doubt is born of an evil desire and is an illegitimate and depraved child. If one does not want to believe in God, his desire may breed an agnostic doubt and feed it into lusty strength. Our doubts, then, like our beliefs, are largely subject to our interests, desires, and wills, and we can make them grow or cause them to wither and die at the subtle bidding of our hearts.

We are not, then, to be surprised at the fact of religious doubt. The nature of all knowledge and especially of religious knowledge makes doubt inherent in the subject so that it cannot be escaped. And let us not think that religious doubt is necessarily dishonest and guilty. It may be profoundly sincere and transparently honest. Many of the most deeply religious and most honest souls have been perplexed with the sorest doubts. Prophets and apostles had their doubts, though they do not often let us see them; and did not a fleeting shadow of doubt fall on the mind of Jesus when for a moment he prayed that the cup of the cross might pass from him? Let not us ministers be alarmed or surprised when we find ourselves troubled with doubt. People usually think that ministers have creeds that fit their minds snugly, like a suit without seam or wrinkle, so as to give them undisturbed comfort, but this is because they do not see into the ministerial mind. The minister may have more doubts than others because he knows more about the difficulties of faith; he has a broader field of knowledge that borders on still broader margins of mystery.

The most beautiful instance on record of how to deal with religious doubt is Christ's treatment of John the Baptist's doubt of Jesus as the Messiah. John had been in prison until he fell into a prison mood. Hope does not burn brightly there, and in that damp and dusky place the world looked dark to John and the checkered shadows on the stone walls turned to ghostly spectres. At length John began to doubt whether Jesus were the Messiah, and he sent a committee to interview him and put the question to him. What did Jesus say? "Go your way, and tell John what things ye have seen and heard." This is a remarkable answer. It contains no harsh judgment upon John, or slightest trace of impatience with him for his doubt. 'Go and tell John the facts,' said Jesus. He did not send word to John that his doubts were damnable and that he should stop thinking and hush his doubts by stifling them to death. This has been a favourite way of dealing with doubt in some quarters. This spirit bids us beware of these troublesome questions, distrust our reasoning powers, and stop thinking. But this is not the spirit of the Bible. Jesus did not stop John's thinking, and mental death is not the cure for our doubt.

Neither did Jesus try to do John's thinking for him. John's question was, "Art thou he that cometh, or look we for another?" Why did not Jesus answer with a plain and positive "Yes"? Why did he not relieve John of all responsibility and perplexity in settling this question by settling it for him? Because this is not Christ's way and it is not God's way. It is a way that presents plausible pleas and attractions. It seems so plain and easy and conclusive, and it has often been tried. The Pope wants to do all our religious thinking for us, and many a Protestant theologian is willing to undertake the same business. Why not have the church fix and finish our creed down to the last letter, and then simply accept it on its dogmatic authority? Because our minds will not let us and God does not want us to do this. Christianity is not a superstition, but a rational religion. God never settles our beliefs for us dogmatically, but he gives reasons for his revelations and bids us prove them for ourselves. " Come now, and let us reason together," is his invitation and bidding. So, on this occasion, Jesus said in effect to John's disciples: ' Go and give John these additional facts and let him draw his own conclusion; I shall not answer his question for him categorically, but I shall suggest to him a line of thought and let him work it out for himself.' He did not tell John to do less thinking, but to do more thinking. Jesus was not afraid of doubts and reasoning in his disciples: he only wanted them to reason enough and to reason their way through to right conclusions.

And so the way out of our doubts is not to think less until we relapse into mental stagnation and death, but it is to think more until we work our way forward into clearer light and larger truth. John took his doubts to Jesus. He did not brood over them in his despondency until he became a confirmed pessimist and agnostic, but he went straight to Jesus, and then he got more light and died in triumphant faith. Let us go to Christ in our doubt and perplexity and consider the facts he gives us, and a fuller intimacy with him will enable us to understand him better, and then we shall find our way through the twilight and darkness of doubt into the light of faith.

And let us exercise the same patience and sympathy with those in doubt that Jesus did with John. The currents of modern thought are flowing through the pews of the church so that there are more doubting hearers in them than the preacher in the pulpit may know or suspect. How to deal with the doubt of our day is one of the preacher's chief problems and responsibilities and is one of the highest tests of his wisdom. He needs to study and understand the nature and causes of this doubt and then face it frankly and fairly. In some instances it springs out of the physical condition of the doubter and is part of his general mood of depression, as was the case with John the Baptist; in other instances it may be due to unspiritual or sinful living, and in still others to entanglement in the sceptical and agnostic thinking and theories of the day. The minister needs to know how to diagnose these various conditions and forms of doubt and to apply the appropriate remedy. In general the preacher needs to beware of treating doubt with dogmatic condemnation and harshness, branding it with a burning mark of guilt, but he should deal with it patiently and sympathetically as an honest state of mind. In too many instances the doubter is driven deeper into his doubt by unintelligent or unsympathetic or unfair treatment from the pulpit. Some of our best informed and most thoughtful hearers are honestly wrestling with doubt and they cannot be browbeaten out of it and forced into faith by dogmatism, much less by blatant ignorance of modern thought. What the doubting questioner often needs is what Jesus sent to John: more facts and light that will give him a larger view and lead him into closer fellowship with Christ. Especially should the doubter be induced to obey Christ as far as his faith goes, and such obedience is often a solvent of doubt. As one walks the path of service his doubts often disappear as mere shadows in his own mind, and he emerges into the light.

It is also important that the pastor should know

how to deal with doubt in private interviews. The long personal conference Jesus held with Nicodemus, who came to him through the shadows of the night with deeper shadows in his soul, is a beautiful instance of how to deal with doubt in private. Nicodemus was troubled about the mysteries of religion, and Jesus did not deny these mysteries, but in great patience he explained to his night visitor the elusive nature of the new birth and smoothed the way for the influential rabbi and secret searcher after truth to become an open disciple. The sympathetic pastor is at times consulted by troubled believers and even by unbelievers, and he should endeavour to win their confidence and meet them on their own ground and lead them into truth and light.

Doubt, then, is a general fact inherent in our thought and not to be escaped in our Christian faith. It may be sincere and honest and should be dealt with, not by condemnation and suppression, but by intelligent and sympathetic treatment. Doubt is a sign of thought and is better than unthinking stagnation, but it is weakness and not strength. It may be good as a temporary state of mind and step towards clearer light, but not as a finality: positive belief is the rightful state of the mind. And when doubt is fairly faced and fought through it often leads to a stronger triumphant faith. Tennyson has finely analyzed and expressed the psychology of honest doubt as experienced by his friend, Arthur H. Hallam, in the familiar stanzas in " In Memoriam ":

> Perplext in faith, but pure in deeds,
>   At last he beat his music out.
>   There lives more faith in honest doubt,
> Believe me, than in half the creeds.

He fought his doubts and gather'd strength,
He would not make his judgment blind,
He faced the spectres of the mind
And laid them: thus he came at length

To find a stronger faith his own;
And Power was in him in the night,
Which makes the darkness and the light,
And dwells not in the light alone.

And Browning has expressed the same thought in
" Bishop Blougram's Apology ":

With me, faith means perpetual unbelief
Kept quiet like the snake 'neath Michael's foot
Who stands calm just because he feels it writhe.

.   .   .   .

Say I—let doubt occasion still more faith!

" And blessed is he, whosoever shall find none occasion of stumbling in me." With these words Jesus
closed his answer to John. They imply that we must
exercise some patience with Christ, that we cannot
fully understand him, that after we have done our profoundest and most sympathetic thinking in relation to
him there will still be an unexplained remainder that
we cannot clear up, that he is bordered with infinitude
that must ever transcend and try our faith. All our
religious thinking must ever be margined and mingled
with mystery. It would be a shallow religion that we
could sound to the bottom; it would be a poor and
pitiful God that we could see through. Some things
relating to Christ we must take by faith; some of God's
ways may ever sorely perplex and pain us. But blessed

is he that is not offended on this account, but rather trusts and worships him the more.[1]

> Let knowledge grow from more to more,
>   But more of reverence in us dwell;
>   That mind and soul, according well,
> May make one music as before,
>
> But vaster.

8. Meditation.—Truth needs to be digested and assimilated, and this is largely effected through meditation, which is a fruitful means of the Christian life. Meditation is fixing the mind on a subject and quietly thinking it over, looking at it from every side and working into its nature and depths until we see it in all lights and relations. It is to be discriminated from mere passivity of mind and reverie or day-dreaming. We may relax our thoughts and let them roam or drift or fly at will, blown about by every wind of chance thought or feeling or caprice; or we may set them to building air castles that are more gorgeous but less substantial than clouds in the sky. Such a state of mind, while sometimes it may be indulged in as a mere relaxation, yet as a habit is useless and mentally weakening. It lures the mind away from the sober realities of life and absorbs it in imaginary diversion that ends in reaction and discontent. As opposed to this idle drifting and empty dreaming, meditation is an active and may be an intense exercise of the mind by which it concentrates its attention and multiplies its associations. It is only by this process that we can know a subject

[1] For a fuller exposition of "How Jesus Dealt with John's Doubt," see the author's *Scenes and Sayings in the Life of Christ*, Chapter XX.

in its principles and digest and assimilate it into our own thought. The raw materials of knowledge pour into our minds through our senses; but these materials can be shaped into our own knowledge only as we lay hold of them by our mental faculties and mould them into form and meaning. As long as our knowledge is the mere repetition and memory of what others have taught us, we do not know anything by our own perception and grasp of understanding. One may commit to memory a proposition in geometry and not have a glimmer of an idea of what it means; only as one comprehends the mathematical principles involved does he perceive the truth and beauty of the proposition.

Meditation goes deeper than this perception of truth and penetrates into its roots and relations by the process of mental association. Any idea or object in the mind is a growing thing that begins to sink rootlets and throw out branches and filaments through the mind and thus relates itself to the entire contents of consciousness. One thought suggests another, as we have already seen, until the whole world of the thinker is organized around the original fact or idea. All the scattered rays of knowledge and experience are focused in this centre until it blazes with light and heat. Then the subject is seen and felt in all its nature and relations and it masters and moves the will.

The quiet reflection of meditation is especially necessary and fruitful in considering our own character and conduct, aims and motives. Out in the world its glare and excitement, competition and temptation, are apt to mislead and confuse our judgment and pervert our ethical vision. Our senses and self-interest and passions sway us and may sweep conscience off its throne. Meditation withdraws us from this outer excitement

into quietness where we can calmly consider our course,
and conscience can be heard. Often we are impetuous
and rash and wrong in conduct, and then in sober
reflection we realize our fault and resolve to restrain
our infirmity and strengthen ourselves against its recurrence, thus growing deeper roots of wisdom and self-
control.

Meditation is the necessary condition of self-
acquaintance. We are in danger of losing touch with
ourselves in the hurry and confusion of the world.
Often we need to retire into solitude and put a finger
on our pulse and look ourselves in the face and see
what manner of persons we are. By close scrutiny and
honest examination we should try our spirits, test
our motives, and endeavour to see ourselves as we really
are.

> By all means use sometimes to be alone.
>   Salute thyself; see what thy soul doth wear.
> Dare to look in thy chest, for 'tis thine own,
>   And tumble up and down what thou find'st there.
>   —GEORGE HERBERT.

Rich inner resources are a fruit of meditation. This
exercise gradually stores the mind with treasures of
knowledge and beauty, ideals and aspirations that
are the strength and comfort of the soul. Some people are so empty that they have no power of self-
entertainment. Left alone, they are instantly discontented and miserable. They have not read anything
or done anything that is worth thinking about. Other
minds are so amply stored with mental and spiritual
treasures that they are their own kingdom and may
be richer than Crœsus in inner wealth. Such people
never can be left alone in empty discontent, for they

are their own best company. This was the experience
of the Psalmist: " My soul shall be satisfied as with
marrow and fatness; and my mouth shall praise thee
with joyful lips: when I remember thee upon my bed,
and meditate on thee in the night watches."

Meditation is necessary to the mastery of life. We
must live our lives inwardly in thought before we can
live them outwardly in action. The architect thinks
his building through from foundation to finish, he puts
it all up in his brain before he erects it in steel and
stone; and such inner preparation must always precede outer execution. The outer action may be brief
and appear sudden, but the inner preparation was
long and patient. The harvest may be gathered in an
hour, but through how many weeks and months did the
wheat silently drink in the showers and sunshine before it ripened into golden grain. The meteor burns
itself out in a moment, but through how many millions
of invisible miles did it gather momentum for that
brief flash of splendour. A great surgeon said that if
he had only three minutes for a critical operation, he
would take two to get ready. Jesus took thirty years
of silent preparation for just three years of work.
If we would be architects and artists in living we
must take time and get ready, grow deep roots of wisdom and strength in meditation, and then we may
throw our branches out and bear ripened fruit in the
world.

Meditation reaches its highest usefulness and finest
fruitage in the spiritual life. The things of the spirit
are best discerned by the spirit in its own inner vision
and reflection. The Bible blossoms out into a new
book in the quiet of meditation. The most familiar
passage may flash and flame out in unexpected light

and heat as we gaze upon it in earnest thought. The
Psalmist understood this psychology when he prayed,
" Open thou mine eyes, that I may behold wondrous
things out of thy law." The minister and teacher especially need to know and practise this art. One should
sit down and meditate on a text or lesson a long
while in order that he may get up and preach or teach
a little while. Meditation ripens all the truths of religion and causes them to bear the fruits of the Spirit.
It carries us into the secret place of the Most High
where we may know God most directly and intimately.
We do not know God best when we are in the urgency
and excitement of action, but when we are in the solitude and silence of meditation. " Be still, and know
that I am God."

> The mountain lake reflects the full-orbed sun,
>   Not when from tempest it finds no surcease,
> But when the last, least ripple's course is run,
>   And its unfretted bosom sleeps in peace.
> The face of God shines not so clear through wind and fire,
> As in the stillness in which broods a pure desire.

9. Truth and Life.—Truth and life are related as
fountain and stream, as fuel and fire, as root and
fruit. Every idea tends to execute itself, and belief
issues in life, faith becomes fact. While our instincts
and practical needs push us immediately into unrea-
soned action, yet our conduct and character are shaped
by our conscious beliefs. As a man thinketh in his
heart so is he, and out of the heart are the issues of
life.

" Truth is in order to goodness." While the scientist
and philosopher may pursue pure truth for its own
sake, the prophet and preacher seek it for practical

ends. They see visions that they may turn them into victories. Religious truth especially is intensely practical, and all its doctrines are intended to issue in deeds. We need to be on our guard against the speculative spirit in religion, studying its facts and spinning theories and carrying on controversies as a purely intellectual interest. Theology may do this in a degree, but even theology needs to beware of this purpose and spirit, lest it lose all flesh and blood and become a bundle of dry bones. Every doctrine in religion has a corresponding duty, and every duty a deed, and the fountain should ever be kept flowing into this stream, the root should be urged into this bloom and fruitage. Few things are so uninteresting and useless as religious doctrines that are not pulsing with life and are only a rattling skeleton. "If ye know these things, blessed are ye if ye do them." "To him therefore that knoweth to do good, and doeth it not, to him it is sin." Knowledge disobeyed is sin, light that increases our guilt. Truth that is not turned into deed and feeling that is not poured upon the will in action wither away and deaden the very capacity of the soul to know and feel, leaving its last state worse than its first. All our religious knowledge and preaching and teaching should flow as an urgent stream into action to turn all the wheels and fertilize all the fields of life.

The deeper and more earnest the conviction the more masterful and fruitful it will be in life. Mighty men have always been men of mighty convictions. Their hearts are fused in the fire of a great faith that forces its way into a great fact. Out of their molten souls have burst flames and poured streams of lava that have burnt and ploughed their way to victory. Paul has shaped all Christian thought because he was fired

by a great faith and said, "This one thing I do."
Luther shook Europe free into liberty because he could
say, "God help me, I cannot do otherwise." A weak
and wavering faith means a feeble and fruitless life.
An indifferent dead faith can have no life-giving power.
"I believed, therefore have I spoken," said the Psalmist, and only as we believe earnestly can we speak
with the accent of certainty and authority; only when
we know the truth with depth and intensity of conviction will it set us free. We should therefore use
every means to feed our faith with truth and feeling
and kindle it into fire that it may burn in our hearts
and force its way through our life and make it throb
with earnestness and power.

Christianity cannot live apart from its truth, any
more than a tree can continue to bloom and bear fruit
after it has been cut off from its root. It is an historical religion, and we cannot give up the Christian
fact and keep the Christian faith. Christianity might
retain its heat for a time after the fuel of truth has
been withdrawn from it, but it would soon begin to
cool and would in time grow cold and dead. The truth
is its life, and only as it lives and grows in the soil of
historic fact and living reality will it continue to bear
leaves for the healing of the nations. Christianity is
no myth or legend or beautiful dream, but a solid
fact of history, rooted in the rocky ledge of Judea,
and we must contend earnestly for its truth and maintain its historic reality, or it will die and disappear as
another iridescent but empty bubble of the human
imagination. But amidst all the vicissitudes and up-
heavals, advancing knowledge and critical attacks of
our modern time, the truth of Christianity standeth
sure. A sublime prophecy is ever being fulfilled:

" Heaven and earth shall pass away, but my words shall not pass away." On this rock of truth our faith rests and the kingdom of God is rising in the world.

IV. WORSHIP

Religion, being our conscious relation with God, comes to its highest and finest form in worship, which is the expression of our sense of the worth of God, or his worthship. The Christian life is rooted in the world, but it also has divine relations; the foot of its ladder rests on the earth, but its top leans against the stars. When this conscious divine relation is cut off or fades out of consciousness, religion falls to mere ethical culture or morals. The theory that " we should live in one world at a time and this world first " is impossible even on the lowest physical plane. If this world were cut off from all other worlds, it would die as though it were struck with a universal blast of lightning or crushed by a cosmic collision. It is the blue sky that keeps the grass green, and the sun shin-ing above us that makes the earth blossom around us. It takes the whole solar system to sustain our bodies, and it takes all the stars in the sky to grow a big soul. This world is too little for our immortal spirits, it does not have elbow room and breathing space for us, and our spirits demand the infinite and eternal. Only God is great enough to match and satisfy our souls, and worship is a universal fact and practical necessity.

1. **Prayer.**—Worship first builds an altar and ex-presses itself in prayer. Prayer is the communion of the soul with God in which it pours itself out in adora-tion, thanksgiving, confession, and supplication.

(a) Such relation to God is just as natural and necessary as a child's speech to its father, and it is an impulse of the human heart that operates with the universality and spontaneity and force of our other fundamental and permanent instincts. We are not now concerned with the theological and philosophical deeps and difficulties of prayer, such as its relation to natural law, but only with its psychological aspects which are the experiences of our consciousness. But these philosophical difficulties, especially the relation of prayer to natural law, need not trouble our faith, for we are constantly answering the prayers we make to one another by using natural laws to serve our own ends. Mr. A. J. Balfour, one of our profoundest philosophical thinkers, in his recent Gifford Lectures, strikingly says: "These difficulties are difficulties of theory, not of practice. They never disturb the ordinary man—nor the extraordinary man in his ordinary moments. Human intercourse is not embarrassed by the second, nor simple piety by the first. And perhaps the enlightened lounger, requesting a club waiter to shut the window, brushes aside, or ignores, as many philosophical puzzles as a mother passionately praying for the safety of her child." [1]

Prayer, then, is grounded in the objective reality of the relation between the soul and God. The faith that our prayers reach God and enter into his plan and that he answers them according to his wisdom and will so that they count for something in life, and effect results that would not otherwise be attained, is the necessary condition of any real prayer whatsoever. The subjective reflex influence of prayer upon the soul is a vital fact, but if we believe that this is all there is in prayer we cannot truly pray at all. This belief or lack of faith turns prayer into an insincere form and

[1] *Theism and Humanism*, pp. 267-268.

hollow mockery. Such an exercise of the mind would give the lie to itself and could only excite despair or a bitter laugh. We cannot continue to believe and practise with the heart what we have rejected with the head. We can no more rise above ourselves in prayer that is only a subjective state than we can lift ourselves to the stars by pulling on the hair of our heads. Such prayer is only a soliloquy, and when its secret is discovered it will cease to be rational and respectable. And so psychology not less than Scripture affirms that he that cometh to God must believe that he is and that he is a rewarder of them that diligently seek him.

(*b*) The objective reality of prayer must be matched by appropriate subjective conditions. Its virtue depends on the state of heart out of which it springs. It is impossible to please God without that faith and love that constitute fellowship. Such faith is the vital artery that binds us to God, and when this is severed or absent the channel of communication is broken. Penitence for sin is another condition of prayer. " If I regard iniquity in my heart, the Lord will not hear me." Any sin cherished in the heart separates it from God and sears it with guilt, and thereby makes true prayer impossible. Humility is also a condition of prayer, for " God resisteth the proud, but he giveth grace to the humble." " Humble yourselves in the sight of the Lord, and he shall lift you up." Humility casts us in dependence upon God and puts us in a mood of heart in which we shall ask only for such things as he will give us.

Brotherly love is essential to prayer, for if we love not our brother whom we have seen, how can we love God whom we have not seen? We cannot ask God to forgive us if we do not forgive others. Any malice, hatred, envy, jealousy, or evil feeling in the heart turns prayer into hypocrisy and acts as a bar to the blessing of God. Patient waiting must also attend our prayer, for the purposes of God often take long time, and we must not lose faith and grow impatient but be of good courage and wait upon the Lord. The most fundamental of all the conditions of prayer is submission to the wisdom and will of God. " Thy will be done " is the explicit or implicit condition of every prayer. It would be intolerable folly and fatality for us to impose our will, so often blind and perverted and selfish, upon the infinite will of God, and therefore we humbly cast ourselves upon him and ask him to grant or refuse our petitions as he sees best. We then accept his decision as infinite wisdom and love and count his very denial as one of his good gifts. Out of a heart of faith and penitence and humility and brotherly love and patience and submission will arise prayer that will be " an odour of a sweet smell, a sacrifice acceptable, well-pleasing to God."

(c) When the objective reality and the subjective condition of prayer thus match each other and combine, the blessing of prayer comes first in its reflex influence. It creates a new inner world, which is one of the deepest and most vital blessings of life. It closets us with God, withdraws and inhibits the attention from distracting things and focuses it upon the object of prayer, and thus kindles it into higher illumination and power. When the attention is turned in prayer upon the greatness of God, it looms upon the soul in overpowering majesty and mystery; upon his goodness, it fills the soul with a new sense of his care and love; upon the soul's own sin, it is seen and felt in its naked guilt and vileness; upon the soul's needs, it cries for help and grace; upon Christ, he is seen and seized as the Saviour. These various objects become vivid points in consciousness, and they in turn kindle the soul with feeling until it may glow with holy emotion, surrender itself in profound trust, experience a sweet sense of forgiveness and peace, subside into deep calm or rise on wings of exultant hope and determination and courage.

Prayer is thus largely communion and meditation in the presence of God. The idea that it is mostly petition, especially that it is begging and teasing God for personal favours, even for material and worldly goods, is psychologically wrong and obnoxious to the reverent soul. We do have a right to carry all our needs, including our business and health and worldly affairs, to God in prayer, but prayer is mainly the soul consciously in the presence of God communing with him and being filled with his Spirit, and thus being calmed and spiritualized so as to see all things in the light of God's wisdom and be strengthened to do his will.

(d) This, however, is not the whole of prayer. Prayer that would stop at this point would fall short of its full condition and fail of its objective answer. The theological statement of the operation of prayer is that the Spirit of God breathes into the soul the disposition and determination to do his will; but the psychological statement of the human side of the same fact is that the soul concentrates its attention into unity and intensity of thought which then pours a flood of feeling on the will and moves it, perhaps with mighty purpose and power, to action. The action is a part of the prayer, its logical continuation and completion. We have never finished a prayer until in obedience we have done the thing we have prayed for.

Prayer is thus no easy lazy way of getting God to hand us favours freely, to bestow upon us goods ready-made, to do our work for us, a short-cut to blessings and an escape from the burden of hard work and the battle of the cross. Rather it is a girding up of our loins for the burden, a call to battle, a way of co-working with God. Instead of releasing us from our duty of work, it sends us right back to our task to enter into it with renewed consecration and intensified energy. The difference is that after prayer we know and feel that God is working for us and in us, and if God be for us who can be against us?

This psychology of prayer is in accordance with Scripture teaching, which constantly connects working with praying, either explicitly or implicitly. " Ask, and it shall be given you; seek, and ye shall find, knock, and it shall be opened unto you," commands which bid us not to stop with asking, but to go on into seeking and knocking. A striking saying on the subject is found in James 5: 16. Translated in the Authorized Version, " The effectual fervent prayer of a righteous man availeth much," and in the Revised Version, " The supplication of a righteous man availeth much in its working," the passage has been translated by Dr. Rendal Harris, " The prayer of a righteous man is of great force when energized." The meaning is plain. We must energize our prayers. Uttered without being energized, they may be only so much vain wishing and empty breath. But when we put into them our energies, turning our wish into work, such prayer " is of great force." God will then also energize our prayer with his omnipotence, pouring his will into the same channel with our will. Prayer, then, does not make God our servant and put him at the mercy of our every

whim and caprice. On the contrary, it makes us servant of our prayers and urges us to work them out with
all our might. It turns our words into sweat and
blood and makes us mighty to the pulling down of
strongholds of evil and in building the walls of righteousness. To pray aright is no light thing, uttering
easy words that drop from our lips as the conventional
words of society. Prayer is hard work, the intensest
energizing of all our powers, the consecration of all
our possessions, the utmost we can give and do, serve
and sacrifice, to work out our prayers into deeds and
fact. This truth was expressed by Cromwell when he
said to his soldiers, "Trust God and keep your powder
dry," and by Dr. Chalmers when he said, "We are to
pray as though God did all and then work as though
we did all." When the will of God and the work of man
thus coincide and flow in the same channel, prayer becomes a fact and force that fills the soul with power
and peace and gives it the victory that overcomes the
world.

When all these conditions are fulfilled, prayer is acceptable to God and sure of its answer. The answer
may not be according to our will, or in the form we
desired, but it will be some better thing than we
asked. Such prayer hides our life with Christ in God
and tunes it all to the music of the Father's wisdom
and will. It sets us afloat on the current of the
divine omnipotence and causes all things to work together for our good. It calms life into serenity and
peace at the centre and gives it power around its whole
circumference. It rolls our burdens on the Lord and lets
us rest in confidence and joy in the Everlasting Arm.
It takes us into the secret place of the Most High,
where we are filled with the divine Spirit, and then

it sends us out strong and victorious to do the work and win the battle of life.

2. Music and Song.—Another element in worship is music and song. Music is the language of feeling, as speech is primarily the language of thought. The heart beats rhythmically. Words are a poor utterance even for the mind. The heart drops such cumbrous means and takes to the soaring wing of song. Music is a voice to its joy and a tongue to its sorrow. When a bliss is born in the soul it instinctively sings, even as the angels sang at the birth of Christ. In sorrow, the first solemn chords of the instrument or notes of the choir let forth fresh floods of grief. How often do we have emotions that we cannot express or even understand, until some touching melody or massive chords give utterance to them, and then we experience relief and satisfaction. No feeling has fully expressed itself until it has flowered into song. Music has a strange power of touching all the million strings in the complex harp of the soul and sweeping it with joy or sorrow. It has charms to soothe the savage breast, it floods the home with melody, it is a fine social pleasure, it expresses our most intricate and refined esthetic emotions, it goes deeper than words and strikes the profoundest chords of the soul, it stirs nations with passion and sweeps soldiers into battle. "Such sweet compulsion doth in music lie" that it puts a soothing or inspiring spell upon us in all the relations and experiences of life.

Music rises to its noblest flights in worship. The Bible is full of song. Moses and the children of Israel broke into song after they had passed through the Red Sea. David, the sweet singer of Israel, with his psalm and harp, is the poet and musician of the Bible, whose

songs are still singing their way through the world.
In the magnificent temple service there was a trained
choir or chorus accompanied with a full orchestra.
Christ was born amidst a shower of heavenly song,
and it is pleasant to remember that Jesus himself
sang. All through the Scriptures we are commanded
to sing unto the Lord; to praise him with harp and
trumpet and organ; to speak in psalms and hymns
and spiritual songs. Finally the book closes with the
pearly gates of heaven left ajar, through which there
floats out upon us the voice of harpers harping with
their harps and singing the new song of Moses and the
lamb.

The pipe organ is the king of instruments in worship. It is a whole orchestra in itself. It combines the
fine silvery strains of the violin, the softness of the
flute, the plaintiveness of the oboe, the assertiveness of
the trumpet, and the deep grandeur of the thunder.
In range and variety, richness and sweetness, colour
and splendour of tone it is incomparable. It blends
perfectly with the human voice. It is suggestive of
devotional moods and aspirations. It lifts the congregation on its mighty wings and bears it along and
aloft. It imparts volume and depth, inspiration and
power to the singing. It is a mighty means of grace,
unloosing floods of spiritual emotion that soothe and
comfort, stimulate and inspire the soul.

And the Christian hymn has had a wonderful mission in singing the church into faith and faithfulness,
service and sacrifice, adoration and aspiration, hope
and courage. When a soul is born into the kingdom
its first impulse is to sing. We have not fully felt the
gospel until we have sung it. The hymn-maker and
organ-builder have helped to express and propagate

the gospel hardly less than the sermon-builder. The poet and musician have their sacred office as well as the prophet and preacher. There is something sacramental in rhythm and metre. Atheism is not singable and produces no songs, but Christian faith instinctively breaks forth into praise. Music has given wings to the gospel, and the gospel has glorified music. Without song the gospel would have been shorn of some of its most powerful pinions, and without the inspiration of Christianity the masterpieces of Beethoven and Haydn would never have been born. Music has touched the zenith of its glory only as it has laid the noblest products of its genius as a tribute on the altar of Christ. Song is as vital a part of worship as prayer; and when the church ceases to sing it will be silent with the silence of death.

More definitely, the office of song in the sanctuary is to praise God. Worship seeks the highest form of expression, which is poetry wedded to music, the rhythm of speech and song. Music is one of the art-paths to God, and in some respects it gives the fullest and freest access to and communion with him. Through its strains our praise is gladdest, our gratitude is richest, our aspirations are holiest; on its wings we are freed from earth-clogs and are borne nearest to heaven and the heart of God.

Song in the sanctuary binds hearts together in Christian fellowship. No other means of expression equals music in its power of kindling common emotions. Christians never get closer together in thought and feeling than when melted into harmony in praise. The hymns of the church are one of its great unifying forces. Creeds have split it into a thousand fragments, but never has it been divided by a hymn. Christians agree in their songs better than in anything else. Few differences of theology have found their way into their hymns. However they divide along lines of doctrine, when they get to singing their hearts begin to beat in unison and their thoughts and feelings blend into fellowship.

Sacred song is also a means of conversion. Music appeals to the better nature in man; it stirs the divinity that is in him. The gospel is never more persuasive and powerful than when it links itself with melody. Many a gospel arrow has been feathered with a song. The gospel of song has converted countless thousands that have remained unmoved under gospel sermons. Revivals are always shot through and through with song. Leading evangelists associate with themselves gifted gospel singers, and thus go " forth by two and two," as Jesus sent out his disciples. When we cannot preach the gospel into men's hearts we must sing it in; or rather we must do both, and speech and song tipped with flames of the Holy Spirit will prove the power of God unto salvation.

Church music, while its artistic qualities ought not to be made the chief thing, ought to be good music, even the best. There is no more virtue in poor singing than in poor preaching. The singing should be congregational. The praise of the sanctuary should not be turned into an entertainment by a few trained performers. We cannot praise the Lord by proxy, and the church should not attempt to compete with the playhouse. There is something wonderfully inspiring in a great mass of voices surging in song. Good congregational singing is a mantle broad as charity that will cover many artistic faults in the choir and also many poor sermons. So long as a church has hearty congregational singing it cannot die. The way to have congregational singing is for the congregation to sing. " Let the people praise thee, O God, let all the people praise thee." It is not necessary to be a trained singer to sing in church. Let the people sing anyway. No instrument is in perfect tune. Noise is the raw material out of which music is made, and a great volume of song will take up and harmonize a good deal of it.

Song in the sanctuary, then, is not a mere embellishment, but is one of the most vital and effective parts of the service. It stimulates the whole Christian life and causes it to blossom and bear the fruits of the Spirit. The church has not yet found out its full power. It is one of our undeveloped resources. We want more singing and better, until the gospel has found its fullest and most joyous expression and the whole earth is vocal with praise.

3. Giving.—Another element of worship is giving. Worship, being only another spelling of worthship, is our sense of worth. The value we put on anything and the price we are willing to pay for it is our worship of it. Thus if we pay two dollars for a book our worthship or worship of that book is two dollars. Expressed in this coarse but not false way, what we pay to God or give to his service measures our sense of his worth to us and is our worship of him. If a man gives two dollars to the service of God when he could and should give ten or twenty or two hundred, that two dollars expresses his sense of the worth of God and he has a two-dollar god. The rich people whom Jesus saw casting into the temple treasury out of their abundance had a cheap God, because they measured his worth at only a negligible fraction of their total possessions, whereas the widow who cast in two pence

had a dear and precious God, because she thought he was worth all she had. Our giving in worship, then, goes deep into our religion and expresses our sense of the worth of God and intensifies all our relations with him.

Giving is a universal fact in all religion, and the heathen far outdo Christians in this respect. The Old Testament legislation taxed the people two tithes for the support of the church and state, besides many other offerings, and the unfaithful people were charged with having "robbed" God "in tithes and offerings." They were urged: "Bring ye all the tithes into the storehouse, that there may be meat in my house, and prove me now herewith, saith the Lord of hosts, if I will not open you the windows of heaven, and pour you out a blessing, that there shall not be room enough to receive it." Jesus watched the treasury of the temple and took note of the gifts of the people, and the collection appeared early in the Christian church. Paul immediately follows his splendid chapter (I Corinthians 15) on the resurrection of Christ with the logical application, "Now concerning the collection," putting behind this offering the tremendous fact and inspiration of this epochal event. Offerings are thus inwoven with the whole Bible in its history and doctrine and are a vital part of Christianity.

Money is obviously necessary for the support of the gospel at home and for its propagation abroad. God is carrying on an immense business in establishing his kingdom in the world, a business compared with which all commercial enterprises are local and small. He must have means to pay the bills, and he calls on us to give our silver and gold, which are his anyway. There is a business side to religion, as well as a religious side to business, and we should put business honesty and promptness into our religion as well as religious conscience and brotherhood into our business. Sometimes the church of Christ is a shame in the sight of the world because of its unfaithfulness or laxness in properly supporting its ministers and churches and in paying its bills. The Lord has need of our money, and we should pay into his treasury according to the systematic and proportional every-member rule laid down by Paul: "Upon the first day of the week let every one of you lay by him in store, as God has prospered him."

But the psychology of giving goes much deeper than the mere commercial honesty of paying our bills. There is a close connection between wealth and worship, gold and grace. Our money is ordinarily our daily service and sacrifice crystallized into gold and silver, our life-blood minted into coin. When we give our money to God we give him our time, our toil, our strength, our sacrifice, our very body and soul, and thus we are literally expressing our sense of his worth to us, or we are worshipping him. We are also giving practical expression to our sense of the worth and needs of our fellow-men and of the power of the gospel to help and heal and save them. And if we love not our brother whom we have seen, how can we love God whom we have not seen? Giving is also one of the richest means of grace in that it expands our sympathies, enlarges our vision, and enables us in a degree to lay down our lives for the brethren, and thus in losing our life we save it. Giving saves us from selfishness and from drying up in all the fountains of the heart and withering into dust.

We thus learn the divine secret, which Jesus brought

from heaven and which he knew as none other ever knew, that " It is more blessed to give than to receive." Getting by giving, gaining by losing, addition by sub-traction,— this is one of the paradoxical laws of the spiritual life. Great souls pour their finest treasures out upon others in lavish prodigality and thereby they enlarge and enrich themselves. The streams they send forth in giving come back to them in mist and rain that keep their lives fresh with dew and their fountains full. It is not a vain promise that if we bring our tithes into the storehouse God will pour us out a bless-ing which there shall not be room enough to receive.

Giving, then, is not an artificial means of promoting religion, much less is it a mercenary scheme of the church for making money and keeping its coffers full, or of the priest for feathering his own nest. Even some Christians look on the collection as a bit of worldly business interjected into the service and intro-ducing a jarring note, and think it would conduce to the spirituality of the worship if it were dispensed with. Sometimes we see in a church newspaper notice or placarded on the front of a church the announcement, " No Collection." It is evidently a bid for attendance, as though the collection were so burdensome or repel-lent that it keeps people away from church. Such an announcement is a reflection on the good sense of peo-ple, and it puts them in a cheap class who would like to sponge their religion off others; it labels them as religious beggars and tramps. People have more re-spect for churches that respect themselves. They ex-pect to pay something for religion as for other benefits; and they very well know that they are welcome whether they are able to pay or not. But there is a deeper objection to such a notice: it forgets that the collection is as much an act of worship as any other part of the service. Paying is as essential in our religion as praying. If we give notice, " No collection will be taken," we may also announce, " The Bible will not be read in this church," " Prayer will not be offered," " The name of God will not be mentioned in this service." God has united getting and giving in his service, and what God hath joined together let not man put asunder.

We commonly think of giving as a duty, that which is due or owed, and this carries with it all the unpleas ant implications of a debt. But we should rise far above this conception and view giving, not simply as a duty and debt, but as a privilege and delight. The Hebrew worshippers blew their trumpets as the smoke of their offerings rose from the altar, expressive of the gladness with which they rendered this sacrifice and service; and we, having passed into the dispensation of the Spirit, should worship God with our offerings with even greater joy. That we by our gifts can give wings to the gospel to send it over the world, that our money gives us an arm and hand by which we can reach around the globe and touch and bless every human being, is a splendid privilege that we should appreciate and that should cause us to blow our most joyous trumpets. This power immensely widens our sphere of service and makes us benefactors of the world; it enables us to do the greater works which Jesus promised us we could do; and it broadens and enriches our life and hides it more deeply with Christ in God. We should leap at such a privilege and find its duty a great delight.

4. **Social Worship.**—An element of special importance in worship is its social nature. While we may

worship God in our private lives and even in solitude,
yet worship reaches its fullest expression in the public
services of the sanctuary. The Scriptures put special
emphasis on the need and duty of such worship and
urge us " not to forsake the assembling of ourselves
together." David was glad when it was church time,
and Jesus " as his custom was went into the synagogue
on the sabbath day." The psychological reason for this
is plain. Religion, while inwardly it is an intensely
individual relation with God, yet outwardly is, as we
have seen, intensely social and contagious. On the day
of Pentecost all the believers in Jerusalem were with
one accord in one place; every one was present, not one
seat was vacant to break with its gap the spiritual current, and all were crowded together in unity of heart to
receive the blessing. Such a congregation is deeply
susceptible to and receptive of spiritual influences. It
is thirsty soil to the rains of grace; it is a powerful
invitation and appeal to the Holy Spirit. God can
pour more of his Spirit, so to speak, upon five hundred or five thousand people than upon fifty or five,
because they are moved if not melted by a common feeling and are thus more susceptible to his grace. If,
then, we want to get the fire of God's grace in our
hearts we must go to the altar where it burns; if we
want as Christians to strengthen our faith and fellowship we must flock together and forsake not the
assembling of ourselves in the house of the Lord.

This answers the question, often raised, whether
there is not religion outside the church and whether
we cannot live the Christian life as well without unit-
ing with the church. We freely grant that there is
religion outside the church, and we wish there were
more of it. We are not in the least interested in deny-

ing or disparaging such religion.   There are men outside the church, making no profession of religion, whose
fine character and conduct put to shame many profess-
ing Christians; just as there are pious heathen men
that excite the wonder of our missionaries, even as
the Roman centurion by his faith drew a wonderful
eulogy from Jesus, and as Cornelius caused Peter to
wonder at the universal grace of God.

Nevertheless, the question still remains, can we be
as good Christians outside the church as in it?   The
question is like asking, Can we have as good harvests
without farming, as good education without schools,
and as good homes without houses?   The great blessings of life are not lying around scattered and loose,
but are organized into definite means and institutions.
One may acquire some education without attending
school and college, but if he wants to get a sound, symmetrical, disciplined education he would better go to
school and get the benefit of its social instruction and
influence.   When Jesus fed the five thousand he had
them sit down upon the green grass in companies of
fifties and hundreds: social organization and fellowship.   If there were any stragglers that refused to sit
down in the ranks and hung around the outer edges
of the crowd, did they get any bread?   The church is
the appointed place where we are bidden to sit down in
orderly ranks and social fellowship to receive the bread
of life, and if we remain out in the wilderness of the
world there is no promise of bread for us.

All the immense and subtle benefits of organization
and social fellowship are realized in the church, and
we deprive ourselves of these and cannot live the Christian life so fruitfully if we cut ourselves off from its
appointed ordinances.   The church is the army of

Christ in which we march under his banner to the music of his call to service, and if we mean to be his soldiers we should get into the ranks and wear the uniform and fight as regulars the good fight of faith. Worship finds its congenial soil and atmosphere for growth and its efficient means of expression and service inside the church, and outside it is likely to wither away.

5. Esthetic Element in Worship.—The esthetic nature is closely related to worship, which expresses itself in beauty as well as in music. This element flowered out in Hebrew worship in the rich fabrics and artistic construction of the tabernacle, " gold, and silver, and brass, and blue, and purple, and scarlet, and fine linen, and goats' hair, and rams' skins dyed red, and badgers' skins, and shittim wood, oil for light, spices for anointing oil, and sweet incense, onyx stones, and stones to be set in the ephod, and in the breastplate "; and in the magnificent temple of Herod that stood with its marble walls and gilded roof flashing in the sunlight, a glittering mass of snow and gold. The temple service, also, was elaborate and splendid, with priests in gorgeous vestments, swinging censors emitting perfumed incense, streaming altars, a great choir with antiphonal choruses, accompanied with a full orchestra. Jesus swept away all this gorgeous spectacle with one wave of his hand as he said, " The hour cometh, and now is, when the true worshippers shall worship the Father in spirit and in truth." But ritualistic worship crept back in time into the Christian church and blossomed out in St. Peter's in Rome, another splendid temple enriched and embellished with all the genius of art and treasures of the world.

Puritanism reacted against this extreme ritualism and beauty in worship and swung to the opposite pole of a plain meeting-house, ugly in architecture, bare of comforts, and mean in its appointments. And the service also was stripped of ritual and musical accompaniment and reduced to unrelieved nakedness. Between these extremes there is a golden mean. Worship should be worthily housed and clothed. A beautiful church, appropriate in architecture, comfortable in its appointments, and rich but tasteful in its adornments, is conducive to the worshipful spirit. And a beautiful service, orderly and chaste and reverent, accompanied with enough ritual to give some symbolic expression to the mystery of religion, is also a means of grace as it strikes deep mystic chords in the soul. Beauty is born of God, all its forms and colours flash out of his heart, it is his own nature exuding through all the beauty of the world. And therefore it should not be excluded from the sanctuary which is his peculiar dwelling-place and fullest revelation on earth, but there it should come to its most perfect and most glorious flower. There is no grace in ugliness, and we should no more let secular life have all the beauty of the world than we should let, in Wesley's phrase, " the devil have all the best tunes."

Yet there is ever some danger in connection with the esthetic side of worship. There is in human nature a tendency to substitute the outward beauty of form for the inward beauty of the soul, the symbol for the spirit. We are disposed to think that because we feel good in the church we are good. The feeling may be due to the comfortable surroundings, or to the spell of the music; even the preaching, sometimes, makes us feel good. But whether we are good or not depends, not on how we feel in the church, but on what we are and do after we go out of the church. The church is the Mount of Transfiguration where we see the glorified Christ, but presently we are to go down upon the plain where there are many sick and troubled folk to be healed and much work to be done. It is the upper chamber where we hold blessed fellowship with Christ and with one another, but it is no place to stay, and presently, as did Jesus and his disciples, we shall sing a hymn and go out; out into the hostile world where our worship will begin its work and its reality be tested. A beautiful service in the church can never take the place of beautiful service in the world; and a picture of Christ, wrought in rich colours in a stained glass window, can never be substituted for the image of Christ in the heart. Leonardo da Vinci swept the golden goblets from the table of his "Last Supper" because he feared that their splendour would distract attention from and dim the glory of the Master Himself, and we should ever be on our guard against the same subtle danger. We should have beauty in the church, but it should be such as will minister grace to us and help to "let the beauty of the Lord our God be upon us."

V. WORK

From worship we pass to work as a means and form of the Christian life. Great emphasis is put all through the Scriptures and in all religious teaching on obedience and work as conditions and duties of the Christian life, and this is true psychology.

1. **For Our Own Sake.**—We are to engage in Christian service, first, as a means of our own life. Obedience or practice is a chief means of knowledge and skill and efficiency in all fields. It may be affirmed, in short, that we do not know anything well until we do it. Theoretical knowledge lacks clearness and certainty

and efficiency until it is transformed into practical knowledge. "Truth is that which works," says pragmatism, and as a rule we do not know a truth until we know it working in experience. We may study the theory of a subject in a book, but we shall not really understand the matter until we translate it out of the book into practice. Book knowledge of astronomy will not make one an astronomer, or of chemistry will not make one a chemist. One can study music as a theory and go deep into its intricate tonal forms and relations and yet not be able to sing a note or strike a chord. Only by long and patient practice can the musician master the art of singing or of playing the instrument so that he can sweep the bow over the strings or his fingers over the keys with astonishing rapidity and accuracy and ease and pour music forth in floods from his soul. Music is thus wrought into the texture of his nerves and becomes his unconscious habit and the instrument becomes a part of his muscular system and an extension of his personality. All art is thus acquired through the persistent drill that translates theory into skill and rules into habits.

This familiar principle applies with special force to religion. Religion as a theory or system of doctrines is set forth in theology and in creeds, and the Christian religion is revealed and illustrated in the Bible. But this truth passes into our religious character and conduct and life only as we act upon it in obedience and service. Faith and faithfulness, reverence and righteousness, patience and peace, goodness and gentleness, sympathy and sacrifice, unselfishness and love, kindness and courtesy become our spirit and speech and unconscious habits only as we constantly practise them. Reading about patience and analyzing its psychology will never make us patient unless we practise patience under provocation. Faith in God as a theory never becomes faith in fact unless we exercise it in the strain and temptation of life. But just as we acquire music or any other art through practice and thus work it into our very nerves, so do we acquire the graces of the spirit and transmute them into automatic habits. Therefore we are bidden: " Work out your salvation with fear and trembling; for it is God who worketh in you both to will and to work, for his good pleasure." While God works his salvation in us we are to work it out; and thus our salvation, while it is God's work, is also the product of our own working. We are to work it into our character as the musician works his skill into his nervous system as a set of habits. Obedience is the great organ of spiritual knowledge. " If any man willeth to do his will, he shall know of the teaching, whether it is of God, or whether I speak from myself." " If ye know these things, blessed are ye if ye do them." We are thus to serve in order that we may be saved, for only through the obedience of service can salvation be realized as a fact.

2. For the Sake of Others.—Salvation is not simply an individual gift and attainment, but it is also a social blessing. We are saved to serve, and we work out our salvation only as we do serve. We can get it only as we give it. In this respect it is like truth and all mental and spiritual goods. Material goods are limited in quantity, and by as much as we give of our store to others we have so much less. If one has a hundred dollars and gives fifty away, he has only fifty left. But if one possesses a truth and imparts it to another he does not have less truth, but more. The act of imparting it to others clears it up and deepens and intensifies

it in his own mind. The teacher is always his own best scholar and is learning more than any other one in the class. In imparting truth it is literally true that it is more blessed to give than to receive, because the process of giving brings in a richer return of mental wealth and power. So is it with faith and patience and peace, with goodness and gentleness, with kindness and courtesy, with sympathy and love, service and sacrifice: as we bestow these fine goods upon others, even upon those who may seem unworthy of them, and even when we pour them forth with spendthrift carelessness and lavish prodigality, we get them back in a multiplied harvest, as the seed buried and lost in the ground returns a hundredfold. In fact, it is only as we give patience that we can get patience, and so with all the fruits of the Spirit: they are social virtues that we can get only as we give them. And so the paradoxical but literal law of growth in the Christian life is: " Give, and it shall be given unto you; good measure, pressed down, and shaken together, running over, shall they give into your bosom. For with what measure ye mete it shall be measured to you again."

The builder of any work is always at the same time unconsciously building himself. The builder of a house is also simultaneously erecting the structure of his own character. If he is putting sound materials and honest workmanship into the house, he is building the same spiritual elements into his soul; and if he is slipping poor materials and dishonest work into the building, he is framing rotten elements into his life. The artist in working at his canvas is at the same time painting the portrait of his character in the gallery of his soul. Every one's outer life returns into and deposits itself in his inner life; whatever he is doing

to others he is doing to himself. The Christian is subject to the same spiritual law. As he builds others up
in faith and righteousness and goodness and peace he
is building himself up in the same virtues. By as much
as he makes others Christians does he become a better
Christian himself. As he transforms others into the
image of Christ he is himself transfigured into the same
likeness. The law of Christian growth is that in saving others we save ourselves, in laying down our life
we take it up again, in losing our soul we save it.
We are not to save others in order that we may save
ourselves: any such selfish motive, however secretly
hidden in the soul, would spoil the beauty and destroy
the reflex blessing of such service; but when we sincerely and with no thought of return lose our lives in
the service of others we get them back more perfectly
wrought into the image of Christ and enriched a hundredfold.

3. **The Call to Service.**—The Christian call to social
service, which began with the beginning of the gospel
and has come down to us through the ages, is receiving
increased emphasis in our day and has opening before
it wider fields and more splendid visions than ever in
the past. " The field is the world " now in a literal
sense, and John Wesley's parish has become the parish
of every intelligent and faithful Christian. This field
begins in the centre of the home and sweeps out through
successive widening circles until it encompasses the
earth. The world has been unified and reduced in size
until it has become a handy and quite manageable
world that we can turn and control almost as we twirl
a geographical globe with our fingers. And so we are
now citizens of the world, cosmopolitans, and the Christian has a field and opportunity of which Paul and the

apostles never dreamed. This unified world is one reason that we can fulfil Christ's own promise and
prophecy, "Verily, verily, I say unto you, He that
believeth on me, the works that I do shall he do also;
and greater works than these shall he do."

Christians are sometimes charged with being too
much concerned with the other world, as though they
were mere dreamers and visionaries that stand gazing
into the sky and looking for the golden city in the glory
land above. They do indeed look for a celestial city
which hath foundations, whose builder and maker is
God, but they are also building a copy of that city
down on this earth. We are even now rearing its
jewelled walls around our horizon and laying its golden
pavements right under our feet. This is the meaning of
all our Christian worship and work. Our preaching
and teaching, schools and colleges, education and sanitation, industrial improvement, civic welfare, political
reform, national righteousness, and our growing international consciousness and conscience, home missions
and foreign missions, what are all these but means of
building the kingdom of God on earth? We are to
cure all the ills of the world and moralize and spiritual-
ize its whole social order. "Holiness unto the Lord"
is to be inscribed on the bells of the horses, and
whether we eat or drink, pray or play, we are to do all
to the glory of God. We are to beat our swords into
ploughshares and turn all the terrible engines of war
into instruments of industry. We are to provide the
means and opportunity of a decent and wholesome and
happy life for every human being. And thus we are to
apply the gospel along all lines so as to cleanse this
world and rebuild it into the beautiful city of God on
earth.

This is the supreme call and splendid opportunity of our time, and it is the greatest and noblest work in the world. We are proud of our national enterprise at Panama in breaking through the backbone of the continent and letting two oceans kiss each other in common trade and travel. But how this great achievement shrinks into insignificance in comparison with the vastly greater enterprise of breaking down all barriers that divide humanity and letting the whole world flow together in one universal sea of brotherhood and prosperity and peace. We are always impressed with the statement that the sun never sets on the British Empire, and yet this empire is only a few red patches on the map compared with this kingdom which envelops the globe around the equator and from pole to pole. This work overshadows all the world, gathers into itself all empires, and is the only world vision that is marching towards victory.

This vision is the tremendous inspiration and power of the Christian life. Any great work tends to make us great, and any small work tends to make us small. A man that would devote his life to carving heads on cherry seeds would presently have a cherry-seed head; but as we climb a mountain the mountain puts its greatness under us, lifts us into a purer atmosphere and wider vision, and imparts to us some of its own majesty and mystery. The kingdom of God is incomparably the greatest mountain of vision in the world; and as we climb it, it lifts us out of our low lives, submerged in the murky atmosphere of the world, into a clearer air and a more splendid prospect; and it especially lifts us out of our little ruts and holes, out of our petty complaints and grievances and aches which are largely subjective and would vanish if we would simply forget them, into the life that is lost in some worthy purpose and noble enthusiasm, into the life that is hid with Christ in God. A life lived on such a mountain has more daylight than there is down in the valleys of the world, it breathes a purer air and is closer to the stars; and the Christians that live there grow taller and stronger, they are larger men with more breadth and brightness of vision, they are more efficient and fruitful in service, and they are more like Christ as he stood upon the Mount of Transfiguration. While the followers of Christ are thus building a Christian world he is fashioning them into his own likeness. " If ye know these things, blessed are ye if ye do them."

VI. Imagination

The picturing power of the mind, that is such a magic wand in the hand of the novelist and artist, is not less potent in the field of religion and in personal growth in the Christian life.

1. **Makes Truth Vivid.**—Imagination makes truth and life vivid by presenting them in the form of mental images and pictures instinct with reality. Religious truth is apt to be abstract and dry: imagination clothes it with flesh and blood and makes it live and breathe. The great Teacher was a master in the use of the imagination in his ministry. His parables were pictures of the truth he taught. The Prodigal Son is a story that makes the truth it embodies as real as life itself. The whole Bible is a picture book of religious truth, and this is one element of its interest and power. We should learn to read the Bible in an imaginative mood, so that its scenes and sayings will start up before us and lay hold of us as present realities. It is through

the gateway of the imagination that these truths enter most deeply and vitally into the soul.

2. **Corrects Faults.**—Imagination helps us to correct our faults. It first enables us to see them, and this is half the battle of winning a victory over them. In the familiar words of Burns:

> O would some power the giftie gie us,
> To see ourselves as others see us,
> It would from many a blunder free us,
> And foolish notion.

Now imagination has this power. It enables us to get out of and look at ourselves and in some degree " see ourselves as others see us." If we will only in the quietness of our own thoughts make a picture of ourselves as we know the reality to be, putting into it our faults of disposition and temper and speech, our failures in duty, all our sins of omission and commission, we shall see something that will be closely like ourselves. The picture will not be all bad, of course, for it will contain much good for which we may be truly thankful. But it will also present such defects as will make it unlovely and blameworthy in many respects and may well give us a sense of humiliation and shame. We may be startled at the sight and feel that we did not know ourselves: if so, it is time to get acquainted. Some persons in the blindness of their conceit and folly are living with fictitious persons and have never seen their real selves. We should make haste to get out of any such fool's paradise into the land of clear vision and reality. This is what the prodigal son did when out by the swine troughs " he came to himself." He saw himself as he was: imagination showed him a photograph of his soul. This seeing ourselves is the first condition of correcting our faults. When we see them our conscience may be pricked with conviction and we will resolve to root them out.

3. Builds Up Christian Character.—In the same way, imagination helps to build us up in Christian character. It has the imperial power of creating an ideal, a pattern of what we would like to be. Let not our ideal be any visionary and impracticable dream, as of great wealth or position or fame: such dreams will make us feverish and discontented and are almost sure to be disappointed and may leave us embittered. Let us keep our ideal well within reasonable bounds, and especially let us construct it of moral elements. We should picture ourselves as we are with our gifts and opportunities and duties and inquire, What should such a person be? Into this ideal let us put truth and righteousness as the foundation elements, the bones of the man we are going to build; then let us put in an intelligent growing mind and a good heart, pure in its purposes and passions, free from selfishness and hatred and meanness, sympathetic and generous in disposition, cheerful and sunny in temperament; then let us put in a strong will that can control all our energies and desires and give us patience and power and peace; then let us put in faithfulness in duty, doing everything we ought to do in the best way we can; finally, let us put in, as the very core and heart of this man, faith in God and a Christlike mind: and the result will be an ideal self. Let imagination construct this portrait carefully and dwell on it lovingly, look up to this heavenly vision, become enamoured and charmed with this better self, see the beauty and blessedness of this nobler soul, and then let us resolve to bend every energy towards realizing it, and we shall grow towards it. Imagination is im-

proving men in every field of achievement by setting up before them higher ideals. Precisely the same process will make us better Christians. Let us set before us an improved edition of ourselves, a more perfect personality, and then work towards it as a mechanic works towards his pattern or an artist towards his vision; let us ever look unto Jesus, the author and finisher of our faith, striving to acquire his purity and patience and peace, his spirit of sympathy and service and sacrifice: so shall we grow into his likeness, and in doing this we shall attain unto our highest and best self.

Let imagination have its perfect work, and it will show us the truth vividly, clear us of faults, and develop us unto a perfect man.

VII. Habit

We have already seen the nature and value of habit,[1] and this principle of our constitution is a necessary and fruitful means of the Christian life.

1. **The Value of Habit in Religion.**—Habit trains us into regular, easy, and accurate ways of doing things, releases us from debate and hesitation, effort and worry, sets us free to attend to novel situations, and lubricates life into delightful smoothness and liberty and joy. Habitual religion is ever the best; religion that has become habit and acts automatically and spontaneously. Jesus " entered, as his custom was, into the synagogue on the sabbath day." He went to church by habit and not by circumstance and caprice; and we shall attain to strength and fruitfulness and joy in the Christian life in proportion as we develop the same spirit and practice.

[1] Pp. 61-63.

We do not do a thing well until we do it without thinking how. No one is a good mechanic who must think about how to hold his tool; and no one has good manners who is conscious of his manners. Not until the hand has forgotten the painstaking processes by which it was trained does it have true skill. The musician must practise long that he may play without practice. Unconsciousness of self is the final touch of perfection. So a Christian grace has not been thoroughly wrought into us until it acts unconsciously. When in vexation we must call upon our patience to come and help us out, we have not yet learned perfect patience. We ought to be patient without thinking about it or knowing that we are patient. When in a matter of conscience we must run after conscience and wake it up and drag it into the case, our ethical sense is not yet well trained. Conscience ought to act without being asked, or our thinking about it. Must an honest man try to be honest? No, he will be honest without trying. Faith that must ever be worked with and prodded into action is a weak faith. When a man must keep working with his stomach and lungs and liver he has a poor set of vital organs; the healthy man does not know that he has any insides. So when we must keep working with our virtues they have not yet been educated into the perfection in which they will act spontaneously. It is true that we can reach such perfection only through long discipline. We must try hard that we may do without trying. Moses " wist not that his face shone." He was filled with the glory of God and then he forgot himself.

2. **Four Rules on Habits.**—Prof. William James has a famous chapter [1] on Habit in which he lays down

[1] *The Principles of Psychology*, Vol. I, Chapter IV.

four rules for the formation of habits, and these apply equally well to our religious life, which covers all life.

(a) The first rule is: " In the acquisition of a new habit, or the leaving off of an old one, we must take care to *launch ourselves with as strong and decided an initiative as possible*." In other words, begin with all your might. When we start in upon any line of conduct with half-hearted decision and effort, we are not likely to go far: hindrances will easily discourage us and turn us back. But when we feel the importance of the new course of action and gather up and concentrate all our energies in the first step, we are likely to start off with such decision and momentum that we shall not lightly be stopped but will keep on. The stronger the explosion behind the bullet, the farther it will fly. This means that we should enter upon the Christian life with our whole mind and soul and strength and burn all our bridges behind us; and we should also enter upon the habitual duties of the Christian life, such as prayer and obedience, with the same whole-hearted and irrevocable decision.

In further elucidation of this rule Professor James says: " Accumulate all the possible circumstances which shall reënforce the right motives; put yourself assiduously in conditions that encourage the new way; make engagements incompatible with the old; take a public pledge, if the case allows; in short, envelop your resolution with every aid you know. This will give your new beginning such a momentum that the temptation to break down will not occur as soon as it otherwise might." These directions all admit of easy translation into religious terms. Three things are here enumerated as means for carrying out this rule. First, intensify the right motives: consider all the facts and aspects of sin and salvation, doctrine and life, faith and fruit; brood over them until they root themselves deep in the heart and grow into their true proportion and power and take full possession of the will and move it with their might; and then we can enter upon the beginning and upon all the duties of the Christian life under such pressure and momentum that we shall not easily be turned back.

The next condition is that we put ourselves " assiduously in conditions that encourage the new way ": that means that we should go to church and prayer-meeting and keep ourselves in a Christian atmosphere under Christian influences. " The use of the means of grace " is the way we ordinarily express this fact; " not forsaking the assembling of ourselves together " is the way the Bible expresses it; " put yourself assiduously in conditions that favour the new way " is the way the psychologist expresses it; and these three mean the same thing.

And the third condition is: " Take a public pledge, if the case allows." In religion, " the case allows." Confession by the mouth is one of the primary duties of the Christian life insisted on in the Scriptures, by no one more emphatically and solemnly than by Jesus himself. Many people think and say, " Why cannot I be a Christian without saying anything about it and without joining the church? " Because the Bible says, " If thou shalt confess with thy mouth, and shalt believe in thine heart, thou shalt be saved," and because the psychologist says, " Take a public pledge." Scripture and science, apostle and psychologist here agree. Such a public pledge is a strong initiative that commits one to the Christian life with such decision and force as will help him to be faithful to the end.

(*b*) The second rule is: "*Never suffer an exception to occur till the new habit is securely rooted in your life.* Each lapse is like the letting fall of a ball of string which one is carefully winding up; a single slip undoes more than a great many turns will wind again." In illustration of this rule President H. C. King quotes from a book on elocution this advice to public speakers: "Dash cold water on your throat every morning when you wash, for 365, not 364, mornings of the year." [1] There are many things in the Christian life to which this rule applies without any exception. Truth, honesty, purity, patience, kindness, love—we are to practise these things always and everywhere, "for 365, not 364, mornings of the year." One single exception in these things lets slip our ball of string and unwinds more than we can wind up in many turns. Every one knows how fatal it is to let the ball of Christian character drop and how hard it is to get it wound up again. The safeguard against this ill result is never to suffer an exception in these virtues, but to practise them three hundred and sixty-five days of the year and twenty-four hours of the day. Rubinstein said that if he omitted his piano practice for one day, he noticed it; if for two days, the critics noticed it; and if for three days, the public noticed it. We should be equally careful of and sensitive to our practise of the Christian graces.

Other things in the Christian life, such as the means of grace, the Bible and prayer and church and prayer-meeting, while they may be omitted in exceptional circumstances when necessary hindrances or other duties interfere with them, yet ought also to be brought under this general rule. Our use of these means of grace ought not to be subject to our convenience and feel-

[1] *Rational Living*, by Henry Churchill King, p. 92.

ing, to the weather and our wardrobe, but they should be attended to by the almanac and the clock. Our rule should be to suffer no exception in these things unless forced upon us by necessity and duty. Such unfailing regularity will fasten the habit of them upon us until they become our spontaneous life and joy.

(c) The third rule is: "*Seize the very first possible opportunity to act on every resolution you make, and on every emotional prompting you may experience in the direction of the habits you aspire to gain.*" This rule warns us against feeling emotions and making resolutions without carrying them out into action. Such wasted emotions and resolutions weaken us so that we respond less promptly and energetically the next time, and finally cannot respond at all. "The habit of excessive novel-reading and theatre-going," says our psychologist, "will produce true monsters in this line. The weeping of a Russian lady over the fictitious personages in the play, while her coachman is freezing to death on his seat outside, is the sort of thing that everywhere happens on a less glaring scale." This is one of the dangers of revival seasons—much emotion and little obedience. This is even one of the dangers of listening to sermons—much hearing and little doing of the word. Some people are so sermon-soaked that they shed all religious truth and do nothing.

So important is the turning of our feeling into action that Professor James says: "Let the expression be the least thing in the world—speaking genially to one's aunt, or giving up one's seat in a horse-car, if nothing more heroic offers—but let it not fail to take place." Act! act! is the urgent admonition of this rule. Do not think that mere fine feelings or good resolutions have saving virtue or any virtue in themselves, but turn these as streams of energy upon the will and set the life agoing in practical obedience and service. No habit has any vitality and strength until it is rooted down in our lives and bears fruit.

(*d*) The fourth rule is: "*Keep the faculty of effort alive in you by a little gratuitous exercise every day.* That is, be systematically ascetic or heroic in little unnecessary points, do every day or two something for no other reason than that you would rather not do it, so that when the hour of dire need draws nigh it may find you not unnerved and untrained to stand the test." Professor James ingeniously likens such asceticism to "the insurance which a man pays on his house and goods. The tax does him no good at the time, and possibly may never bring him a return. But if the fire *does* come, his having paid it will be his salvation from ruin. So with the man who has daily inured himself to habits of concentrated attention, energetic volition, and self-denial in unnecessary things. He will stand like a tower when everything rocks around him, and when his softer fellow-mortals are winnowed like chaff in the blast."

This rule warns us against indulgence in relaxing a habit after we have acquired it. We must keep our habit "in condition," as the athlete keeps himself in condition by gratuitous exercise every day. One of our most frequent and most subtle temptations is to be governed by our sense of ease and relax our habits when we think we are safe in them. Philip Gilbert Hamerton, in his delightful book on *The Intellectual Life*, remarks that if we once take to excusing ourselves from duty on the ground of our feeling, "we will find that kind of inspiration coming pretty often."

But we are never safe in relaxing habits and must keep up their tonicity by exercising them on the margin of effort where they still require of us some unpleasant, if not painful, exertion. This means that we should do some things—for example speak kindly to one who does not like us or whom we do not like, or go to prayer-meeting on a wet night—if for no other reason than that we are determined to keep ourselves in good ethical condition and maintain our habits at their best.

These are the rules of a master psychologist, who says their "ethical implications are numerous and momentous," and applied to our Christian life they will develop in us such habits as will make it regular and certain, smooth and delightful, fruitful and masterful.

VIII. CHRIST IN US

We have not yet reached the real root of the Christian life. Paul possessed and expressed this root when he testified, "Christ liveth in me." The Spirit of Christ had taken possession of Paul so as to become his deepest disposition and dominant motive. Whatever Paul was thinking or doing, however great or small, he was acting out his Christian disposition and doing the work of Christ in the world.

1. **Negative Aspects of the Christian Life.**—This enables us to define the essence of the Christian life, and first to discriminate it negatively from certain means to this end.

(a) The Christian life does not consist in the observance of religious forms. Keeping the Sabbath, reading the Bible, going to church and offering prayer and singing hymns are not Christianity and do not in themselves make a Christian. They are useful and even necessary means to this end, but they are no more the Christian life itself than ploughs and harrows are wheat and corn. These are the external forms and means of religion, but they may flourish in full bloom and ostentatious display, as among the Pharisees, and yet have no genuine Christian spirit and fruit. It may be easy and congenial for us to wear these trappings of religion on the outside of our lives and let our hearts remain unchanged in selfishness, even as the inner corruption of whitened sepulchres. This has been the most common danger and disease of the church from the time of the Pharisees to this day. But the Christian religion is not an external application, like a face powder, but must be taken inwardly and pass into the blood.

(b) Again, the Christian life does not consist simply in knowledge about Christ. We put great emphasis upon the duty of searching the Scriptures that we may grow in the knowledge of Christ, and this emphasis is put in the right place, for this truth is a vital means to the Christian life. Yet we should not confuse such knowledge with the Christian life itself. Knowledge of music does not make one a musician. The most eloquent writer on the art of painting that ever lived was John Ruskin: yet Ruskin himself was no painter. He knew how pictures ought to be painted, but he could not paint one himself. So we may know how the Christian life ought to be lived and yet not live it ourselves. One of the most finished and beautiful Lives of Christ ever written was the work of Renan, a French sceptic. We might know enough about Christ to write his Life learnedly and eloquently, and yet not have Christ in us.

(c) Nor does the Christian life consist simply in moral education and culture. Polishing a piece of coal

will never transmute it into a diamond, and the finest
moral polish that can be put upon human nature will
not change the sinful heart into saintliness. A lion
may be tamed and trained until it seems as innocent
and harmless as a kitten and as obedient as a child;
but it is a lion still, and at the smell of blood will be
as savage and bloodthirsty as when it crouched in its
native jungle. So a course of moral education and conventional ethics may tame human nature until it seems
innocent and beautiful; but it is unregenerated human
nature still, and on proper occasion or provocation will
develop all its original evil. Nothing can come out of
the heart that has not first been put into it. Christianity first puts Christ in the heart, and then the Spirit
of Christ rules in and over it and issues in all its
streams.

(d) Deeper still, the Christian life does not consist
merely in imitating Christ. It is true that he is our
perfect Pattern, and imitating him is one of the most
vital means of the Christian life. Yet this imitation
is not to be the mechanical imitation of outward rules
and habits, but the inward emulation of spirit and
life. No amount of external imitation will make us
Christians, just as tying oranges on a tree will not
make an orange tree. We might imitate the outward
appearance of Christ's life closely, even going to the
length of wearing seamless robes or washing one
another's feet, as some have done, and yet be as far
from him in spirit as the inner corruption of a
sepulchre is from its outer whiteness. The outward
imitation of Christ turns the commandments into har-
ness straps that simply restrain and fret us, whereas
these commandments should be the inner laws of our
own nature and operate as spontaneously as do the

physical laws of the body. The Pharisees carried the principle of outer imitation to its logical perfection. Their religion was reduced to petty external rules. Nothing was done freely from the heart, but everything had to be done by outer regulation and constriction. As a consequence their religion was all on the outside as a show and sham, a rotten interior glossed over with external respectability. Christ tore away this system of superficial appearance and mechanical constraint and introduced inner reality and liberty.

2. **Positive Aspects of the Christian Life.**—The Christian life in its positive nature consists in having Christ within us, and then we spontaneously live as he lived.

(a) To do anything well we must have its nature within us. We are told that every important Greek vase has been measured vertically and horizontally with precision altogether admirable and the results published in four large volumes. "Yet," says Ruskin, "English pottery remains precisely where it was in spite of all this investigation. Do you fancy a Greek workman ever made a vase by measurement? No, he dashed it from his hand on the wheel and it was beautiful. And a Venetian glassblower swept you a curve of crystal from the end of his pipe; and Reynolds swept a curve of colour from his brush, as a musician the cadence of a note, unerring, and to be measured, if you please, afterwards, with the exactitude of law." [1] Why could these men perform with such marvellous accuracy and ease these rare feats which other men cannot do with the most elaborate measurements and painstaking imitation? Because these things were in them. The artistic nature in them shaped the vase on the wheel

[1] *The Eagle's Nest*, p. 120.

and threw the colour on the canvas with the unconscious ease and perfection of instinct. It is easy for anything to act according to its own nature. It is easy for sugar to be sweet, for the sun to shine and the grass to grow. So it is easy for a Christian to be Christlike when Christ liveth in him. If the root is right, every leaf and blossom will be of the right shape and colour and the fruit will have the proper flesh and flavour. If Christ lives in us all our thoughts and deeds will be the fruits of the Spirit.

(*b*) Complete self-surrender of the heart to Jesus Christ is the secret of such a life. Paul had made this surrender and hence he could say, " I live; and yet not I, but Christ liveth in me." No special temperament or genius is needed to receive this gift and attain this life, but it may be possessed and enjoyed by the humblest soul. Mr. Beecher tells us that about the finest Christian he ever knew was an old negress who had been a slave. Eight or ten children, one by one, had been snatched and sold away from her, yet her patience and forgiveness towards her oppressors were remarkable. " She stood as a trunk with branch after branch torn off; but the topmost boughs were bright with blossoms, and the light of heaven rested on them." [1] Christ lived in this humble soul. And if we will surrender ourselves to him in the same faith and faithfulness he will dwell in us so that we each one can say, " I live; yet not I, but Christ liveth in me: and the life which I now live in the flesh, I live by faith of the Son of God, who loved me, and gave himself for me." Then the Christian life will flow out of us as a stream from its fountain and as light from the sun.

[1] *Sermons*, Vol. I, p. 142.

IX. Discipline

Our account of the growth of the Christian life would not be complete, even from the point of view of psychology, without some mention of the ministry of discipline. Temptation, trial, and sorrow have a large place in our Christian life. However these things in their roots may be intertwined with sin as their cause, yet when rightly resisted or borne they are the means of strong and rich character. The human spirit never thrives well in constant warmth and sunshine. Cold and storm have a part to play in developing the deep roots and tough fibre of strong souls. The greenhouse with its artificial heat and protection rears tender blooms that quickly wither, but oaks grow out in the open and are cradled in hardship and rocked by storms. The world is thickset with difficulties and dangers, disease and disaster, and it is the mastering of these that makes men. A world all upholstered with safety and luxurious comfort and ease would not make vertebrate souls. Temptation tries and develops men in courage and might and enables them to mount on the steps of victorious deeds to the crown of mastery. Jesus came out of the temptation in the wilderness a stronger man and Saviour than he was when he went in.

Sorrow chastens the human spirit into beauty that cannot otherwise be acquired. It may be the mother of faith, submission, and peace. Pearls are the product of the suffering of the shellfish, and out of its agony the human soul secretes some of its finest gems of character. Tears are great teachers; their bitter, briny drops may be transmuted into telescopic lenses that enable us to see things beyond the horizon of our earthly vision. We do not see the things of time and eternity in the right light until we see them through our tears. Great souls nearly always wear crowns that have been fashioned in the fires of great sorrows; and those that have escaped this severe discipline usually exhibit some lack of character. The music of the world would be robbed of much of its finest beauty and greatly impoverished if its minor notes were stricken from its chords. " If I could make you suffer two years," said an eminent teacher to one of his pupils, " you would be the greatest contralto in the world." Masterful faith in God is not attained until we can exclaim, "Though he slay me, yet will I trust in him." Even the Son of God was made perfect through suffering, and we cannot reach this high prize through any easier process. Often must the outer things of life perish in flames of loss and sorrow that the inner spirit may be renewed and chastened into perfection. God causes all things to work together for our good and transmutes pain into peace, suffering into submission, ashes into beauty, and a spirit of heaviness into a garment of praise.

> Had he not turned us in his hand, and thrust
> Our high things low and shook our hills as dust,
> We had not been this splendour, and our wrong
> An everlasting music for the song
> Of earth and heaven.

X. Character

1. **The Nature of Christian Character.**—The outcome and final end of all this growth in the Christian life is Christian character, a perfect personality, " a completely fashioned will."

The scientific ideal of the perfect man is expressed in Huxley's well-known definition of education: " That

man, I think, has had a liberal education who has been
so trained in youth that his body is the ready servant
of his will, and does with ease and pleasure all the
work that, as a mechanism, it is capable of; whose
intellect is a clear, cold, logic engine, with all its parts
of equal strength, and in smooth working order; ready,
like a steam engine, to be turned to any kind of work,
and spin the gossamers as well as forge the anchors of
the mind; whose mind is stored with knowledge of the
great fundamental truths of nature and of the laws of
her operations; one who, no stunted ascetic, is full of
life and fire, but whose passions are trained to come
to heel by a vigorous will, the servant of a tender
conscience; who has learned to love all beauty, whether
of nature or of art, to hate all vileness, and to respect
others as himself." [1]

The Christian ideal of the perfect man as set forth
in Scripture includes the same elements: a pure,
healthy body ("a temple of the Holy Spirit"), disciplined into servitude to the will ("I bring it into sub
jection"), a developed mind, a noble heart, and an
obedient will, all combined into symmetry and harmony, a full-statured, broad-visioned man living in full
fine relations with men and with God. These elements are pictured as " the fruit of the Spirit," " love,
joy, peace, longsuffering, kindness, goodness, faithfulness, meekness, self-control."

The Bible not only gives us a portrait of the perfect
man, but also sets before us the Living Reality in him
who " is holy, guileless, undefiled, separated from sinners, and made higher than the heavens," perfect in all
the powers and graces of manhood, the Son of man
and Son of God. All ministries and means of grace
[1] *Lay Sermons*, pp. 34-35.

are given unto us " for the perfecting of the saints, unto the work of ministering, unto the building up of the body of Christ: till we all attain unto the unity of the faith, and of the knowledge of the Son of God, unto a full-grown man, unto the measure of the stature of the fulness of Christ." In so far as we are filled with the spirit of Jesus Christ and are like him we have reached the final end of the Christian life and have attained its fine blossom and full fruitage.

The Christian, then, is no narrow or deformed or defective man, that lacks any essential element of the fullest and strongest and finest manhood. He has no right to be ill-proportioned and misshapen, in any respect unlovely and repellent, round and rich on one side and shrivelled and mean on another; but in him all manly qualities, the physical and the spiritual, the intellectual and the emotional, the passive and the active, meekness and virility, kindness and courage, faith and works, should be combined and blended into harmonious symmetry and strength and fruitfulness. He should be a citizen of this world in all of its interests and also a citizen of heaven, loyal to its laws and imbued with its spirit, with his eyes on the earth yet ever following the gleam of the heavenly vision. He should be " filled unto all the fulness of God," and stand as tall and beautiful as Christ himself. This is the ideal Christian life towards which we should ever strive.

2. **Is Character a By-Product?**—Is perfection of personality to be sought directly as a personal end, or only indirectly through social service? Is it right to cultivate the self? We sometimes hear advice to the effect that self-cultivation is mistaken in theory and bad in practice. Even so eminent an educator as Woodrow Wilson is quoted as saying, in an address

to the National Council of Boy Scouts, that "character is a by-product," and that "a man who devotes himself to the development of his own character will succeed in nothing except making a prig," and that "if you set to work to make character because you love yourself you will make an ass." This is strange talk to come from a schoolmaster, for is not the whole process of education from the kindergarten to the university a cultivation of the self? Are we not to build up a good body, a disciplined mind, and a noble heart? Is not "a man to examine himself" and see wherein he falls short and bring himself up to a higher standard? Are we not bidden to "love thy neighbour as thyself"? Unless we first cultivate the self we shall have nothing of worth with which to serve others. True love of self is simply appreciating and guarding and developing our own worth and right and dignity, and such self-love must precede other love, we must get a soul before we can serve. Of course we must be on our guard against conceit and selfishness and morbid self-consciousness; and of course we can develop and cultivate the self only as we also serve others, for development of personality is not an isolated but a social process, and we are to use our developed and cultivated selves in the service of others; but this fact does not annul the complementary fact that self-development has its necessary place in our life and is our primary duty. In stating a double-faced truth we ought not to emphasize one side at the expense of the other, but keep both in their due place and proportion and thus preserve the full-orbed sphere of life.

3. Individuality in Christian Character.—We have already remarked on the individuality of character,[1]

[1] Pp. 65-68.

and we must leave large room for this vital fact. Christian life, being the fullest development and highest form of life, is subject to the widest differentiation and the greatest variety of types. All the infinitely varying elements that enter into the constitution and development of the body and the soul are reflected in the individuality of the personality. The temperaments, sanguine and choleric or phlegmatic and melancholy, give to it their tone and colour. And so we have every type and variety of Christians, intellectual or emotional, practical doers or meditative mystics. Some specially exhibit one grace or activity in the Christian life, and others are marked by some other characteristic.

The Bible characters that crowd its gallery with their portraits are remarkable for their sharp individualities. Abraham and Moses, David and Job, John and James, Martha and Mary, Peter and Paul, stand out like etchings. And Christian history exhibits the same kind of portraits. Athanasius and Augustine, Luther and Calvin, Wesley and Whitefield, Edwards and Finney, are as distinct as mountain peaks that notch the sky each one with its own particular shape. Christian thinkers and leaders to-day also have their own special gifts and work, and all the millions of Christians are marked each by his own individuality. We still have Peters and Pauls, Marthas and Marys in the church, and many new types of Christians are produced to meet the needs of our modern time. As God never quotes himself in nature but casts each planet in its own mould and paints every sunset and flower petal with its own shades of colour and puts a distinctive mark on every leaf, so he never repeats himself in fashioning Christians into the likeness of

Christ, but gives them gifts differing and causes them
to differ as one star differeth from another star in
glory.

We are strongly disposed to look with some doubt or
suspicion or envy on this variety of gifts and to think
that other people ought to be like us, as though we
were the perfect pattern and model. We regard our
church, our creed, our mode of worship and type of
Christian character as the perfection of orthodoxy,
and may think that to differ from us is a dangerous
and guilty thing. There are sectarians who would put
the whole world through their own little theological
machine and bring people out all the same size, shape,
and colour, just like a machine that cuts nails or
makes buttons. We see such tendencies in small religious sects that impose upon their members narrow
and rigid rules governing their creed and forms of
worship and even their manners and dress. Of the
Quakers, most excellent people, Charles Lamb said
that " if they could they would paint the universe in
drab."

But God has not built the kingdom of grace, any
more than the kingdom of nature, on lines of uniformity. He has given us gifts differing and shaped
every body after its own pattern and cast every soul
in its own mould. Our infinitely varying elements of
personality are divinely given and are to be respected
and appreciated each for its own peculiar worth and
work, use and beauty. God wants all kinds of people
in his world and church and kingdom, and that they
may all find easy entrance and warm welcome and
abundant hospitality he has built his city with twelve
open gates, and we should rejoice to see people of every

type of individuality crowding through all these en-
trances into his kingdom.

Our levelling sectarian ideas would work an enormous impoverishment of the world, stripping it of its
variety and picturesqueness and beauty and reducing it
to a dead level of monotony, like a flock of sheep or
blackbirds. It would be a poor and pitiful, dull and
dreary world, if other people were all like us, whatever our type and gifts may be. Variety is the spice
of life, and all the beauty and joy of this many-
coloured world grow out of our diversity of gifts.
More disastrous still, uniformity of type would vastly
lower the efficiency of Christian service, for the principle of special gifts, with the resulting division of
labour which so enormously increases production in
industry and art, is equally efficient and fruitful in
religion. It is because " God hath set some in the
church, first apostles, secondly prophets, thirdly teachers, then miracles, then gifts of healing, helps, govern-
ments, divers kinds of tongues," that we can carry
on the varying activities of the Christian life and build
the complex kingdom of God in the world. One can
preach and another teach, one can sing and another
pray, one can write books and another write songs, one
can train the children in the home and another in the
school, one can labour in the gospel at home, and another can go as a foreign missionary. Let us not, then,
envy or disparage or despise one another. " For even
as we have many members in one body, and all the
members have not the same office; so we, being many,
are one body in Christ, and severally members one of
another. And having gifts differing according to the
grace that was given unto us, whether prophecy, let us
prophesy according to the proportion of our faith; or

ministry, let us give ourselves to our ministry; or he that teacheth, to his teaching; or he that exhorteth, to his exhorting: he that giveth, let him do it with liberality; he that ruleth, with diligence; he that showeth mercy, with cheerfulness."

The same principle may be extended to our denominations and to various Christian organizations such as the Young Men's Christian Association. They each have a special character and mission. A denomination is a large group of people that have common thoughts and sympathies in Christian faith and service. It is generally best that such people should flock together and go into the kingdom on the same side. This conduces to order and harmony and efficiency. In the Cathedral of St. John the Divine in New York, around the apse are arranged seven chapels in each one of which worship is conducted in a different language. It would not conduce to the intelligibility of the service to remove the dividing partitions and merge the polyglot congregations into one; and yet they are all gathered under the same roof and are parts of the same great cathedral. So our denominations may be viewed as chapels in which groups of Christians worship in somewhat different accents of faith and order; yet they are parts of the same grand cathedral and worship the same Christ. No doubt there are too many dividing partitions. Some of these have been taken down, and others are growing thin and fragile and are about to crumble; but some of them may long endure, at least in the interest of efficiency.

There is, however, one deadly danger in connection with denominations: and that is, that each one will think that it has the only true gate into the kingdom, whereas John saw twelve gates open day and night, three on every side, so that from whatever direction any weary traveller might come he would find an open gate. We may well pity the blindness of that bigotry that can see no gate but its own. This narrow spirit is waning, and there is growing that broad spirit that rejoices to see the people come from the north and from the south and from the east and from the west and enter into the common kingdom of our Lord and Saviour Jesus Christ.

There are thus wide room and great need and use for individuality in the Christian life and service. God loves variety and has scattered it in the richest profusion over all his works. He who makes one star to differ from another star in glory and puts a distinctive notch in every leaf will not repeat even the most perfect soul or the most beautiful saint. Having made us each one after a special type, he breaks the mould and fashions the next one after a different pattern. He has infinite resources and never does the same thing twice, and hence the endless diversity of his works. It is by ever varied individuality that he keeps his world from stagnation and fixity and death and rejuvenates it in ever new forms of life and beauty and joy; for

> God fulfils himself in many ways,
> Lest one good custom should corrupt the world.

4. **Christian Society.**—The full and final outcome of Christian growth is Christian society, the kingdom of God on earth. This society begins in the home and broadens out through widening circles in the church and community and state and nation until it sweeps the great circle of the earth. Its final realization is a redeemed humanity in a world of universal justice and

peace and brotherhood and spiritual blessing, a Christianized social order. Though a kingdom, yet it is also a democracy in which all are kings and priests unto God. Gifts differing will ever remain, and these will give birth to differences in service and reward and to different social classes, but these will all be united in the deeper unity and democracy of Christian brotherhood. Prophets and apostles caught foregleams of this coming universal kingdom. " And the ransomed of the Lord shall return, and come to Zion with songs, and everlasting joy upon their heads: they shall obtain joy and gladness, and sorrow and sighing shall flee away." Jesus declared that " there shall be one fold, and one shepherd," and St. John saw the holy city descending out of heaven from God and the nations entering into it. We are now building this city and the weary world waits and longs for it. War may seem to be overturning and uprooting its very foundations, but such destruction often precedes construction, and amidst the convulsion are being laid deeper and more solid foundations of a permanent world kingdom of brotherhood and love.

What is the final end and finest flower of our vast splendid civilization? Not our great cities and buildings and banks, our marvellous inventions and multiplying wealth, much less our warships and engines of destruction. These material things may be only the rank soil out of which will grow scarlet blossoms of enervating luxury and pride, social injustice and vice, blossoms that will wither into dust. The highest outcome of civilization, the end for which all things else are means, are good people. Lowell said that the finest flower of our civilization is a group of cultivated people engaged in friendly conversation. This is the Christian ideal. "Ye are my friends," said Jesus to his disciples. And what is heaven? Perfect society raised to its highest power. "But ye are come unto the city of the living God, the heavenly Jerusalem, and to an innumerable company of angels, to the general assembly and church of the first-born, which are written in heaven, and to God the Judge of all, and to the spirits of just men made perfect, and to Jesus."

CHAPTER VII

THE PSYCHOLOGY OF THE SERMON

PREACHING is persuasion. It is the proclamation of the gospel in speech so as to persuade hearers to believe upon and follow Jesus Christ. It is not teaching, or lecturing, or entertaining, or acting, though each or all of these in varying degrees may enter into it. Its object is to enlighten the mind so as to kindle and inspire the heart and thereby decide and energize the will to act; it seeks to convert men and make them Christians in character and conduct, spirit and service.

The psychology of preaching is the application of the principles of psychology to this art so as to attain its practical purpose. All the powers and means and motives of the preacher should converge to this one point as their burning focus and sovereign end. The preacher above all other men should be a practical psychologist, a master of the art of ruling the human soul.

We have made incidental application of our subject to the art of preaching during the course of these chapters, but we are now to gather it up and concentrate it upon this one point. The psychology of preaching involves the whole subject of preaching in homiletics and delivery and really covers the entire course in the theological seminary and goes back into the college and into all the preceding life; but in this chapter we

290

can only glance in a suggestive way at the application
of psychology to the sermon.

I. The Parts of the Sermon

The sermon is the chief tool of the preacher, and
therefore he should first study and know how to fashion
it. A primary object of the preacher is to gain and
hold the attention of his hearers so that he may convince their minds and move their wills, and we shall
consider the psychological construction of the parts of
the sermon with a view to this end. No matter how
orthodox a sermon may be, if it does not have the
quality of interest, if it does not obey the laws of the
mind so as to enlist the attention and work conviction, it will fail of its purpose. Every part of the sermon as well as the sermon as a whole should be so
constructed and pervaded with the quality of interest
that it will hold the minds of the hearers from beginning to end.

1. The Text.—The very first words of a discourse
are of critical importance, almost making or marring
it at the start, and the text is the tip of the sermon,
the point of its spear. Some texts at once attract attention and awaken expectation, and others fail to
excite interest and may create a sense of disappointment as having been worn threadbare and exhausted.
A text should have unity, point, suggestiveness, and, if
possible, freshness. These qualities are more likely to
be found in a short text, and as a general rule the
shorter the text the better. A short text is easily re-
membered and it may strike and stick in the mind like
an arrow. A long, loosely jointed text, or one that consists of several verses gathered from different parts of
Scripture, is likely to lack unity and point and to be

confusing. Even the passage on which an expository
sermon is based should be reasonably short and have
compactness and unity, but the text of a topical sermon
is best when it is a single verse or clause or phrase or
even word, which concisely states or suggests the subject. Of course many familiar well-worn texts must
be used, but an unusual text makes a fresh appeal to
the mind. Some preachers have a kind of genius for
finding good texts, for the good texts have not yet all
been found. Horace Bushnell exhibited this genius
when he took for his great sermon on " Unconscious
Influence " the text, " Then went in also that other
disciple " (John 20: 8). The preacher should study
this art and learn to look for the gleaming point of
light in a verse, as a diamond hunter is ever keenly
watching for the sparkle of light in a stone.

2. The Topic.—Even more important than the text,
as regards interest, is the topic or subject of the sermon, which should have the quality of arresting and
holding the mind. To be interesting a subject should
be worth while, it should concern us, it should be
timely, and it should be attractively stated.

(a) The subject of a sermon should be something
worth while. There should be sufficient magnitude and
mass in it to give the sermon weight and momentum.
Trifling matters, petty rules of behaviour, commonplace platitudes do not have sufficient bulk and substance for pulpit discourse. Such things may be treated
incidentally in a sermon, but are not large enough for
its central subject. Sermons as a rule should have
large themes, subjects of momentous importance. No
other field of discourse so abounds in great subjects.
Religious principles run through all life and out
through the universe up to God, and the preacher

should know how to connect his subject with these cosmic relations. The mind is instinctively attracted and aroused and impressed by great things, and the preacher should enlist the aid of this psychological law by hitching his sermon to the star of a great subject.

(b) In the same line, the subject should be one that concerns us. It should be a matter that comes home to every one's business and bosom. The modern pragmatic test of truth is, What difference does it make to us in our conduct? If it makes no difference at all, then as far as our conduct is concerned it is just the same as though it were not true. The same test may be applied to our sermons: what difference do they make to us in our living? If no difference, or if we cannot see or feel the difference, then what use are they and why preach them? We have all heard sermons on theological incomprehensibilities or on outworn and obsolete aspects of doctrine or polity that we felt did not concern us in the least. It made no difference to us whether they were true or not. This is the root of the objection to doctrinal sermons: the people see no use in such sermons and so find them dry and dreary. But if the preacher can make doctrinal sermons practically useful by hitching them right on to daily living, the people will hear them gladly. The author once heard a sermon on the intercession of Christ with the Father in heaven. For half an hour the preacher carried on an imaginary description of some mysterious process that was going on up in heaven and never once did he touch the earth and the common mortals that were listening to him. He was talking about something that they could not understand and that he knew nothing about, so that for half an hour we were enveloped in a fog of mystery. It was simply impossible to be interested in such a sermon. This is what is the matter with a good many of our sermons: they are up in the air and far away in a misty theological region and do not come down to the ground. They do not get into our hearts and lay hold of our daily life. They may be true in a sense, but they do not concern us, and hence are not interesting and efficient. No other subject lies so close to life and goes so deep into the heart as religion, and we should learn to see such aspects of it as have this vital element of practical usefulness.

(c) Sermon subjects should be timely, adapted to their day, and often to the current events of the day. A sermon that could have been preached as well in the ninth or nineteenth century may not hit the mark in the twentieth century. A Christmas sermon would be strangely out of place and would only create amusement on the Fourth of July, and a patriotic discourse suitable for the Fourth of July would jar the sensibilities at a communion service. Sermons should be opportune to the season of the year, the state of the congregation, and the events of the day. Every minister knows he can preach sermons in a revival season that he could not preach so well at other times: the soil is then prepared for them; there is a state of interest to receive them. Great public events, such as the San Francisco earthquake or the sinking of the *Titanic*, call out sermons that take advantage of the common thought and feeling, and such sermons, taking the tide at its flood, may rise to the occasion with tremendous power. And yet the preacher may go too far in this direction, and preachers that are always preaching on current events may tire the people because they are simply pouring upon them out of the pulpit the same

stuff with which they have been drenched through the
hose of the newspaper during the week.

(d) And the subject should be attractively stated. A
conventionalized, commonplace statement of a subject
may doom a sermon to deadly dulness before it is born.
Such a subject first spreads its stupefying influence
over the mind of the preacher while he is making the
sermon, and then it chloroforms the congregation while
it is being delivered. On the other hand, a fresh live
subject, or one stated in apt, suggestive, and striking
terms, wakes up the mind of the preacher and then it
wakes up the congregation. Great preachers usually
have a genius for finding or making suggestive and
attractive subjects. One realizes this when he runs his
eye down the list of topics in a volume of sermons by
Phillips Brooks or Dr. W. L. Watkinson. Who would not
like to hear a sermon on Phillips Brooks's " The With-
held Completions of Life," or on Dr. Watkinson's " The
Splendid Isolation," or " The Hidden Sackcloth "?
In looking over the list of subjects of sermons in the
Saturday newspaper one is instinctively attracted by
some and repelled by others. A good subject is a sermon half done. It almost creates its own sermon,
unfolding as naturally and inevitably as a seed into its
flower. A preacher should spend much time and study
in getting his subject into good shape. Cut out superfluous verbiage and condense it into a compact and
telling phrase. See that it just hits the mark. Shape
and smooth and feather it like an arrow. Hammer and
polish it until it has the sharpness and glitter of a
sword. Tune it up until it sings. Listen to it and see
that it sounds well. Get it out of the beaten dusty
track into a fresh bit of meadow or forest or up on a
new mountain top. Get a subject that is alive with

interest, and then it will excite the interest of the congregation.

Of course there are dangers at this point. Every
sermon cannot have a striking subject, and there must
be many on commonplace themes. In such cases it may
be well not to advertise or mention the subject and let
it come out in the sermon. The preacher should not
strain after original subjects and make extravagant
and fantastical ones. Sensational subjects may be an
offence and abomination. They may violate every principle of propriety and advertise the preacher's conceit,
shallowness, and spiritual irreverence and impertinence.
Yet in avoiding this extreme and abuse we should not
fall into slovenly subjects, but ought to give our themes
careful attention and get them into the best form.

An interesting subject, then, is the first element of
an effective sermon, and such a subject is one that is
worth while, that concerns the hearers, is timely, and is
attractively stated.

3. The Plan.—The next vital element in an efficient
sermon is the plan, and a good plan is one that has
unity, logical order and cumulative power.

(a) A sermon should have unity, or one idea or principle should run through it as a spinal column or
trunk artery. If it is divided and scattered into dis-
connected ideas it will divide and distract the attention
of the hearers and lose interest. Little matter how
good its parts are, if they do not cohere into unity they
are not likely to concentrate and hold the attention.
Many a sermon that contains good things is not a good
sermon, and a sermon may contain many interesting
things and yet not be an interesting sermon. It would
sometimes puzzle hearers to assign a subject to a sermon, and possibly to do this would puzzle the preacher

himself. Sermons that thus wander around through a miscellaneous field and jungle of ideas in which the preacher is going everywhere preaching the gospel and not finding it anywhere cannot hold the attention of the hearers. The preacher who is jumping around like a grasshopper cannot expect his people to follow him in his gymnastics. But a preacher who travels along a straight road to a goal will lead and draw his congregation after him.

(b) This unitary subject should unfold in its logical order. It should be linked like a chain, or unwind like a rope, so that each link will lead directly to the next link and the rope untwist into its own strands. When the transitions in a sermon are abrupt and unrelated, marking no advance in development, they jar the mind and throw its interest off the track. The most ignorant mind is instinctively logical and feels the necessity and value of order. When the preacher violates this psychological law he is likely to pay the penalty of having an inattentive congregation. Old-fashioned sermons had heads, but some modern sermons have no heads or head at all. A sermon should have heads or divisions, though they need not always be announced. The higher animals all have skeletons, though they do not wear them on the outside. Our sermons should be vertebrate and not a jellyfish mass or mess, and the vertebræ should be articulated in their right order, and thus they will follow the laws of the mind and enlist interest.

(c) And a sermon should have cumulative power. This is likely to result from unity and logical order, but it needs to be looked after. A sermon that is most interesting in the beginning and weakens in the middle and breaks down at the end is a poor sermon, however logical it may be. The sermon-maker should therefore watch this point and arrange his plan and materials so that it will grow in interest and culminate in a climax. Many an otherwise good sermon ravels out into loose threads at the end or is diluted down into thin watery stuff. Save the best things till the end. Start low down, but rise to a summit that will give a mountain view of the subject, and then the final impression will be good.

A unitary, logical, and cumulative plan helps the sermon in the making as it grows upon the mind and attracts all kindred associations. All that the preacher knows and has accumulated in his experience will grow around such a skeleton as its flesh and blood. It helps the hearers in grasping and following it, as it slips into the logical grooves in their minds. And it greatly helps the preacher in the delivery of his sermon as it unwinds like a rope, each part suggesting the next; and thus he can preach it, not by memory, but by a process of reproduction by which it constantly re-creates itself.

4. **The Introduction.**—Nothing should come in immediately before the sermon in the way of announcements or other talk. Announcements, when verbal, should be made at an earlier point in the service. When the minister rises to preach he should read his text and begin. The audience at this moment is in a state of expectancy, and any other matter, especially a verbose stream of talk about miscellaneous affairs, will distract and may ruin attention. A preacher may kill his sermon by giving his congregation " that tired feeling " before he begins. The introduction should, as a rule, be short and strike the subject or point of the sermon quick. Dr. T. De Witt Talmage was crude and

lurid enough in the matter and rhetoric of his sermons, but he had a genius for introductions. He nearly always struck his subject in the first sentence, and that sentence was a graphic, epigrammatic statement. Long introductions wear the hearers out while the preacher is getting ready to begin. The most common introduction is usually the poorest, namely, the kind which consists in telling the story of the context and simply padding it out with prosy language or watering it down in a sea of words. The people generally know the story, probably the preacher has read it to them only a few minutes before, and they should be credited with human intelligence. Of course the context must sometimes be explained, but this should be done briefly and graphically, and often it can wisely be let alone. While the preacher is wandering around in his introduction, many a hearer must feel like calling out to him, "Play ball." Let the sermon start right off the bat. Every sermon is interesting in the beginning in the sense that the preacher has the attention of his congregation, and if he catches this interest at its first tide he may hold it and it will lead him on to fortune. But if the preacher wears out this fresh initial interest or dulls its keen point and loses the attention of his audience in his introduction, he may have lost his chance. It is wonderful what a preacher can do in the first five minutes. The author once sat down in a church just as the minister was announcing his text and a clock on the wall pointed to eight o'clock. After the sermon had been going on a good while, as it seemed to the hearer, and he began to feel weary as the preacher was wildly reaching around after ideas with none in his neighbourhood, a glance at the clock showed that it was only five minutes after eight. In five minutes he wore out the attention of his casual hearer. On the other hand, the same hearer, sitting in Dr. Parkhurst's church in New York, had no sense of time. A short crisp introduction introduced a sermon all electric and alive with interest. A sermon is just as long as it seems. A prosy sermon is long at fifteen minutes, and an intensely interesting sermon is short at an hour. Great pains should be taken with the introduction to make it short, graphic, and interesting, leading by a few steps or a single straight step into the subject. The entrance to a house should bear some proper proportion to the house itself and not overshadow it or be a long tortuous approach. The visitor wants to get quickly through the vestibule into the bright warm interior. Hitch the subject close up to the text, come to the point at once, strike the iron while it is hot, start the sermon off with a good strong shove and give it momentum, and then it will go.

5. The Body of the Sermon.—The development of the subject follows the introduction and carries out the plan. It states each head or progressive stage in the unfolding subject, shows its logical relation to the whole, supports it with proof, and illuminates it with illustrations. It puts flesh on the bones of the skeleton and fills it out with blood and breath. Care should be taken to state facts accurately and have the arguments sound and the illustrations pertinent.

The argument of the sermon should appeal to the mind in a train of reasoning, presenting facts and putting them together in such relations that they will lead to a logical conclusion. This truth should then be pressed upon the conscience and emotions so as to stir up the feelings of sin and guilt and repentance, of duty to God and faith in Christ, of the obligation and worth and reward of righteousness and the beauty and blessedness of holiness. It should awaken early tender associations of religious training and memories. It should penetrate into the deepest feelings and instincts of dependence on God and yearning for a heavenly Father. These emotions should then be poured as a flood upon the will to move it in decision and action. This is the true psychological order in preaching. Preaching which first and simply aims at arousing feelings by playing on the heartstrings with tender memories or exciting scenes or strong fears or ecstatic hopes may create a brain-storm of excitement and frenzy, but it will quickly subside and leave a burnt-out state of soul as hard and dead as cold lava or ashes, the last state worse than the first. Feeling that grows out of fact, emotion that is kindled in the heart by conviction of truth in the mind, has deep roots and will endure. Such feeling is fed by the permanent supply of fuel in the truth and continues to energize and move the will. The argument of the sermon should keep this practical point in view and concentrate all its facts and illustrations and logic on this end.

6. **The Conclusion.**—The conclusion should bring the message of the sermon to its climax and leave it at its highest point of interest and efficiency. It should gather up all its separate parts and compact and sharpen them into one point and press this point home in one final stroke. It should send the people out under the spell of a great thought or vision that will lead them on to victory.

The conclusion should come as soon as the sermon is done and not be continued in prolonged uncertainty. A college student is credited with defining an oration as consisting of three parts: " the introduction, the body, and the peroration. The introduction is what you say before you begin; the body is what you say; and the peroration is what you say after you are done." The definition applies to many a sermon. The introduction is sometimes what the preacher says before he begins. He fears he will not have enough material to fill out the time, and he wanders around, tramping over the context and, incidentally, over the congregation, until he really begins. And then the conclusion of many a sermon is what the preacher says after he is done. Many a preacher does not know when he is through and keeps on talking. He may not know that he is done, but his hearers do. The preacher that several times says, " One word more," or intimates that he is through and then continues for five or ten minutes more, deceives his audience and might be arrested for obtaining their attention by false pretences. Having given them the prospect of welcome relief he should keep his promise and give them what they want. Many an otherwise good sermon has been spoiled by the last five or ten minutes of it. It lacked terminal facilities, and superfluous prolixity ran it into a ditch. It is all the better when the conclusion comes with unexpected suddenness. It is far better that the sermon should end when the people wish it would keep on, than that it should keep on when they wish it would end. It is better, in approaching a precipice, to stop too soon than too late, and the same principle applies to a sermon. The conclusion should never be left ill prepared and vague in the preacher's mind with the hope that some inspiration will come to him at the end, but he should have the conclusion well shaped out and sharpened in his mind and at the proper moment drive it home and stop.

These parts of a sermon have been considered from the point of view of psychological interest, and this interest grows right out of the substance and spirit, foundation and framework of a sermon, and is not a superficial veneering or paint put on the outside of it, or an artificial device or trick, or flower or tinsel of cheap ornamentation that is tied on it. It is a subtle quality or spirit that pervades the whole of it; not foam on its surface, but effervescence that bubbles up out of its depths and gives pungency and relish to every portion and particle of it. The bloom of the grape is not painted on the outside but is secreted from within, and the fragrance of the rose comes from its root. And so an interesting and efficient sermon is one that has a worthy subject, attractively stated, logically unfolded, and effectively applied, and that begins at the beginning and quits when it is done.

II. General Characteristics of the Sermon

There are some general characteristics of the sermon that have much to do with its interest and efficiency.

1. Style.—Prominent if not foremost among these is style. The preacher should not only have something to say, but he should also know how to say it. There are therefore few things that a preacher should more assiduously strive to master than an effective style. Words are his tools, and he should learn to use them with expert accuracy and ease, force and efficiency. Some of the elements of effective pulpit style are lucidity, simplicity, conciseness, force, and beauty, and we shall briefly consider several of these.

(a) The primary quality of good style is lucidity, the clearness and ease with which language is understood. The preacher should speak so as to be instantly understood, and when he does not do this he probably does not understand himself. There was in one of our theological seminaries an Armenian student who had poor use of English and was in the habit of saying in answer to a question, " Professor, I have that in my mind, but I cannot express it." One day the question was, " What is a vacuum? " and after thinking a moment the student answered, " I have it in my mind, Professor, but I cannot express it." When a preacher thinks he has something in his mind which he cannot express, he probably has a vacuum in the place where his idea is supposed to be.

The object of language is to convey thought from one mind to another, and it should do this with the least friction and loss. Of all the many books that Herbert Spencer produced the ones that will probably live longest are not his ponderous volumes on philosophy and sociology, but two small ones, his essay on " The Philosophy of Style," [1] and his little book on *Education*. His essay on style goes to the root of the philosophy of style by showing that the one principle that explains all the rules on the subject of good style is economy of effort in understanding the thought expressed. After enumerating a number of these rules, such as simplicity and brevity as opposed to verbose and involved sentences, the use of Saxon words and avoidance of parentheses, he says: " On seeking some clue to the law underlying these current maxims, we may see implied in many of them the importance of economizing the reader's or hearer's attention. To so present ideas that they may be apprehended with the least pos-

[1] Published separately and also in his *Essays*, Vol. II, pp. 333-369.

sible mental effort is the desideratum towards which
most of the rules above quoted point. . . . A reader
or listener has at each moment but a limited amount
of mental power available. To recognize and interpret
the symbol presented to him requires part of this
power; to arrange and combine the images suggested by
them requires a further part; and only that part which
remains can be used for framing the thought expressed.
Hence, the more time and attention it takes to receive
and understand each sentence, the less time and attention can be given to the contained idea; and the less
vividly will that idea be conceived." " Let us then
inquire whether economy of the recipient's attention is
not the secret of effect, alike in the right choice and
collocation of words, in the best arrangement of clauses
in a sentence, in the proper order of its principal and
subordinate propositions, in the judicious use of simile,
metaphor, and other figures of speech, and even in the
rhythmical sequence of sentences." The whole essay is
of inestimable value because it analyzes the psychological laws and qualities of style and thereby brings
all its rules under one root principle.

The preacher therefore should carefully study the
matter of choosing his words and arranging their order
and constructing his sentences and paragraphs so that
the thought will slip through them into the hearer's
mind with the least friction and loss of meaning on his
part, leaping from the speaker's to the hearer's mind as
light shoots from the sun to the eye. He should read
over and listen to his own sentences to see whether they
express his thought with this clearness and ease. Practice will improve and perfect this power of lucid expression until mind will speak to mind with almost
instantaneous directness. This quality of style diverts

the attention from the style itself and concentrates it upon the contained thought. Style should be like the sash and leads in a window which occupy as little space as possible so as to let the more light through; so style should be so lucid as not to hinder or obscure the thought, but let it through in unobstructed clearness.

(b) Another vital element in pulpit style is force. The thought may be clearly expressed so that there is no mistaking its meaning, but it does not strike and stick in the mind. It has no cutting edge like a sharp tool, or biting power like an acid, but it rolls off the mind like water off a roof. Verbosity and prolixity and commonplace prosiness are fatal to force, padding out and deadening sentences with their cushions of superfluous words. Effort should be made to eliminate unnecessary words and phrases and to condense sentences into compact form and sharp points. Care should be taken to place the emphatic word in a sentence so that it will have the greatest force. A sentence should end well, not ravelling out into loose, vague words, but rather ending in a knot so that it will crack like a whip. It is true that all the words and sentences in a sermon cannot be equally emphatic, and there is such a thing as making the style too uniformly forceful, which keeps the hearer's attention on a strain and presently defeats itself. There should be great variety in the style of a sermon, ranging from the low levels of commonplace narrative to the peaks of imaginative vision or of eruptive power. This relieves and varies the attention and keeps the interest fresh. A sermon made up of a string of epigrams and figures of speech would grow tiresome, just as a dinner of spiced condiments would pall upon the appetite.

Force should be distributed so that at times it will spread itself out in narrative leisure and ease, and then concentrate itself into brilliant epigrams and explosive aphorisms and strike tremendous blows.

(c) Still another element of effective pulpit style is beauty. Beauty is such a harmony and exquisite propriety of good qualities in an object as pleases our esthetic sense. It is not a mere ornament that could as well be dispensed with, but is an element of utility. " Beauty," says Victor Hugo, " is an added service." Thought that is wrought out into logical consistency and application is a beautiful product, and its proper expression shares in and reflects this constitutional beauty. The proper beauty of style, therefore, is not the external adornment of flowery writing, but is inherent in the thought. An idea does not reach its fullest and finest expression until it has been edged with beauty, or until beauty exudes from its whole substance. Thought instinctively seeks for and incarnates itself in choice diction, fitting figures and illustrations, the diamonds of speech in which it can flash forth its proper forms and colours. When so expressed thought is far more efficient, ministering to the esthetic nature and calling more of the soul into activity than unadorned prose.

The minister should study this art and acquire the knack and habit of using speech that has form and finish and is jewelled with beauty. He needs to be on his guard against meretricious forms of beauty, flowery sentences and grandiloquent words. He should ornament construction and not simply construct ornament. Beauty of style should come from the thought, as the scarlet flush of the peach comes from its stone core, and the colour of the cheek and the splendour of the eye from the blood. We should first take care of our ideas to get them into clear and consistent shape, and then we can express them in beautiful speech. Lucidity, force, and beauty are three chief elements in an effective pulpit style.

2. **Illustrations.**—Illustrations are vital and vivid points in the sermon, and in nothing do great preachers show their genius more than in this art and power. An illustration is a concrete instance of a general principle, a diamond that shows what carbon is. The general principle may be abstract and vague and hard to grasp; carbon as a chemical element is difficult to visualize, but a diamond glows and flashes with light and everybody can see it. A sermon that has no illustrations is likely to be abstract and dry, but one that is thickset with the diamonds of concrete instances of its general principle or doctrine will sparkle with interest.

The poorest illustrations are stories, especially those that are dragged in, screaming, by the hair. Great preachers are chary of them. Phillips Brooks never used them, and one will look for them in the sermons of Dr. W. L. Watkinson, one of the greatest masters of illustration of our day, in vain. Stories are apt to be unreal, of doubtful authenticity, and probably coloured up by the preacher himself, and the hearers begin to have a suspicion that they never happened. An incident out of one's personal experience, or an historical reference or event of definite date, may be very effective, but a mere story-teller in the pulpit is likely to be a shallow preacher, preaching thin and watery sermons.

The best illustrations are picturesque instances of the principle being presented from nature, science, art, literature, and daily life. A preacher with a homiletic instinct and seeing eye finds tongues in trees, books in the running brooks, sermons in stones, and good in everything. All nature glitters with them as thick as dew on the morning grass, and they stare the preacher in the face. The most effective illustrations grow out of life and are concrete bits of daily happenings. Nothing is so interesting to man as man himself, and so a sermon should have little abstract reasoning but should be crowded full of the living reality and warm breath of human life. The painter always puts some evidence of human presence in his painting to give it human interest, and every part of a sermon should have in it the red blood of the human heart. Human life is the best illustration of life, and therefore the most real and vital illustrations are usually drawn from life itself.

Illustrations out of cyclopedias of illustrations, "canned" illustrations, are generally stale and lack real aptness and are to be left in the can and the can kept out of the study. Illustrations should spring right out of the subject and be fresh instances of it, like blossoms out of a rosebush, and should not be tied on to it from the outside, like artificial flowers on a tree. And a good illustration as a rule is like a tack, short and sharp, with a point that goes right in and sticks. An illustration that is long and complicated may become tedious and it distracts attention from the subject itself and may thus defeat its own end. In fact, illustrations should never be introduced for their brilliance or beauty or for their own sake, but only as they contribute to the clearness and interest of the subject. The best illustrations are not those that come marching into the sermon blowing a trumpet or beating a bass drum, but those that crack like a rifle, and then the bullet speeds to the mark and the work of the illustration is done.

3. **Slang and Humour.**—Some preachers try to make their sermons interesting and popular by sprinkling them with slang and language from the street. Some even go down into the gutter and into saloons and dens of vice and drag out the most vulgar and degrading expressions, and their sermons reek with such language as with garlic. Such fictitious interest is a flash in the pan, and not the steady shining of a light. Few things are more irreverent and offensive in the pulpit than such coarse and vulgar language, and such preachers soon run their course and find their level, though occasionally a man of genius can offend and bear the burden of his offence; yet even he would be stronger without such encumbrances. The pulpit, however, should not be monotonously dignified and starchy, but should at times be unconventional and free and may even occasionally be made vivid and vital with a bit of slang. Slang is often picturesque speech in the making, and many a slang word or phrase, picked up out of the street or gutter, has become classical and in time sparkled as a diamond in the king's English. Colloquialisms are often effective in the pulpit, and any tool of speech that does good work is to be used. There is said to be slang in the Greek New Testament, and a preacher with good judgment will know how to use this effective instrument without passing the borders of propriety and taste.

Humour also has its place and use in the pulpit. There is humour in the Bible, Jesus used it, and it is a universal principle running through life and must have its place, we must think, in the mind of God. A sermon should not be too solemn, at least every sermon should not be, especially with long-faced sanctimoniousness. The funereal air and tone of the pulpit have done much to make it unpopular, especially have they made it chilling and repellent to the young. Religion is good cheer and joy and has affinity with all bright and pleasant things, sunshine and flowers, music and gladness. We ought to take our religion seriously, but not too seriously. It has a lighter side which should not be refused its place or neglected. A dash of humour in an illustration or phrase will often relieve the strain of a sermon, relax the feelings, and give the hearer a sense of rest and a fresh start. And, besides, humour and sarcasm and irony are often most effective in putting points or answering objections or exposing fallacies, as is often seen in the Bible itself. Great preachers generally have a sense of humour and infuse its effervescence and sparkle into their sermons. Spurgeon and Beecher were full of humour, and it bubbles up out of their sermons and gives them freshness and zest. Of course humour ought not to be used so as to raise a broad laugh and destroy the sense of reverence and worship, but within proper bounds it has its place and power in a sermon and helps to preach the gospel.

4. Imagination.—The imperial power of imagination is a magic sceptre in the hand of the preacher that can wield it, and every preacher can learn to use it in some degree. The first business of the preacher is to lead his hearers into a knowledge of the truth, and he will succeed in this only as he gets them to visualize or realize it. There is, of course, but little opportunity for presenting religious truth through the senses. The Protestant preacher has no images or holy relics to show. Only to a very limited extent can material ob-

jects be brought into the pulpit to illustrate spiritual
truth, though pictures and moving pictures are being
used in some pulpits and may have a large use in the
future. Being shut off from the vividness and power
of direct presentative knowledge, the next best thing
the preacher can do is to use representative images in
making spiritual truth clear and vivid. To a considerable degree the preacher must deal in general propositions, abstract conceptions: these, as we have seen, are
the weakest and least interesting, the dryest and dullest kind of knowledge, especially to untrained minds.
The preacher must try to brighten up and intensify,
enliven and enrich these abstract conceptions with
imagination so as to turn them into concrete living
images. The difference between the interesting
preacher, who keeps every eye awake and sparkling
with eager attention, and the uninteresting, dry
preacher, who puts everybody into a dull, drowsy state,
is found just at this point. The one sends through the
minds of his hearers a stream of living images, unrolls before their imaginations a panorama of pictures,
and the other sends through their minds a series of
abstract propositions that simply sound solemn. Such
solemnity is closely akin to somnolency.

The use of the imagination in preaching opens a
large subject, and we can only touch it at a few points.
Psychologists classify the forms and functions of the
imagination in various ways, but for our purpose we
may divide them into the creative, the illustrative, and
the verbal.

(a) The creative imagination is the highest form of
this faculty and puts forth the most splendid products.
In its creative activity the imagination takes the raw
materials of the world and works them up into new

forms of structure, thought, and beauty. The poet
weaves them into musical lines and fairy visions, the
artist spreads them on his canvas in forms of loveli-
ness, the musician tunes them into grand chords and
sweet melodies, the architect builds them into mighty
cathedrals that have in them some of the majesty and
mystery of mountains. The psychological poet, such
as Shakespeare or Browning, uses his imagination in
penetrating into the profoundest depths of the human
soul and bringing its secrets to light. The orator uses
it in framing his thoughts into mighty orations that
sway vast multitudes and shape nations and ages.

The preacher may use this creative imagination with
wondrous effect Great preachers almost without exception have been endowed with princely imagination,
and they have often used it in its creative activity.
Mr. Beecher would often throw scenes in the Bible and
religious truth into dramatic form and act them out
with overpowering effect. Mr. Moody had considerable creative imagination by which he could enter into
the heart of Scripture scenes and sayings and reproduce them so that they stood out in lifelike reality.
For instance, listen to this passage from one of his
sermons:

"I can imagine that when Christ said to the little
band around him, ' Go ye into all the world and preach
the gospel,' Peter said, 'Lord, you do not really mean
that we are to go back to Jerusalem and preach the
gospel to those men that murdered you?' 'Yes,' said
Christ, 'go, hunt up that man that spat in my face;
tell him that he may have a seat in my kingdom yet.
Yes, Peter, go, find that man that made that cruel
crown of thorns and placed it on my brow, and tell
him I will have a crown ready for him when he comes

into my kingdom, and there will be no thorns in it. Hunt up that man that took a reed and brought it down over the cruel thorns, driving them into my brow, and tell him that I will put a sceptre in his hand, and he shall rule over the nations of the earth, if he will accept my salvation. Search for the man that drove the spear into my side, and tell him there is a nearer way to my heart than that. Tell him I forgive him freely, and that he can be saved if he will accept salvation.' "

This realistic bit of dramatic description brings this scene before us and gives us a sense of the forgiving grace of Christ that no amount of abstract statement or logical reasoning could do. Phillips Brooks possessed this power of dramatic imagination in a rare degree. His biographer, Prof. Alexander V. G. Allen, in describing one of his great sermons, remarks: " The subtlety of the spiritual imagination that enabled the preacher to enter into the mind of Christ had the effect of reproducing the scene, as though Christ himself were standing in bodily presence before the congregation. What had taken place those centuries ago was repeating itself in the consciousness of many on that Sunday afternoon." [1]

Such imagination is a gift that few possess. Genius is a native endowment and cannot be acquired. For a plain unwinged soul to try to soar in such flights of imagination in the pulpit is sure failure and folly. It is only a step from the sublime to the ridiculous, and many a preacher has taken this step in trying to be dramatic. It is true that the ordinary preacher may have a dramatic vein in him, and it is well for him to cultivate it and use it judiciously, but this is a point

[1] *Life and Letters of Phillips Brooks*, Vol. II, p. 123.

where ambition tempts us to o'erleap ourselves, and we need to keep well inside our limitations.

(b) Illustrative imagination consists in seeing truth in various forms and using a familiar and vivid form to throw light on a less familiar form. Almost any truth ramifies the whole universe and turns up myriad manifestations that may seem to have no connection with one another, but are really different aspects of the same thing. Imagination traces these hidden links of relation, brings distant and disparate things together, and uses one thing to illustrate another. Thus Newton leaped from the apple to the moon, saw in that falling apple all the worlds falling to their centres, and bound the whole universe into unity. The philosopher and poet and man of imagination will take any common truth and trace it far and wide through the complex web of the world and in the most hidden and unexpected places will show its gleaming thread. If we cannot see and understand the truth in one of its aspects he will show us the same truth in another aspect which is more visible and vivid, and then we see it. This is the philosophy of illustration, which is so great a power in the hands of the preacher. Spiritual truth runs down through roots and rocks to the core of the world and out through all worlds and up to God, and so any spiritual truth can be shown to us in material form in which it becomes visible and tangible. Things on earth are copies of things in heaven. The spiritual truth that may be abstract and shadowy, hard to see and feel, may thus be made as real to us as the sights and sounds of the material world.

Jesus was a master of illustration, and it was this that made his preaching picturesque and interesting so that the common people heard him gladly. His parables are bits of dramatic imagination which, if nothing else could be said about him, would rank him with the great dramatists. These parables make religion as real as our everyday life and will never lose their charm and power. But Jesus also sent out a decree that all the world should be taxed to furnish illustrations for his teaching. The fish in the sea, the flower by the wayside, the grass of the field, the vineyard on the hill, the birds flying in the air, salt and sunshine, bread and water, the lost sheep in the wilderness and the lost coin in the house, all familiar things preached the gospel for him as he spoke, and the commonest thing became luminous and eloquent with spiritual truth under the touch of his hand. He thus brought religion home to the business and bosoms of his hearers and made it as real to them as their sowing and reaping, their baking and their building. He caused their imaginations to dress the truth up in these everyday clothes, and then they recognized it and grew familiar with it.

This is still the business of the preacher, and illustrative imagination is still one of the most effective means of doing it. Religious truth is not a kind of truth that stands aloof and remote from the rest of life, but is just the plain principles of common life run up to their highest expression and application. Faith in God is the same principle as faith in man, and obedience to him as the obedience of a child to its father or of a soldier to his general. The common things of life are thus the truths of religion in a lower and more familiar form, and this enables us to use the lower as illustrations of the higher. Imagination catches these familiar facts of daily life and sets them in its light and then they glow with higher meaning and are seen to be copies of things in heaven.

The preacher that abounds in true and striking illustrations is making spiritual truth visible and tangible, picturesque and beautiful, so that it is as real to his hearers as business and bread. He is sending a series of pictures through their minds that not only are pleasing to them but keep them alive and alert and make the truth stand out before them in living reality. Every preacher knows how a congregation gives increased attention to a good illustration; the reason is that just at that point they begin to see the truth; imagination has kindled it in their minds into light and heat and they feel its power.

(c) By verbal imagination is meant the ordinary process of image-making in the mind by which it forms pictures of things and thoughts. Our words nearly all have, or originally had, an image of some material thing at their root, and these etymological pictures are often striking and beautiful. Lady means the loaf-giver, the daughter is the milker, and to be astonished is to be thunderstruck. These images at the roots of our words have in many cases been covered up and lost, and now the words are only arbitrary names for us; but when we dig down to their roots we find their colours still fresh and beautiful. Primitive language was thus more picturesque and vivid than our abstract speech. But hosts of our words still retain this image-making power, and these are the most effective words in making our speech colourful and forceful. All names of concrete things, such as horse, tree, mountain, are of this nature and create pictures in the mind. Such words as red, green, scarlet, river, sea, shore, sky seem to brand themselves on the brain; whereas abstract words, such as virtue, generalization, relativity, create vague impressions that are but dimly perceived and felt. The use of language is thus a constant exercise of the imagination which brings a series of pictures before the mind.

In all writing and speaking the aim should be to put in as many as possible of these picture-making words. In telling anything we should first try to see it vividly and then tell it so that others will see it also. For instance, Macaulay wants to tell us that history has little to say about the common people, but he does not put it in this general abstract form. He says: "History is silent about those who held the plough, who tended the oxen, who toiled at the looms of Norwich, and squared the Portland stone for St. Paul's." Here we see the men holding the plough and cutting stone for St. Paul's Cathedral, and the picture stands out vividly before us. Carlyle tells us that Sir Walter Raleigh was executed "on a cold, hoar-frosty morning," and this bit of description helps us to realize the scene. The poets, of course, have this power in the highest degree and it is the very soul of poetry. What a picture of Ruth in a foreign land Keats gives us in two lines:

When sick for home,
She stood in tears amid the alien corn.

Or what a picture of the setting sun does Coleridge draw with a few swift strokes in the "Ancient Mariner":

The sun's rim dips; the stars rush out;
At one stride comes the dark.

How sharp and clear and startling are these descriptions, how every word tells. The remarkable effect is largely achieved through the verbal imagination embodied in the very words.

This diffused imagination, while it is not so princely in its power as the creative, or so showy as the illustrative imagination, is yet of high efficiency in imparting to style the qualities of lucidity, freshness, and force. It makes every page picturesque, every line alive. Such language lives and breathes and speaks to every sense. The preacher needs above all other men to think in concrete terms, clear-cut images, that will create pictures in the minds of his hearers so that they will see the truth. His language should be saturated with imagination, and then he will flood their minds with currents of living thought. Such a preacher must necessarily utter many general truths and abstract conceptions, but the stream of his ideas will be brightened and intensified with concrete images that will be so many luminous points in it that will irradiate the whole course of thought. His imagination will be constantly using verbal images and shaping picturesque phrases that will turn the minds of his hearers into a gallery of truth.

5. The Spirit of the Sermon.—The sermon has a subtle spirit or soul that has much to do with determining its persuasive power. The truth-seeking spirit of honesty and candour should pervade it in all parts. The preacher should beware of exaggeration and misrepresentation of every kind and degree. His spirit and style of argument should be such as will beget confidence in his mental and moral trustworthiness. There should be as little as possible of the controversial spirit in his sermons. It should never appear that he

is mainly bent on proving himself right and others wrong. In stating the position of opponents, he should be scrupulously fair and state their views as they would state them themselves. In dealing with doubt he should be sympathetic and tender and follow the example of Jesus in dealing with John the Baptist's doubt. He should be especially on his guard against the dogmatic spirit and dictatorial air that settles everything by his own ipse dixit. If Jehovah could condescend to say to refractory Judah through the prophet Isaiah, " Come now, and let us reason together," and if Jesus could constantly and patiently reason with his hearers, how much more should the preacher stand down on a level with his people and speak to them as a brother man in the spirit of candour and humility.

The protection of the pulpit that hedges the preacher around with its sacredness is one of his dangers. The teacher and lawyer and most public speakers are subject to interruption, contradiction, and correction on the spot; and this tends to make them careful in their statements. But the preacher in the pulpit is in a bombproof. No one can strike back at him or would think of interrupting him. As a consequence he can do as he pleases: twist texts, garble quotations, misrepresent opponents, use illogical reasoning or fallacious illustrations. To make a statement striking or give brilliancy to a point he can strain the truth. He has everything his own way and can carry it with a high hand. He can make personal allusions and hits and grow sarcastic and spiteful. He feeds on his own dogmatism and grows intensely overbearing. He leaves no room for difference of view. To doubt him, one would think, is to doubt God. Said Senator Carpenter of Charles Sumner: " He identifies himself so completely with the universe that he is not at all certain whether he is a part of the universe, or the universe is a part of him. You will soon see the Sermon on the Mount revised, corrected, and greatly enlarged and improved by Charles Sumner." The preacher is in danger of acquiring a touch of this spirit, and he should guard against it by cultivating the spirit of honesty, reasonableness, sincerity, humility, and truth.

The sermon should throb with a spirit of reverence, of loyalty to Christ, and of a passion for souls. The hearers should feel that the sermon comes from the soul of a friend whose heart's desire and prayer unto God is that they may be saved.

III. MANNER AND DELIVERY

The manner of the preacher and the delivery of the sermon are vital factors in the psychological efficiency of preaching, and they are briefly touched on in this connection only as they are related to this point.

1. The Manner of the Preacher.—The dress and behaviour of the minister in the pulpit should be such as not to attract attention to themselves and thereby distract it from the sermon. The preacher should be quietly and becomingly dressed. If a gown is not worn, conventional dress is best, neither extremely in fashion nor out of it. Anything that suggests either slovenliness or foppery is out of place and offensive in the pulpit. The preacher's behaviour should be reverential and worshipful. He should enter the pulpit and sit down, having made all his arrangements for the service beforehand. Some ministers as soon as they enter the pulpit grow restless and get busy with all sorts of things. They turn and give directions to the organist or choir leader, go down and consult an elder or give

orders to the janitor, or they are seen selecting hymns and Scripture passages, and if a visiting minister is in the pulpit they strike up a conversation with each other. All such things are out of order and distracting to the congregation and to the spirit of worship. The minister should make all his preparations before entering the pulpit and should then reverently conduct the service. To be restless and fidgety and fussy, running about after many things, is as improper and disorderly in him as in anybody else, and he should be the first to do " all things decently and in order."

2. The Delivery of the Sermon.—The delivery may be three fourths of the sermon, and this involves the whole art of elocution. For the sake of completeness a few hints are offered. The general rule governing delivery is the same as Herbert Spencer's principle regarding style—namely, it should convey the message to the hearers with the least effort and loss of meaning on their part and with the greatest effect. This means that everything is to be excluded from the delivery that hinders the conveyance of the thought and that distracts attention from the sermon to its delivery. The best delivery is that which is least observed and leaves the most mental energy for attention to the thought of the sermon. All mere mannerisms that only attract the attention of the hearers to the delivery and perhaps offend their judgment and taste are psychologically wrong.

(a) The primary virtue of delivery is distinctness. The speaker should make himself heard, or there is no use in his speaking at all, and he may only aggravate his audience. Distinctness of utterance means clean-cut enunciation of the syllables, especially of the consonants, so that they will leave the mouth of the speaker as clearly defined words. Distinctness is not loudness of voice, for often increased loudness only increases the indistinctness so that the more sound the less sense. Some ministers mutilate and muffle their words, especially the last syllables, so that they are clogged up and smothered back in the throat, whereas the words should be ejected through the teeth and lips as the sharply minted coins of speech. Other ministers clutter up their sentences with hems and haws and other unnamable grunts that appear to be a way of filling up vacancies in the stream of speech while they are trying to think of the next word or idea, and these raucous noises not only injure distinctness but are very offensive. Any one with a little care can learn to speak distinctly, and this will enable a voice of very moderate power to be heard in the average church auditorium.

(b) Varying modulation by which the delivery is adapted to the varying thought is the next virtue in pulpit speech. One of the most common, as it is also one of the most fatal, faults in pulpit delivery is the monotone in which the preacher drones away with little change of pitch and emphasis. The wonderful instrument of the human voice is thus robbed of its variety and music, as though a violin had all its range and richness reduced to monotonous and exasperating sawing on one string. This singsong utterance quickly kills attention and has a strange soporific power that soon tells on the most pious deacon. The delivery should change in its level of tone and degree of emphasis with every change in the thought. Narrative or unimportant passages can be hurried up and more emphatic passages can be slowed down in speed. Emphatic words should always stand out by increased

stress or other modulation of the voice. Parts of the
sermon may be calm and smooth as a limpid stream,
and other parts may become charged with feeling and
power as a flood in its fury. The preacher need only
listen to his own thought and give natural expression
to it, and his delivery will largely take care of itself.

(c) Pulpit delivery has changed in our day from the
former rotund and grandiloquent oratory to a conver-
sational style of speech. The minister is a man with
a message, and he should simply speak to his hearers
as he would to friends. Oratory that gets high and hot
and waxes eloquent and tears passions to tatters is
out of date, and the people want to be spoken to with
directness and simplicity. The greatest preachers are
masters of this style of address. Of John McNeill it
is said: " He speaks as though he were talking to men.
He is not lacking in oratorical graces, but he does not
appear to be thinking of anything but his theme and
audience. There is a self-consciousness which is charm-
ing, and an absence of all unnatural and artificial mannerisms that is winning. Mr. McNeill is in the pulpit
the same talker that he is in the parlour." [1] Mr.
Beecher was a master of this style of delivery, and it is
ever the most popular and effective.

" All great art is simple. The ability to be simple,
honest, and truthful is the supreme measure of the
artist. Fine elocution is worse than fine writing.
There must be no stiltedness, no straining for effect.
The primary questions for the reader to ask himself
are—Do I realize this passage? Do I see every scene
as if I were there myself? Are the characters about
which I read and whose words I quote really men and

women? Do I simply and directly express the activity of my own thinking, my own imagination? Do I reveal the experience of my own heart in response to the truth?"[1]

(d) As to gestures, the fewer, down to a low limit, the better. The preacher that is constantly sawing and pawing the air and flinging his arms about and gesticulating violently is not controlling himself and is distracting attention from his subject to his gymnastics. Gestures are proper and may greatly facilitate conveying the thought of the sermon; gestures may even be eloquent, and so may pauses, for silence is as necessary and may be as significant in speech as sound; but these aids are effective only when they are kept in restraint in the background and do not become a show in themselves. Studied gestures, the mechanical raising of the arm as angular and awkward as though it were a wooden arm moved by some hidden machinery which we can almost hear creak, self-conscious gestures, are bad. The best gestures usually grow out of the thought and may be quite unconscious. "Give me something to say," says Emerson, "and hands and feet will take care of themselves." No amount of violent gesticulation will cover the nakedness of an empty sermon, but one full of thought will usually find its own proper expression. Both delivery and gestures are rooted back in the mind, and the first and most important thing is to fill the mind, and then let its contents gush out. This does not mean that no attention is to be given to these arts, for they should receive the most painstaking care, but they are to be kept

[1] *Vocal and Literary Interpretation of the Bible*, by S. S. Curry, p. 319. This is one of the most suggestive and best books on reading the Bible, and its principles also apply to speaking.

hidden in the thought. Anything in the manner, delivery, or gestures of the preacher that attracts attention to these aids distracts attention from the sermon and detracts from its efficiency.

CHAPTER VIII

THE BROADER PSYCHOLOGY OF PREACHING

THE psychology of preaching as considered in the preceding chapter was confined to the sermon and its delivery. But there is a broader psychology of preaching than that of the sermon, and this is the general soil of the minister's culture and personality out of which his sermons grow, and the tracing of the psychological roots of preaching will take us down into this subsoil. The study of the Bible, of theology, and of homiletics is the lifelong work of the minister, and it is assumed that he is always a systematic student in these fields. But a sermon grows out of much more than these special studies or the particular study of the text on which it is based. Every sermon springs out of the whole life of the man that preaches it. As every seed draws on the soil and the shower and the sun so that it takes the whole solar system to make a single grain of wheat or blade of grass, so every sermon sinks its roots down through all the years of the preacher and is the outgrowth of his total experience. Or as a river is composed of drops that have fallen out of the sky over many thousands of square miles, so a preacher's sermon is composed of multitudinous drops that have fallen out of his whole life. Mr. Beecher was right when he said it took him forty years to make a certain sermon, though he spent only a few hours on its special preparation.

One of the poorest ways to make sermons is just to study texts and sermons and nothing else. The experienced preacher in time finds that his sermon making becomes subordinate and incidental to his general study. Everything he reads or does, however trivial, is sure sooner or later to crop out in a sermon in some illustration or turn of thought or phrase or word, Ruskin said that he would use the devil himself, if he could catch him, for black paint; and so the preacher can use everything, however unrelated or unpromising it may seem, in his sermons. Hence the importance to the minister of that broader culture which will form the rich soil out of which good sermons can grow. A barren soil is sure to raise poor sermons. A small man cannot preach a big sermon because he does not have the breadth and depth of experience out of which a big sermon can come. The minister that is constantly broadening his brain and enriching his heart through general culture is engaged in the best preparation for sermon-making. A book on any subject, however remote it may seem from his preaching, will add something to the richness of the soil out of which his sermons grow.

The minister, then, should live a broad life and strike his roots down through many strata. He should send out a decree that all the world shall be taxed in the interest of his intellectual life and his sermons. He should beware of wearing down into narrow professional ruts, but should range widely and freely over the world. He should have hobbies on which he can ride far away from his pulpit, and then he will bring back unexpected materials for his proper work. Every minister must choose his own general studies and hobbies, those that appeal to his aptitudes and tastes, but there are several of these fields that no minister can afford to neglect.

I. The Study of Nature

The first of these is the study of nature. The natural sciences are especially fruitful fields for the minister. They open the book of nature, that older bible that rolled from the hand of the Creator ages before Moses wrote and David sang. Astronomy has ever been a favourite science with the theologian and preacher, as it displays the Creator's mighty plan and power, and the beauty and grandeur, majesty and mystery of his creation in all the wonders of the skies. This study will not only immensely widen the preacher's conception of the universe, but will broaden his thoughts on all subjects, and it will stimulate his imagination and give him many of his best illustrations. Geology is another science that is a rich field for the minister, as it turns up the rocky leaves of the globe and enables him to decipher the hieroglyphics which record its long and wonderful evolution. The study of science draws the minister off from his professional studies and gives him a liberal education; it disciplines his mind in the scientific spirit of truth-seeking and stores it with rich materials for his sermons.

It is the study of nature in the open, however, that we wish more especially to commend to ministers. In field and forest, stream and rock, he can study nature at first hand and become an expert in some natural science, such as geology or botany, and this has proved an opulent mine for many a minister.

A fruitful means of the broader culture for the ministry is the systematic exercise of walking. In these days of electric cars and automobiles, and now of the airship, we are almost in danger of losing the use of our legs. While it is said in the Scriptures that the Lord delighteth not in the legs of a man, it is nowhere written that we are not to delight in them ourselves. Walking is a form of recreation that requires no expensive apparatus and is never far away. The average minister in a few minutes can get his feet off the pavements down on the green grass of the fields and into the soft leaves and mellow loam of the forest. Such walking at times may be brisk and carry us with vigorous strides along the roads and over the hills, so as to stir the blood and send it leaping in a ruddy tide through all the arteries and veins, and again it may be a lazy loitering and dreamy drifting through fields and forests, so as to let nature whisper her secrets to us lovingly and let her wine soak in through our pores. What are some of the advantages of such walks to ministers?

1. Good Health.—First, good health. A sound body is the physical basis of a sound preacher and a good sermon. A sick preacher with a torpid liver, dyspeptic stomach, sallow complexion, whining voice, dejected look, and pessimistic air will preach a sick sermon that will make his congregation sick. But ruddy health is contagious and will radiate from the sermon and infect the people. The minister's study, stuffed with stagnant air, is one of his dangers. He should therefore breathe and work and live in pure air. A walk in the open of two or three hours once or twice a week will oxygenize his blood, renovate all his organs, shoot splendour into his eyes, and plant roses in his cheeks. It is a bath in God's universal health. Long enough has the preacher been a pale, anemic man, panting for breath and appealing to the sympathies of

his female parishioners while incurring the pity if not
the contempt of his men. He, too, needs to be a man
with stout bones, red blood and deep lungs, a manly
man in body as well as in soul; and to be such a man
he should take care of his health and drink deep from
nature's own springs.

2. **Intimate Acquaintance with Nature.**—A second
result of such recreation is intimate acquaintance with
nature. We soon begin to grow acquainted with the
fields and woods, and the birds will greet us as friends;
we shall experience a thrill of pleasure in the spring at
the first robin's note or the first flash of a bluebird's
wing. The flowers will speak to us in their own language and the trees grow familiar in leaf and bark.
Every season and day will have its own charm, and
stormy weather, when the wind and rain slap the skin
into a glow of health, will be as enjoyable as a June
morning. All this will open a new field of education
and pour a fresh stream of illustrations into our minds.
Earth and sea and sky, forest, vine, and flower will
become eloquent with spiritual truth, and we shall
embroider our sermons with quotations from nature as
Jesus did. A lover of nature can hardly be a dry
preacher. Bits of green grass and blue sky, bird notes
and flower blossoms will creep into his sermons and
give them freshness and charm.

3. **A Good Thinking Shop.**—Nature in the open is a
good thinking shop for the minister. The fresh air, the
lofty dome of the sky, the far horizon, the solitude and
silence have a strange stimulating and fertilizing influence on the soul. They often clear up our minds,
smooth out our perplexities, and put us in our best
moods. Problems often solve themselves, we know not
how, when we are in communion with nature. Our

best thoughts often then come flocking around us and build their nests in our brains and in our hearts. We see things more clearly in the pure air and have broader visions on a hilltop. Trials that loom large upon us down in the murky atmosphere of the valley grow petty up on the summit, and duties that were drudgery below shine out in splendour as they are transfigured on the heights. The hilltop cures us of many of our worries by encircling them with a wider horizon and overshadowing them with a vaster dome. Perspective is needed to give right proportion and value to life, and we get a larger and truer scale of measurement on the unhampered summits than down in the cabined valley. The great world then imparts to us some of its spaciousness and serenity. We seem nearer to God in the solitudes of nature where we can hear his still small voice more clearly than where cross the crowded ways of man.

> A restful calm steals through the wearied soul
>   When, drifting lazily, in dreamy mood,
>   Through flowery field and tangled, leafy wood,
> We merge the self in nature's larger whole.
>
> The fevered pulse, when bathed in this deep stream
>   Of pure serenity and silent power,
>   Forgets the gnawing worries of the hour,
> And feels its throbbings soothed to peace supreme,
>
> When nature's vast unplumbed environment
>   Flows round our restless fragmentary life,
>   Submerging all its sense of pain and strife,
> The heart swells full with pure divine content.

And thus life in the open helps to cleanse the blood and sweep cobwebs out of the brain and pessimism out of the heart and to ripen and enrich the sermon for Sabbath morning.

II. The Study of Literature

Passing from nature to human nature, a second field for broader culture for the ministry is literature. Reference is especially made to what De Quincey calls the " literature of power," or that which moves the emotions. It includes poetry, fiction, essays, and miscellaneous writings, " belles-lettres," as the French call them, or beautiful writings. A book on any subject, however, such as history or science, which is pervaded with imagination and has distinction of style, may rise to the level of literature. It is a good plan for a minister to select one author at a time for his study and read his works through, and thus he will gain his point of view, grasp his line of thought, and absorb and assimilate his ideas into his own blood. What are some of the fruits of such study?

1. Discipline in Thought.—First, discipline in thought, especially in the knowledge of human nature and life. If the minister is ignorant of the human world in which he lives and which he is endeavouring to move and mould, if he lives in an isolated cell of his own, he will fail to connect with his work and be a monkish misfit in the world of men and be impotent to do them good. Of course he should immerse and soak his soul in the actual world and study human nature at first hand. But the study of literature will be a fruitful discipline at this point. Great literary writers are, first, great thinkers. No mere ornamentation of style, no feathery plumes on the arrows of their words, would send them singing through the world if they did not put behind them big explosive ideas.

Their style does not make their thoughts, but their thoughts make their style. To learn to write and speak we must first learn to think. Too many people, including some ministers, are trying to say something without first getting something to say. The great poets, novelists, essayists, are men of profound insight into human nature and life. They have steeped and saturated themselves in the world. They know what is in man. They have anatomized the human soul. There is hardly a question of importance that does not have light thrown upon it in the pages of such writers as Emerson and Carlyle and Ruskin. Even when they are wrong they are half right, and whether right or wrong they are always immensely suggestive. The study of such authors shows us how great minds think and tends to beget the same power in us. It lets us see the world through their eyes and gives us a deeper and richer insight into it.

2. Discipline in Feeling and Imagination.—A second result of the study of literature is a fruitful discipline in feeling and imagination. The preacher is after the feelings of his hearers, for these are the motors that move the will. Literature is preëminently thought shot through with emotion. The great literary writers have not only thought deeply but have also felt intensely. Their souls have glowed and flamed with emotion, and at times their pages burst into volcanic fire. Reading literature charged with pure deep emotion is the best education for the feelings. It develops them in strength and sensitiveness and trains them in that delicacy and refinement that we call taste. The masters of literature are also men of powerful imagination. They see visions of beauty and unveil the splendour of the world, often hidden from us, before our

eyes. Shakespeare sets the whole world in the light of his imagination and we behold wondrous things. Victor Hugo can make us see the lock on a prison door so that we shudder at it, or describe the awful havoc created by a cannon torn loose from its moorings on the deck of a warship so that we instinctively feel like escaping from the monster as it pauses and " meditates " for the next spring upon its victims. We have seen the power of the imagination in the hand of the preacher, and we can acquire this gift in some degree from those who have it in princely measure. By reading great literary authors we can catch some of this luminous power. Shakespeare and Victor Hugo will receive us as scholars, and while they never can endow us with their genius, yet if we study them patiently and sympathetically they may give us at least a hint of their secret.

3. **Discipline in Style.**—A third result of the study of literature is discipline in style. Style is not thought, but it is the dress that makes it attractive or the power that drives it home. Knowledge is steel in the bar: forceful expression is the same steel in a keen polished blade. Knowledge is electricity diffused in the cloud: vivid expression is the bright swift flash. Knowledge is the bullet: style is the powder that sends it to its mark. Wonderful is the power of a striking sentence; phrases have made history. When Napoleon said to his soldiers, " There are no Alps," he thereby in effect levelled those icy heights and carried his soldiers over them. When Lincoln said, " This nation cannot endure half slave and half free," he put a charge of powder under the institution of slavery that blew it to pieces. Daniel Webster's simple statement of a case was said to be its strongest argument. The masters of literature

are masters of style. Their pens drop jewels " that on the stretched forefinger of all time sparkle forever." They dip their brushes in all the colours of the rainbow and paint pictures. They say things so that we can see them, and they suggest more than they say. They compress great thoughts into single sentences and think in thunderbolts.

One secret of their power that we may learn from them is the compression of thought into the fewest words possible. The force of an idea is often inversely to the number of words that express it. Multiply the words and the idea grows thin and loses force; condense the words and the idea gathers energy. One of the commonest faults of writers and speakers is their verbosity. One could go through their speeches or sermons and by striking out words and compressing paragraphs double the strength and sharpen the points of their ideas. Young writers and ministers especially should be merciless with the pen in correcting their productions. Slaughter the adjectives. Count every word struck out so much thought gained. Instead of big words with little ideas rattling around in them, use short words and let the thought lap over at the ends. Take the short-cut to your meaning. Avoid tedious explanations and come to the point. Leave the long complicated sentences to the Germans. De Quincey says that a German would realize his ideal if he could write a book in one eternal sentence, and Mark Twain says that a German newspaper often goes to press before it reaches the verb. The long sentence is apt to grow obscure and break down of its own weight. A short sentence goes to the mark like a minnie ball. Proverbs and aphorisms, the slowly crystallized diamonds of speech, are brief. The famous sayings of men, the happy hits of the orator, the telling sentences of an article or sermon, are short and sharp. Old Cotton Mather could be terribly prolix himself, but he left one bit of advice that should keep others from imitating him: " Be short."

The great literary writers are constantly showing us that the simple truth told in the most direct words, adorned only with choice diction, is the most effective as well as the most beautiful style. John Stuart Mill, that master of simple, forceful English, once wrote the sentence, " This is a very strong statement," and then struck his pen through the word " very." A friend, seeing the manuscript, asked why he had done this. " Because," said Mr. Mill, " I wanted to make that statement as strong as I could." To his mind the sentence, " This is a strong statement," was a stronger statement than the sentence, " This is a very strong statement," and he was right.

In studying literature we fall under the influence of these great writers and acquire their modes of thought and expression. Such reading makes us acquainted with our faults and sets before us high ideals. It begets in us the literary sense so that we instinctively feel when a sentence has the right swing to it or ends effectively. It enlarges our vocabulary and enriches it with graphic phrases and figures of speech. And it is not by mere imitation that we acquire from good writers elements of their style, but by a process of assimilation, or induction as an electrical current is generated in one coil by a current in a parallel coil. Style is catching. If we will persistently read these masters and steep our minds in their modes and moods of expression we shall absorb some of their spirit and art.

III. The Study of Philosophy

A brief section is here introduced on the value of a special line of general study, and philosophy is chosen as an example, though some other field of thought could be made to serve the same purpose. There is danger that the minister may fall into the habit of browsing around in the fields of lighter literature as a mere indulgence and luxury and thus weaken the stern habit of solid study. Philosophy cannot be charged with being a thin and weakening intellectual gruel, for it is understood to be the profoundest and most strenuous field of thought. It is true that it suggests to some minds only a maze of words " weaving their eternal dance before us," as Matthew Arnold thought, or a world of mist and mud. Yet philosophy, so far from being confusion worse confounded, is, in Prof. James's well-known words, " an unusually obstinate attempt to think clearly and consistently," and in the words of Prof. Charles E. Garman, " Philosophy is simply intelligence at its best." The minister obviously wants to think clearly and consistently and to have intelligence at its best.

Philosophy is an attempt to reach the ultimate principle of things, the one underlying reality out of which all the forms of the universe arise, the single taproot that bears all the buds and blooms of the world. One branch of philosophy finds the ultimate reality of the world unknowable and ends in agnosticism, another finds it in matter and ends in materialism, and another finds it in spirit and ends in some form of idealism, and idealism divides into impersonal pantheism and theism. Our philosophy is thus our unified and total view of the world, what we think of it as a whole in its nature, order, and purpose. Every thinking man has some such notion of the world, however dim and confused or wild and irrational it may be, and thus every one is a philosopher whether he knows it or not, and we can no more escape from thinking in terms of philosophy than we can escape speaking prose. The only question, then, is not whether we shall be philosophers or not, but whether we shall be good ones or bad ones. The minister must be a philosopher, and it remains for him to decide which kind he will be.

It is not meant to affirm or suggest that every minister should or could become a philosopher, for something depends on personal aptitude and circumstances; but it is meant that as a general study philosophy is specially suitable and profitable to a minister, and a few reasons for this view will be briefly stated.

1. **Mental Discipline.**—The preacher should study philosophy, first, as a mental discipline. Such discipline is one of his constant needs, as intellectual laziness with its resulting stagnation is one of his dangers. His preaching then wears down into a rut in which every sermon jogs along in the same old way. His people know just what he is going to say on any text because he has said it all before, and so they are tired before he begins. Like the antiquated doctor who has long been left behind by the wonderful progress of his science and simply keeps handing out the same old quinine and calomel pills, this out-of-date preacher keeps preaching technical doctrines in the same forms and phrases in which our fathers preached them and never makes them speak in new accents. It is this fatal mental stagnation that more than anything else carries preachers over the dead line before their heads are grey.

The cure for this microbe of mental "sleeping sickness" is solid, systematic study, especially of great subjects that discipline the minister's mind and enlarge his world. Of course his main studies are the Bible and theology and all the subjects that directly relate to his work. But out in the field of broader culture philosophy takes a high place. It is admittedly one of the greatest, if not the greatest subject in the world. Its master students and exponents have ever been the profoundest thinkers of the ages and have written their names high on the scroll of fame. Their masterpieces, from Plato's *Republic* and Kant's *Critique* to more modern works, though they may be read only within a narrow and select circle, are yet among the most enduring monuments of literature and are milestones in the march of human thought. However abstract and remote they may seem in their ideas and expression, yet they have passed into the intellectual blood of the world. To study these books, or a few or one of them, so as to master it will expand the brain and clear the vision of any man, but especially the minister. It will put iron into his blood and strengthen him for all his studies and all his work.

2. The Use of Philosophy in Preaching.—The preacher should study philosophy, second, for its use in preaching. It is not meant, of course, that he should take technical philosophy into his pulpit and preach its speculations. This would be an amazing thing to do and would only confuse and bewilder the people. The business of the pulpit is to proclaim the gospel, and it should not preach anything that does not contribute to this end. Nevertheless, there is great use in the pulpit for the philosophic spirit and for philosophic methods and aims. The object of philosophy, as we have seen,

is to see the world as a whole; and hence the philosopher is ever seeing the whole in each part and each
part in its relation to the whole.

Now this bears on preaching in two ways. First, in
the matter of illustrations. The whole art of seeing
illustrations consists in an exercise of the philosophic
mind. The philosopher sees the whole universe in every
part and particle of it, the sun in the dewdrop and
the heavens in the atom; and so the philosophical
preacher sees the general principle he is presenting in
every common thing and daily experience, and thus
makes the earth and air and sea and the lives of the
people illustrate and preach the gospel to them, as
Jesus did. He takes the principle of sacrifice, for example, and traces its scarlet thread, dipped in sacri-
ficial blood, through the entire web of the universe, as a
red strand is woven into every rope in the British navy.
The study of philosophy is a constant exercise of this
insight, and more than anything else it will enable the
preacher to see how any general principle manifests
itself in myriad forms, and thus he will see the whole
world aglitter with illustrations of any subject. The
poet sees the same thing, but the poet and the philosopher are deeply akin.

A still deeper use of the philosophical mind in preaching is in bringing every truth into relation with the
whole world and with God. The philosopher sees that
every atom of the universe is connected up with every
other, so that to understand one atom in all its relations we would need to understand the universe. This
is what Tennyson means when he says that if we could
understand a flower in its crannied wall we " would
know what God and man is." The application of this
philosophical principle to preaching is plain: all the

truths and duties we present should be set in a divine
light in their relation to the world and to God. One
of the dangers of preaching is that it will deal with
small subjects in a small way. Some sermons have
trifling themes that yield no larger results than petty
rules and platitudinous moral advice. Every sermon
ought to have a broad base, deep as eternity, and a
summit that lifts its hearers into the celestial blue.
This does not mean that every sermon should be a great
effort with an ambitious theme. Such efforts are likely
to fall flat. There must be many sermons on common
subjects that keep close to the ground of daily experience. Nevertheless, the philosophic preacher will connect every subject, however ordinary and lowly, with
its cosmic and divine relations so that it will be seen
to be a thread running through the whole fabric of
the universe and a strand running up to God. This
principle will lift everything out of triviality into eternal significance. It will make the smallest things great,
and every common duty shine with celestial light.
Every preacher does this in some degree, but the
philosophic mind of insight greatly increases this
power.

3. The Foundation of Theology.—A third reason
why the minister should study philosophy goes still
deeper into this subject and can only be indicated in
this connection. Philosophy is more fundamental than
theology and furnishes its foundation and framework.
Every theologian is first a philosopher, and every problem of theology has its roots down in philosophy. A
minister's philosophy, then, will have architectonic influence in shaping and colouring his theology; his
philosophical skeleton cannot be concealed, but will
inevitably show through his theological flesh. If he

does not have any definite philosophy or does not know what his philosophy is, so much the worse will it be for his theology: it will be infected by the unsound or confused philosophy that necessarily lies latent in his mind. Hence the great importance to a minister that he get hold of a consistent and solid philosophical system that will be a sure foundation and framework for his theology.

4. **An Objection Answered.**—The objection may be raised at this point that philosophy is a confused and cold abstract theory that will not warm the pulpit but will rather tend to chill it and may even send its temperature below the freezing point. Many preachers, it may be said, even the best ones, pay little or no attention to technical philosophy. The really great preachers, such as Spurgeon and Beecher and Phillips Brooks, are great poets rather than philosophers, men of imagination and emotion with pictorial and persuasive power rather than of logical and metaphysical analysis and argument. What the preacher needs, then, is not more philosophy but more imagination, emotion and spiritual earnestness and zeal. A philosophical preacher, it may be said, would be the last kind of a preacher a congregation would be willing to call and the first they would run away from.

The general answer to this objection is that the philosopher and the poet are not antagonistic but closely akin. They have the same fundamental type of mind, that of insight into the central nature and totality of things, so that they see the whole in each part and each part in the light of the whole. It is this power that gives the poet his vision and his fertility in illustrations, so that in the flower in a crannied wall he sees the whole system and secret of God and man.

and in the meanest flower that blows he discerns thoughts that are too deep for tears. It is precisely this power that makes the great preacher, and the great preachers always are genuine philosophers, though they may be untrained and unconscious ones. And philosophy is not antagonistic to emotion that springs from clear and consistent thought, though it is unfriendly to and will smother emotion of the fanatical and ranting kind. The proper effect of thought is to kindle emotion and not kill it. One reason why the poet feels so intensely is that he sees so deeply, and the philosopher can feel intense and rich emotion for the same reason. The picturesque power and overflowing emotionalism of great preachers are not dried up but are deepened and fed by their philosophical insight.

The preacher, then, need not fear that his study of philosophy will chill his heart and clip his emotional wings: rather it will kindle his heart with greater warmth drawn from the central fires of the world and give him more powerful pinions. When he sees with philosophical insight he will know that the universe is back of the truth he is presenting, that the stars in their courses are fighting for it, and he will feel that if God be thus for it, who can be against it? Philosophy is not a chilling abstraction, but is full of kindling thought and emotional power. It will not make a thin cold preacher, but will tend to broaden his brain and fire his heart and make him a flaming apostle. It will help him to speak with such vital conviction and earnestness as will tend to convince and move others.

There are many other means for the broader culture of the minister, and the ones considered are only illustrative. One of the most vital of these is the minister's own spiritual life, his private devotion and meditation.

The thin soil of a superficial careless devotional life cannot afford much depth of earth to sermons, and they will be weak with the poverty of the inner life out of which they grow. The minister must first know Christ before he can preach him, and he should dwell much with him in secret, and then he may come forth from his presence with a glowing heart and transfigured face to speak that he does know and testify that he has seen.

The minister, then, is not wasting his time in following extraneous pursuits in studying nature and literature and philosophy and other means of general culture. While such avocations may not yield immediate materials for the next sermon, they are yet constantly dropping seeds and fructifying influences into the minister's mind and heart and thus enriching and mellowing them as fertile soil out of which good sermons will surely grow. This broader culture is the well-stocked storehouse out of which the minister can draw illustrative material for his sermons or out of which will swarm throngs of associations to give them fulness and richness. The lack of this general culture makes many a preacher a narrow and illiberal man, who is not only unacquainted with, but suspicious of, if not hostile towards fields of truth beyond his range, and this not only makes his sermons ill-informed and poor, but shuts him out of the sympathy of the broader minds in his congregation and may expose him to their criticism and sometimes to their pity and contempt. All human knowledge and culture lead to religion, as all roads ran to Rome, and the minister who is widely travelled on the great highways of the world will come to every sermon and service with rich treasures of thought and feeling, as bees return to their hive burdened with golden sweets from many fields, and this will greatly increase his resourcefulness and power.

IV. The Power of Personality

All the points in the psychology of preaching hitherto considered, the construction and delivery of the sermon and the broader culture that underlies it, taken together do not fully account for a preacher's power. He may have all these qualities in a considerable degree, and yet not be an efficient preacher. In fact one may be finished almost to perfection in these points and yet lack the vital element of power, being " faultily faultless, icily regular, splendidly null." One sometimes hears a preacher who is so precise and finished and finical that one almost wishes he would violate some rule of propriety so as to show the genuine wood beneath all his veneer and varnish and polish. It would be a relief to have him drop his fine rhetoric and simply blurt out something that would strike and stick. On the other hand, a preacher may be deficient at many of these points and seem to violate most of the rules and to be a law unto himself, and yet may move multitudes and draw many into the kingdom. Wherein lies this great difference and secret in preaching?

1. **Personality the Master Force of Life.**—It lies in the personality of the preacher. Personality is the master force of human life. It is this that makes the great statesman, general, orator, preacher, artist, or leader in any field of action. It was by the force of personality that Demosthenes swayed Athens, Cæsar mastered Rome, Paul drove the wedge of the gospel into Europe, Luther created the Reformation, and Napoleon dominated all the kings of his day. It was the personality of Columbus that, amidst the cowardly

fears and appeals and threats of his sailors as they
cried out against the terrors of the unknown sea, held
the prow of his vessel ever westward, every morning
keeping it in the track of the sun and every evening
driving it deeper into the night. It is personality that
makes great discoveries, writes great books, paints great
pictures, achieves great triumphs and heroisms, and
writes names high up on the roll of fame. Almost every
great human achievement is the lengthened shadow of
some great personality. Personalities are the mountain
peaks of history that mark the culminating points in
the range of events and lift the level of their region.
A man of small personality, then, cannot preach a great
sermon, and a man of great personality, though he may
preach a small sermon, will yet put behind it such
driving power that it will seem great and will have a
great effect.

2. What is Personality?—What, then, is personality? Like many other great and vital things it cannot
be shut up within the verbal boundaries of a definition;
it is atmospheric and elusive, it cannot be accurately
analyzed and enumerated and weighed in all its elements. It is highly complex and subtle, it is largely
spirit, it is something plus over and above the analyz-
able elements of a man. Often we cannot tell what
the secret of a powerful personality is, and perhaps the
man himself does not know.

Personality consists of the native endowment of a
man developed into discipline and power. The native
endowment is by far the larger part of it, and to this
nothing can be added by education and effort. Heredity
does more for us than we ever can do for ourselves. As
seven-eighths of an iceberg is submerged under the sea,
so seven-eighths of a man's personality is immersed in

the blood of his heredity. The bulk of his body, the breadth of his brain, the volume of his blood, his stock of vitality, his brawn and breath, and the power of his mind, the warmth of his emotions, the strength of his will, and all the subtle elements that shape and colour his individuality and give it distinction, these basic constituents of his personality are selected and mixed and tempered for him in his birth and have roots running back through countless generations.

Genius is born, not made; and so is personality. In this respect we start out with so much inherited capital which we cannot increase. We are given the potency of a certain type and degree of personality, and by no possibility can we add one cubit to our stature or make one hair white or black. No amount of education or effort can make a Shakespeare or Milton out of a common mortal, or a Henry Ward Beecher or a Phillips Brooks out of an ordinary preacher, any more than lead can be transmuted into gold or a pebble into a diamond. At this point we must accept our fate and stay within the mould in which heredity has cast us.

This fact, however, is by no means discouraging, for native endowment must be developed and disciplined into its fullest proportions and powers, and here is a large field in which our own sovereignty must create ourselves. This is the meaning and aim and effort of all our education from infancy, and the process is not finished and does not cease with our school and college days but runs on through all life. The building up of our personality must be carried on within the limits of our native endowment, but these limits leave us plenty to do. The tallest redwood that now bathes its summit in the sun three hundred feet above the ground might have remained as a germ in its seed, and the greatest genius that ever lived might have remained undeveloped and died unknown as only a bundle of splendid possibilities. Few persons have developed themselves up to their limits, and there remain in us resources that have not yet been touched, deeps we have not yet tapped. The preacher, then, is not to bewail his personality as though he were given a hopelessly poor tool with which to do his work, but he is to take stock of himself and develop his resources and work his personality up to its highest point of discipline and efficiency.

3. **Points in Efficient Personality.**—Taking up, now, in detail the matter of developing and controlling our personality we should look after and endeavour to intensify the following points:

(a) The body is the physical basis of personality. The vitality and vigour of the body enter largely into the clearness of the mind, the width and warmth of the sympathies, the flight and vision of the imagination, and the decision and force of the will; and in the minister they have much to do with the construction and delivery and power of his sermon. The minister therefore should develop and take care of his body so as to keep it in fine fettle, in harmony and tune, as a physiological and psychological factor in his preaching.

(b) The personality of the preacher should be unified in body, mind and heart so that all his powers will be compressed into one channel and flow in one forceful current. This means that the preacher should not be divided by conflicting conditions, thoughts, and pursuits. If he is preaching one thing while he is thinking about or troubled over another thing, his attention and whole personality will be divided. If he has mixed up business with his ministry, he is in great danger of diversion from his calling. "This one thing I do," said Paul, and he concentrated all the powers of his great personality into his ministry, and this made it one of the gulf currents of history. The minister should strive to free himself of distractions, to lay aside every weight that besets him, and to focus all his powers and purposes into one burning beam of consecration.

(c) Unconsciousness of self is another element in power of personality. Perfection is not reached in any human art or pursuit until it has passed beyond self-consciousness and is lost in its object.

> Love took up the harp of Life, and smote on all the chords with might,
> Smote the chord of Self, that, trembling, pass'd in music out of sight,

Until the self is thus so smitten that it passes into the music of life, its self-consciousness distracts the unity and spoils the harmony and weakens the power of the soul. The preacher is specially subject to this law. If while preaching Christ Jesus he is conscious of himself, if he is charmed with his own manner and message, if he is posing as a performer or actor to exhibit his own brilliance and wit, if he is seeking to attract attention to himself and elicit the praise of his audience, he may have his reward, but he will not save souls. "No man," says Dr. James Denny, "can persuade an audience at the same time that he himself is clever and that Jesus Christ is mighty to save." He may do the one thing or the other, but not both: for the two things are psychologically opposed and the one will exclude the other. The preacher must, with Paul, determine not to know anything among his people, save

Jesus Christ, and him crucified, and when in this obliteration of self his own personality passes out of sight he will have unified power. " Unite my heart to fear thy name."

(*d*) Intensity is another element of power of personality. Some personalities are by nature and habit dull and uninteresting; they are alkaline in nature and give a negative reaction, they are bromidic and soporific; others are bright and enlivening; they are acid in nature and give a positive reaction, they are effervescent and contagious. Much of this difference is temperamental, but it is not wholly beyond our control. An intense and lively personality depends on deep convictions that readily flush the feelings and infect others. The preacher needs to be a live and contagious personality that he may infect and stir his congregation; and he should therefore think deeply and earnestly and cherish intense convictions that kindle his soul into glowing heat, and then his personality, instead of being dull and depressing, will be vivid and vital.

(*e*) The deepest power in the personality of the preacher is the Christlike spirit. His aim is to persuade men to be Christians, but he cannot give what he does not have; if his own spirit is an unlighted torch he cannot touch into flame other souls. A worldly preacher cannot make Christlike people. All other gifts and attainments, body, mind, imagination, brightness and brilliancy, rhetoric and eloquence, cannot round out the personality of the preacher and give him genuine power if he have not the spirit of Christ. He may be popular and seem powerful for a while, but his day will be short. On the other hand, if a man of moderate abilities and entire consecration has the spirit of

Christ, unified and sincere, with a passion for saving souls, he may not be a great but he will be a highly efficient preacher. Sinners will be drawn to him and the people will love him and flock around him as they thronged around Christ. Only goodness can create goodness, and many a preacher by the simple goodness of his heart and life makes his people good; and in the day of reward his crown may flash out with stars surpassing in glory the crown of a more popular preacher.

Bodily vigour, unity, unconsciousness of self, intensity and Christlike goodness are points that the preacher can cultivate and intensify and thereby more fully develop his personality and raise it to its highest degree of power.

V. THE PREACHER AS A PROPHET

The object of preaching is to put men under the spell and power of the great eternal verities and sanctities of the Christian life. The preacher must therefore be a seer who can first discern these verities as majestic visions and unveil their glory to men so that they will charm and capture them. The things of the spirit loom up over the things of the flesh, but the great world is largely blind to them, and " where there is no vision, the people perish." The preacher must be a prophet who can first see, and then get others to see, the visions of life.

Standing on the summit of a mountain spur in Colorado the author once saw a glorious sight. Off to the west lay the main range of the Rocky Mountains, running north and south in full view for two hundred miles. The planet was wrinkled into those giant billows of rock that rose above the sea at some points nearly three miles high. Their summits and sides were flecked

with the foam of unsullied snow, splendid white visions
with their bases buried in the molten heart of the globe
and their peaks plunged into the sun. The sight gave
one a sense of power and grandeur, majesty and mystery that almost impelled one to break forth in a shout.
And yet the question arose in the mind, What use is
that mountain range? No grain of wheat or blade of
grass ever grows up there and no foot ever treads those
icy heights. Cubic miles of rock and billions of tons
of snow are heaved up in those ridges: why all this
waste? No waste, but great use in many ways. He
who built all things knew what he was doing in pushing up those summits and planting them on their im-
movable foundations. They are storehouses of life. All
summer long those vast snowdrifts spin themselves
into slender rills, which dissolve into iridescent mists
and weave exquisite bridal veils around waterfalls and
gather into rushing roaring cataracts and rivers and
flow out over the plains in irrigating streams. Denver
is a daughter of those snows. Vast populations suckle
life from those immaculate breasts. Those snowy summits fling far and wide meadows and orchards, towns
and cities, turning deserts into gardens and peopling
them with teeming populations. Not only so, but those
rocky ribs of the earth play a great part in the life of
the whole continent, determining the course of winds
and rivers, reaching up with their giant icy hands and
squeezing the moisture out of the clouds and pouring
it upon distant plains and breathing their fresh vitaliz-
ing air over the whole land. Level those barren
heights and cities would perish and the Mississippi
Valley would in large part become a desert. Everything in nature is beautiful in its time, and those gi-
gantic ridges, that we may have thought useless, are

the shining hills of God whence he sends down streams
of life upon the earth.

The spiritual verities and eternities of the world are
such mountain heights. To dim worldly vision they
may seem cold and barren, yielding no fruit or profit
and tempting only visionary eyes and foolish feet. But
the preacher is to see them with a prophet's eyes, and
to him they are to loom up over all the earth as majestic
mountains of God, the mother of all life and beauty and
blessedness, the fountain of streams that are for the
healing of the nations and the satisfaction of the deepest thirst of the human soul. He is to see them so
vividly that he can unveil their presence and precious-
ness and power to other eyes, and bring men under
their spell so that they will be mastered by their might
and drink of their streams and live on their life. With
such a vision the people will not perish but will live,
and the whole earth will grow green and the wilderness
and the solitary place shall be glad, and the desert
shall rejoice and blossom as the rose. This is the high
calling of the minister, no other surpasses it in greatness, and all things else he should count as loss that
this one thing he may do.

CHAPTER IX

THE PSYCHOLOGY OF TEACHING

THE application of psychology to preaching in the preceding chapters applies for the most part to teaching with little more than a change in the terms. Preaching and religious teaching have much in common. Both seek to impart truth so as to move the will and mould the character and life. They therefore make use of the same fundamental means and differ only in subordinate points. "The relation between preaching and teaching is very close, and it is often hard to distinguish between them in our Lord's ministry. The preacher addresses a larger company of people than the teacher, and they in turn listen to him silently, without asking questions or taking part in the discussion. He deals with general principles of truth, as a rule, without discussing the processes by which they have been developed, or the facts on which they are based; and his purpose is to inspire and incite to action rather than to instruct. The teacher, on the other hand, usually speaks to a small number of people, who ask questions and take part in the discussion. He deals with facts and processes which the preacher leaves out or takes for granted, and his purpose is to imbed the truth in the mind rather than to inspire and arouse. Measured by this standard, there were not many occasions in our Lord's ministry when he played the part of a preacher. There are a few outstanding days, like that one in Galilee when he delivered the Sermon on the Mount, when he preached in a way that lifts and thrills us to this day when we read it. But generally he is among the people, talking to them, asking them questions and playing the part of a teacher. During the last year of his ministry he withdrew himself from the crowds, as a rule, that he might be with his disciples alone to teach them." [1]

The religious teacher thus stands close to the preacher and to the Master himself in his work. In this closing chapter, which has principally in view the work of a Sunday school teacher, it will not be necessary to go over the ground that has already been covered, and the subject will be treated only from some general points of view.

I. Definite Aims in Teaching

In *The Theory and Practice of Teaching,* by Edward Thring, one of the leading headmasters and foremost educators of England in his day, the volume being one of the wisest, wittiest, and most suggestive books on teaching that can be found, the title of one of the chapters, for the author is delightfully unconventional in style, is " Run the Goose Down." " Many a teacher," he says, " runs about mentally just as if he was trying to catch geese on a common. There is the flock assembled in a reasonably compact body. He makes a dash into the middle, of course missing his victim; and off they go in all directions, he after them, first chasing one, then another, till the flock has ceased to be a flock, and he, all out of breath, is no longer in reach of any of them. Run one goose quietly into a corner, run him

[1] *Learning to Teach from the Master Teacher,* by John A. Marquis, D.D., LL.D., President of Coe College, pp. 4-5.

down, is the first rule in catching geese; and a good rule, too, whether in classroom or on common." The author then proceeds to apply this rule to a number of points in teaching, such as picking out faults and correcting them one at a time, seizing vital points in the lesson and dealing with them thoroughly, and so on. The simple rule, " Fix on your goose, and run him down," he says is of marvellous practical power.

The art of education is advancing, and teaching in the Sunday school should keep pace with this progress. In truth, this teaching should not only compare favourably with that in the day school, but it ought in some respects to be better, more personal, sympathetic, and vital. It is becoming a specialized art and must be studied as such. Success in any work depends on plan and purpose and concentration of effort; on knowing where to begin and how to go through; what points to deal with thoroughly and what points to pass over lightly; on having a definite program in mind and sticking to it. Seizing a piece of work at the wrong end, or dashing into the middle of it and trying to get hold of it all over at once, rushing at the whole flock, only results in distraction and confusion. Success depends upon having our work well in hand and keeping cool; on knowing what we are going to do and doing that one thing; on picking out our goose and running it down. This principle applies to the preparation of the lesson, the handling of the lesson before the class, its application to life, and to the whole course of the teacher's work.

II. THE PREPARATION OF THE LESSON

Teaching demands preparation as certainly as preaching, and a good lesson can no more be extem-

porized than a good sermon. The idea that just anybody can teach a Sunday school class is as unreason-
able and foolish as that just anybody could step up into
the pulpit and preach. The teacher's preparation, like
the preacher's, is rooted down and back through his
whole life. All his knowledge and experience will enter
into his teaching and make it rich or poor according as
his general culture is deep or shallow.

The preparation of the lesson first takes in a general
view of the context and course of the lessons. A topical
lesson usually includes a passage of ten or fifteen verses
and is one of a series running through a book or books
of the Bible. It is obvious that the teacher must have
some knowledge of this general background and framework of the lesson. Not only should the intervening
chapters be read, but the general history should be
studied so as to give a clear view of the whole course of
events. The class also should engage in this study and
have this general knowledge. This enables teacher and
scholar to fit the particular lesson into its place
and study it in the light of the larger scene.

Next comes the preparation of the lesson itself. The
first thing is to look over the passage as one looks out
over a landscape and sees its striking features. There
is nearly always a central thought or picturesque scene
in a lesson to which all its lines converge; one thread
that will unravel its whole web. Such a plan usually
lies on the surface of the passage, and if the teacher
finds it for himself, even though it is not the best outline, yet it may be the best for him. This outline should
be engraved like a sketch map on the teacher's mind.
Get hold of this, imbed it firmly in the memory, and let
other points fall into subordinate places. It is a mistake to try to teach everything or to make all things

equally important in a lesson. One can find all the deep things of theology in almost any verse, just as a scientist can find all the wonders of the universe in a pebble. It is almost as important to know what not to teach as to know what to teach; to keep many incidents and thoughts in the background and push a few prominent ones into the foreground; to let the flock go and run one goose down.

In the light of this outline the teacher should carefully study the lesson, reading it over thoughtfully, fixing the meaning of its words, tracing the logical links of the passage, comparing it with other Scripture, and endeavouring to recreate in his own mind the scene and thought as it lay in the historian's mind or before the prophet's vision. He should endeavour to dissolve the crystallized words in his mind so that they will melt back into the original meaning of the Scripture writer and saturate his own soul with the same truth. This is the psychology of words, as we have seen,[1] and by this means the teacher is first to fill his mind with the words of the lesson and find that they " are spirit and are life."

The principle of association [2] and the process of meditation [3] play an important part in this preparation. Association causes all the kindred ideas in the mind and down in the subconsciousness to flock around the lesson and pour their fuel into its fire. Meditation stimulates association and brings out all its resources. And thus as the teacher's mind plays around and broods over the lesson and works down into its depths it opens out and begins to disclose points of light and grows luminous until the whole lesson seems to be ablaze with new meaning and beauty and power. The

[1] Pp. 228-234.   [2] Pp. 32-35.   [3] Pp. 229-233.

most familiar verse or word may suddenly glow and sparkle as a diamond. It is thus the teacher's eyes are opened and he beholds wondrous things out of the lesson. When the teacher's mind is thus illuminated and his soul absorbed by the Scripture he is ready to teach with contagious interest and enthusiasm.

The help of a good commentary will be needed to clear up difficulties in the lesson. But never mind about trying to explain all the obscure things in the lesson while preparing it. It may be well to run one or two difficulties down, but there are many things in every lesson the teacher can afford to let go. A few points studied thoroughly will give the teacher a sense of confidence and command over the lesson that will be better than much superficial reading.

Lesson helps are a good thing, but like every good thing they may be misused. They may lead us away from the study of the Bible into miscellaneous reading about the Bible; sometimes they so overlay the lesson that we cannot see the woods for the trees. They are apt to overload our minds with a mass of undigested information; and their chief mischief is that we may let them do all our thinking for us and get no ideas of our own. Better far that we read less, and think more; depend less on the knowledge of others and more upon our own study and thought. One can really teach only such truths as by reflection and experience he has made his own. The raw materials of coal and coke and limestone and ore that are poured into the top of the blast furnace melt down through its burning heart and come out at the bottom in a glowing stream of molten metal; so should all the materials of Scripture study pass down through the heart of the teacher and come out as living streams of experience and then he can go before his class and speak that he does know and testify that he has seen.

III. The Teacher Before the Class

When the teacher appears before the class his part is that of a leader. He is not a lecturer to take up all the time with a general discourse on the lesson; much less is he there to show off the knowledge he has gathered in his preparation. The good teacher never tells all he knows, and he gives the impression that all he says is only a hint of what he might say. The sun never lets all its light shine. Emerson says that we never quite respect the man that tells us all he knows; and the teacher that talks so much that no one else can say anything is likely to lose the respect of his scholars. The impression of reserve power is often one of the greatest factors in the influence of a preacher or teacher. The hearers of Phillips Brooks often felt what tremendous things he could say if he would only let himself out. The teacher needs to restrain himself with this wise reserve and not say too much. He is not a monologist and should not monopolize the time. It is just as important to know how and when to close the mouth as to open it, and the teacher whose mouth is always running has yet to learn one very vital point in the art of teaching. The wisdom of the teacher is rather to be measured by what he can get his scholars to say than by what he says himself.

The teacher, equally with the preacher, needs to be on his guard against any dogmatic and dictatorial air in conducting the lesson. He should have positive views which he should assert with decision and earnestness, but should not seek to impose them on others by mere authority. The fullest freedom and liberty should be invited and encouraged in the way of discussion and differences of views. It should be open to any scholar to ask any question in connection with the lesson, and when the teacher cannot answer it he should frankly say so, and such confession, instead of injuring the standing of the teacher, may rather increase confidence in him. Such questions may be referred to the class, and if no one can answer them they can be reserved for further study and report. Such a question can often be referred to some member or members of the class for this purpose.

The teacher will encounter views that he may not think correct or Scriptural or orthodox, and while he may be positive in expressing himself on such points he should not infringe on the independence and liberty of mind of the scholars. Anything like browbeating and suppressing differences of views and doubts is as ill-advised and unjust and fatal in its consequences in a Sunday school class as in the pulpit. Of course much depends at this point on the age of scholars, but scholars of any degree of maturity should have their independence and individuality of mind respected. The teacher should be among his scholars as a comrade, even as a servant. The preacher stands on a platform at a higher level than his congregation, but the teacher is usually down on the floor with his scholars, and this is significant of a closer personal relation in which the teacher and the scholars are workers together in learning the truth.

The whole personality of the teacher counts at this point, and his vital influence as a teacher will depend more on what he is than on what he says. He may not always be able to clear up difficult points in the lesson and may make mistakes, but if he wins the confidence and love of his scholars he will be a good teacher for them and he will win their souls.

IV. The Art of Questioning

The lesson must be held well in hand by the teacher, or it will drift about and run into all kinds of discussion and get into confusion. There should be considerable liberty in this direction, but it is best to confine the lesson to the outline and cluster the questions around the main points.

Questioning is a fine and often a difficult art. We might think that anybody could ask a question on any subject, but it may take as much knowledge to ask a good question as to answer it. It takes an expert lawyer to put the right questions to a witness, and there is equal need of expert questioning in teaching. Socrates, the greatest teacher of antiquity, was simply a walking interrogation point, going around asking men questions. With a few simple and apparently innocent and easy questions he could puncture and expose the empty ignorance of the most conceited sophist and reduce him to pitiful helplessness; or he could draw out a sincere seeker after truth and lead him into clearer definitions and larger views. Socrates had a theory that all knowledge lies latent in the human mind and that all that is needed to draw it out is a series of questions to bring it to remembrance. In a remarkable passage in the "Meno" he questions a slave boy as to what he knows about a right-angled triangle and draws out of him the knowledge that the square of the hypothenuse is equal to the sum of the squares of the other two sides. This complex proposition is a stumbling-block to many a high school or college student, but this slave boy under simple questioning knew it. It is a wonderful feat in pedagogy, and shows what skilful questioning can do.

Another master in the art of questioning was Jesus, the divine Teacher. Much of his teaching was carried on by asking questions. Often instead of asserting a truth on his authority he would submit it to his hearers with the question, " What think ye? " or " What man of you " would not do so and so? He thus, like Socrates, drew the truth he was teaching right out of the minds and bosoms of his hearers. He appealed to their own experience and made it confirm his own teaching. When the Pharisees and Scribes were trying to entangle him with their cunningly devised questions, he often turned their own snare into a net with which he caught them and reduced them to helplessness. His dialectical encounters with these enemies are among the most remarkable features of his ministry. His lessons were conversations in which question and answer were the means of instruction.

There are two points in the art of questioning which the teacher needs to keep in mind. One is that the question should be adapted to the knowledge of the scholar; it should find a point of contact with and fit into the scholar's state of mind. If it is addressed to his ignorance and is unintelligible to him, it will only bewilder and confuse him. But when it enters fhe mind as a seed that finds its appropriate soil it will quickly take root and grow up; it will call forth the latent resources of the mind; all the scholar's associations will flock to the question to help answer it. This is the principle of " apperception " already explained.[1] The scholar hears each question through his existing knowledge or total state of mind, and therefore a good ques-

[1] Pp. 29-30.

tion will appeal to this content and arouse it into
action. The secret of Socrates's success with the slave
boy was that he kept constantly appealing to what the
boy did know and thus drew out of him what was
latent in his mind.

Another closely allied principle is that of the individuality of the mind of each scholar.[1] The minds of
the scholars may look very much alike to the teacher,
but a deeper look discloses endless and profound differences even in a graded class. A question is not the
same question to any two scholars, but it arouses different associations and meanings in their minds. The
teacher is disposed to standardize his teaching and expect it to fit equally all the minds in the class. But as
he grows acquainted with them he will begin to note
their individualities and adapt his questions to their
varying states. In time the practised teacher will learn
instinctively to know and respect, and adapt his teaching to, the individual knowledge and state and needs of
his scholars.

A question should be definite and clear and yet it
should not answer itself. Of course the teacher must
ask many questions having obvious answers, for he
should catch the dullest minds in his class. A good
question reaches after principles and suggests thought
and stirs up interest. It strikes the mind and makes
it ring as the clapper strikes the bell. All the difference between good teaching and poor may consist in the
questions asked. Therefore the teacher should study
this art and practise writing out questions that bristle
with points and prick the mind with attention and
interest. The preparation of such questions may be an
important part of the preparation of the lesson.

[1] Pp. 65-68.

V. The Use of Imagination and Illustration

What has been said as to the use of imagination and illustration in preaching applies with little change to teaching. The lack of the power to make a subject interesting is as fatal in teaching as in preaching, and the teacher must make every effort to save the lesson from being dry and dull and to brighten it up with interest; and one of the chief means to this end in teaching as in preaching is the use of imagination and illustration.

The lesson usually contains a scene and this should be put before the class as a picture. The Bible is a highly picturesque book, full of oriental action and colour, and the teacher, as well as the preacher and every reader, should endeavour to see it in this light, and this will make its spiritual truth vivid and bring it home to us. For the smaller scholars the lesson may be told as a story, which will set it on the stage of the imagination, and the same effect should be produced with all grades. A lesson consisting of a parable or miracle in the gospels or a dramatic scene in the Old Testament is more than half taught when it is simply seen and realized by the imagination. The teacher should cultivate the insight and power of seeing the picture in the lesson and so telling or suggesting it, it may be as a mere sketch in a few broad strokes, that the class will see it also.

The author once heard a teacher describe how he got some small scholars in a school he was visiting to realize the height of a mountain. The lesson was about a mountain the height of which was given as fourteen thousand feet. This teacher saw that the children had no slightest conception of such a height, it was a mere

meaningless name to them, and they were dull-eyed and
indifferent. The visiting teacher, who was the super-
intendent of the district, took the class in hand. There
was a mountain just out through the window about a
thousand feet high, which was familiar to the scholars.
The teacher had the children look at it, and then told
them to imagine another mountain a thousand feet high
shoved up on top of it; then he told them to imagine a
third mountain a thousand feet high shoved up on top
of these two; and he kept on until he had seven mountains piled up in this way. Then he took a daring
leap. He asked the scholars to imagine two such mountains each seven thousand feet high and then to lift
one of these up and put it on top of the other: there
was a mountain fourteen thousand feet high! By this
time the eyes of the children were sparkling with interest and their heads were dizzy with the height of that
mountain, which they now saw almost as plainly as
though it were before their vision. Imagination showed
it to them and gave them a vivid sense of its towering
height, and it was a great teacher that enabled them to
see it. Every teacher, whether in the day school or the
Sunday school, can cultivate this art and do much
by this means to visualize and realize the lesson.

Illustrations are means to the same end. A remarkable feature of the Bible is that it always seems to be
a contemporary book, paralleling the principles and
events of our day, so that it reflects our life, and our
life illuminates and explains it. This enables us to find
illustrations lying thick around us that show us its
teachings in living operation, and the teacher, like
the preacher, should cultivate the art of seeing and
applying these illustrations. Lesson helps and com-
mentaries supply many illustrations, but the ones the

teacher finds himself will probably be the best in his hands. Sometimes a striking illustration can be found of a statement or scene in the lesson that will make it flame before the imagination. When Isaiah, to illustrate the greatness of God, exclaims, " Behold, he taketh up the isles as a very little thing " (40: 15), the teacher can give an account of the explosion of the isle of Krakatao, near Java, in 1883, in which a mountain a cubic mile in volume was literally blown into dust and scattered on the winds around the earth, the explosion being heard a hundred and fifty miles away, sending waves across the Pacific that rolled in destruction upon South American coasts, and reddening the sunset skies for more than a year. Such an impressive event enables us to understand more vividly how God " sitteth upon the circle of the earth," and picks up islands as pebbles and blows them away as dust. The resourceful teacher will be on the outlook for good illustrations and may keep notes of them, and by this means he can make every lesson interesting and keep his class alive and alert.

VI. Getting the Scholars to Work

An important part of the teacher's work is to get the scholars to work. It is not the business of the teacher to do the scholar's work for him and keep him passive while he pours truth into his mind. This may be easy and pleasant and even entertaining for the scholar, but it is really doing him an injury. Because the teacher is keeping the class interested with his stories and lively personality and talk, he may think he is doing good work, whereas he may be doing the poorest kind of work and even work that is worse than none. The object of teaching is not simply to impart information, but to develop the mental faculties of the scholar so that he can get information and test it and produce thought for himself. Mere knowledge is only the food that is placed in the mental stomach; the food must be digested into intellectual blood and brain, into thought power, or it will do no good and may even do harm. The teacher is to teach the scholar how to see facts and relations, grasp principles and apply laws for himself. It is not his office simply to teach his own opinions and beliefs, pouring the contents of his mind into the moulds of his scholars' minds, but to teach them how to use their minds so as to form their own conclusions and beliefs. He is not interested so much in what they think as in how they think. Dr. Thomas Arnold moulded a generation of English boys into noble men, not by imposing upon them his intellectual and moral beliefs, but by imparting to them his intellectual and moral processes, his honesty and humility, his candour and sincerity, his patience and charity of mind. He aroused their whole mental and moral nature and developed it into independence and power of action, and this made his boys men, many of whom afterwards sat in the seats of the mighty.

Referring again to Plato's Dialogue "Meno," in which Socrates taught the slave boy the proposition in geometry, we see that it is a psychological masterpiece of teaching because Socrates did not tell him anything as ready-made information, but rather set the boy's own mind to work so that he saw each step of the process for himself. Let us listen to the dialogue between Socrates and the boy as it starts off:

Soc. Tell me, boy, do you know that a figure like this is a square?

Boy. I do.

Soc. And do you know that a square figure has these four lines equal?

Boy. Yes.

Soc. A square may be of any size?

Boy. Certainly.

Soc. And if one side of the figure be of two feet, and the other side of two feet, how much will the whole be? Let me explain: if in one direction the space was of two feet, and in the other direction of one foot, the whole would be of two feet taken once?

Boy. Yes.

Soc. But since this side is also of two feet, there are twice two feet?

Boy. There are.

Soc. Then the square is of twice two feet?

Boy. Yes.

Soc. And how many are twice two feet? count and tell me.

Boy. Four, Socrates.

The dialogue runs its course and comes to this conclusion:

Soc. And that is the line which the learned call the diagonal. And if this is the proper name, then you, Meno's slave, are prepared to affirm that the double space is the square of the diagonal?

Boy. Certainly, Socrates.

Soc. What do you say of him, Meno? Were not all these answers given out of his own head?

Men. True.[1]

[1] Jowett's *Dialogues of Plato*, Vol. I, pp. 256-260.

This is great teaching because it is stimulating the boy's own faculties to see things and follow them out to their logical conclusion.

Now this general principle applies to teaching in the Sunday school as well as in the day school and university. The teacher is not set over the scholars simply to tell them what to believe about the lesson. This would often be the shortest and easiest way out of the matter, but it would accomplish little or nothing. The teacher should aim at getting the scholars to work the lesson out for themselves. This means that they should study the lesson before coming to the class, and to get back into the scholar's preparation of the lesson and see that it is done is part of the teacher's work.

In handling the lesson before the class the teacher should not be too forward in bringing out the points and applications of the lesson, but should draw these out of the scholars themselves. Every means should be used to encourage the scholars to do their own thinking and form their own conclusions. Even children should be taught not as parrots but as persons. The teacher should respect the minds and mental rights of his scholars, and they should be taught to feel their intellectual responsibility and to respect their own judgment. Any spirit in the teacher that discourages and suppresses independent discussion and thought is a mistake on the part of the teacher and may be a serious injury to the scholar. It is possible by such means to plant the seeds of doubt in young minds and send scep- tics right out of our Sunday schools. While of course any irreverent and rationalistic spirit should not be suggested, yet scholars should be encouraged to search the Scriptures, whe‡her these things are so, and to try the spirits, whether they be of God.

" Sayest thou this thing of thyself, or did others tell it thee of me? " (John 18:34), was a searching question put by Jesus to Pilate, and the same question goes to the root of our knowledge and of our scholars' knowledge. Do we know these things pertaining to salvation of ourselves, or did others simply tell us of them? If we do not know them of ourselves, we know nothing as we ought to know it. Then our knowledge is second-hand, report and rumour, and not first-hand, personal, experimental knowledge. So our scholars should know the truths of Scripture, not because they have been told about them, but because they know these things of themselves, having grasped them in their minds and realized them in their experience.

VII. The Teacher's Interest in the Scholar

There is something deeper in teaching than question and answer, the impartation of knowledge and intellectual stimulation, and that is the spirit of vital sympathy and fellowship that should bind the teacher and scholar together. If they sustain only an external official relation, it will yield little profit to either and may be attended with unpleasant friction and even galling bondage. The Sunday school teacher especially should be interested in the scholar and be enthusiastic and absorbed in the work. If teaching is only a perfunctory duty to him it will be drudgery; but if it is interesting and inspiring it will be a delight.

This opens a wide subject in itself on which only a few suggestions can here be made. The teacher should study not only his lesson but also his scholars; he should study their characters and circumstances, get

into the secret of their lives, and the study will develop
unexpected interest and even fascination.

All people are interesting when we have the insight
to see into them. It is sometimes thought that the mass
of human beings are a dull plodding crowd and that
only a few bright minds are worth our notice. This
is a great mistake. Nothing is uninteresting if only
we have eyes to see it. Ruskin wrote one of his noblest
lectures on the yellow iron stain he saw on the marble
rim of a fountain in the town where he had been invited to speak. Huxley has a profound lecture on a
" Piece of Chalk," and a French author has written an
entertaining volume on *The Story of a Stick*. If these
things properly studied are interesting, how much more
so are men and women and children. Men of genius
see this and base their art upon it. Ruskin says of
Turner: " One hour he is interested in a gust of wind
blowing away an old woman's cap; the next he is painting the Fifth Plague of Egypt. A soldier's wife resting
by the roadside is not beneath his sympathy; Rizpah
watching the dead bodies of her sons not above it.
Nothing can possibly be so mean that it will not interest his whole mind and carry away his whole heart."

The fictitious characters that move across the pages
of a novel whom we follow with such interest are just
such persons as move around us in real life; only the
novelist has the genius to see their interesting traits
and portray them for us. Sir Walter Scott said that
there is romance enough in every life for a three-volume
novel. So we are not to think that we are to go far and
hunt for some exceptionally bright person to find one
worthy of our sympathy and study, but just take the
next man or woman or child and study that life, get
into its inner experiences and secrets, and there will

be unearthed an unexpected wealth of fascination. Your next-door neighbour may be just as interesting as the Queen of England; at least she is more accessible. If we were to take the first little ragged urchin we meet in the street and could get into his heart and see his thoughts and plans, his joys and sorrows, his originalities, the unique things in that little breast that never were before, we would see that which would fascinate us and teach us great lessons, throw us into laughter or fill our eyes with tears.

This interest inherent in every individual life, even in the most commonplace one, is vastly heightened by the immortal and infinite worth of every soul. Personal gifts and traits of originality, interesting individuality, and even genius are superficial and unimportant in comparison with the deep and lasting worth common to all men. " One ruddy drop of human blood the surging sea outweighs," and any humblest child embodies worth surpassing that of all the jewelled coronets of the world. The sculptor or painter commits his ideas to and spends infinite toil upon perishable materials, he is only shaping crumbling stone or colouring frail canvas, but the teacher of a child is shaping immortal spirit and helping to produce a portrait of a soul that will outlast the stars and be set in the gallery of eternity. If we can have some appreciation of the infinite value of our scholars we shall at least take such interest in them as the artist does in his evanescent work and build ourselves into their souls. No teacher knows what he is doing, how far into the future he is reaching when he is training a child. An old German schoolmaster always took his hat off to each new boy that came into his school, never knowing what elements of genius might have been mixed in his newly moulded brain. When Erasmus came out of that school his prophetic instinct was justified. Never despise a child, for in it sleeps some of the omnipotence and worth of God.

Teachers, study your scholars. Get into their inner life and explore their individuality. You will thus get interested and even absorbed in them and your duty may be transformed and transfigured from drudgery into delight. The very stupidest pupil in the class will richly repay you for your sympathy and self-sacrifice. The dull boy's mind is always the wise teacher's problem, and he may teach you as much as you can teach him. You will learn to love your scholars and begin to see their unique and immortal worth, the divine possibilities in them. You will look on them, as Jesus looked on men, as the children of the Father. Then you can teach them and have an influence over them, and the vital touch of your life on their lives will be the means of imparting to them the Spirit of Christ and making them his.

VIII. Leading Scholars to Christ

What is it for? is the final test to which everything must be brought. What is the object of all our work in the Sunday school? It is not mere instruction and education, as it is in the day school. It is conversion to Christ and training in Christian character and life. Teaching the Word of God is a very important means, but it is only a means, to this end. The seed of truth is sown in the minds of the scholars that it may spring up in Christian fruit. The teacher is to lead his scholars to Christ. This is the definite and final end on which he should concentrate all his teaching and prayer and influence.

This end should dominate the work before the class, and yet it should not be made too obtrusive. The personal application of the lesson requires wisdom and tact. It is not wise to be constantly forcing a spiritual application out of every fact and detail. It is possible thus to make the subject of personal religion distasteful to scholars and defeat the very end of teaching. Yet the instruction should always have a practical drift and suggest personal duty. The Christian life should be presented in its true light as life more abundant, full of liberty and joy, and not as a narrower life which always wears the sombre aspect of restriction and gloom. It should be presented as a duty, but as a glorious duty and privilege which is the fullest and richest life and most joyous blessedness.

In order that we may make our class work effective and lead scholars to Christ, we must endeavour to reach them individually by personal word and influence. Jesus found Philip and Philip found Nathanael: that is the way the kingdom started and has been extending ever since; each convert found the next, and thus the golden chain has lengthened down to our day when some one found each one of us. Jesus in healing people generally touched them; he singled them out and came into personal, vital relations with them. When he was about to feed the five thousand, he did not attempt to deal with the multitude as an unorganized mass, but he had them sit down in ranks of hundreds and fifties: he cut up his work, he had the people arranged so that he could get at them one by one. In our preaching and teaching we too often seem simply to throw the bread out upon the multitude, the congregation, or the class, instead of handing it to them one at a time. We need to get close to our scholars in personal and private relations in which we can get them one Ly one.

The teacher as surely as the preacher is called to convert souls and develop them in the Christian life. Any lower view or frivolous spirit in a Sunday school teacher that fails to see or interferes with this mission is pitiful blindness and failure. The teacher is to seek by prayer and pointed application of the truth and personal private word and influence to lead each scholar to Christ. He should have a passion for souls that will be a deep, secret, impelling power and transfiguring spirit in his work. He that winneth souls is wise. Then and not till then will the final end of Sunday school teaching be realized, and the teacher will have the reward and joy of his work.

We have come to the end of our study. Science only takes the old and familiar things of the world and gives them new meaning and application, but we still have to make the application, and they will serve us only as we rightly use them. Psychology has not given us any new forms and forces in our religious life and work. It has only opened up the laws and workings of these things and enabled us to understand them a little better. They are still full of the deep things of God's Word and world, margined and mingled with the mystery of all life. However much we may study and understand the things of the spirit, our increased knowledge will do us good only as we translate it into obedience and experience. Psychology cannot save us; only the grace of the Lord Jesus Christ can do this. Though we understand all psychology and have not love, we are nothing. Let us appreciate and appropriate what psychology has taught us and continue to study our religious life and work in its growing light and gain all the insight and efficiency we can in this field of truth. But let us above all grow in grace and in the knowledge of our Lord and Saviour Jesus Christ, that we may grow up into him in all things, till we all come in the unity of the faith, and of the knowledge of the Son of God, unto a full-grown man, unto the measure of the stature of the fulness of Christ.

Now unto the King eternal, immortal, invisible, the only wise God, be honour, and glory forever and ever. Amen.

BIBLIOGRAPHICAL NOTE

As a suggestion to any students and readers that may wish to pursue this subject further a few books out of the large and rapidly growing literature of the subject are here named:

(1) The works of William James hold a foremost place both in general and in religious psychology. His *Principles of Psychology* (New York: Henry Holt and Co. Two volumes, $5.00) is still a leading authority and is wonderfully informing and interesting, even for the general reader. His *Varieties of Religious Experience* (New York: Longmans, Green, and Co. $3.50) is one of the most important contributions yet made to the psychology of religion. It gathers illustrations of religious experience from a wide field and comments on them with penetrating suggestiveness. His *Will to Believe* (Longmans, Green, and Co. $2.00) also contains much psychological and philosophical matter on the subject of religious belief of unusual interest and value.

(2) *The Study of Religion*, by Morris Jastrow, of the University of Pennsylvania (New York: Charles Scribner's Sons. $1.50) is a study of the historical origin and nature of religion and its relation to philosophy, psychology, ethics, and other fields of thought and life. It prepares the ground for the special study of the psychology of religion.

(3) *The Psychology of Religion*, by Edwin Diller Starbuck, of the State University of Iowa (Charles Scribner's Sons. $1.50) was one of the first books in this field in which Professor Starbuck was a pioneer investigator. His book covers only the psychology of conversion, of which it makes a thorough inductive study. Facts were collected on the questionaire method, and on the answers received from several hundred persons giving their experience in conversion inductive conclusions are based. It is still one of the best books on the psychology of conversion.

(4) *The Spiritual Life*, by George Albert Coe, of the Union Theological Seminary, New York (New York: Fleming H. Revell

379

Co. $1.00), and also his *Religion of a Mature Mind* (Revell. $1.35) are early and still valuable contributions to the subject. Professor Coe entered upon the study of the psychology of religion almost at the same time with Professor Starbuck, and the two were fellow-pioneers in this field.

(5) *The Psychology of Religious Experience*, by Edward Scribner Ames, of the University of Chicago (Boston: Houghton Mifflin Co. $3.50). This is one of the most elaborate general works on the subject. Part I sketches the history and method of this science; Part II traces the origin of religion in the race; Part III treats of the rise of religion in the individual; and Part IV deals with the place of religion in the experience of the individual and society. It is one of the ablest books on the subject, but the author holds very liberal views on religion.

(6) *The Psychology of Religious Belief*, by James Bissett Pratt, of Williams College (New York: The Macmillan Co. $1.50). Part I develops the psychological factors of belief; Part II traces the historical origin of religion; and Part III, on the " Present Status of Religious Belief," discusses the development of religious belief in childhood, the types of belief in mature life, and the value of God.

(7) *The Psychological Phenomena of Christianity*, by George Barton Cutten, a Baptist pastor and educator (Charles Scribner's Sons. $2.50). There are thirty-two chapters in this book, each of which treats by itself some aspect of the religious life, such as the religious faculty, revivals, conversion, worship, prayer, throwing on them the light of illustration and experience gathered from a number of pastorates. It is a suggestive popular treatment of the subject.

(8) *The Philosophy of Christian Experience*, by Henry W. Clark (Revell. $1.25). " Not twice in a generation does one meet with so valuable an analysis of experimental religion as Mr. Henry Clark gives us in his ' Philosophy of Christian Experience.' "—Marcus Dods.

(9) *Christian Psychology*, by James Stalker, of the United Free Church College, Aberdeen (New York: George H. Doran Co. $1.25), is an elementary outline of psychology with applications to Christian faith and life. It would be a good book for a beginner in the study of general psychology.

(10) *The Psychology of the Christian Soul*, by George Steven,

an Edinburgh Presbyterian pastor (George H. Doran Co. $1.50). The author treats the religious life as a process of education and traces its development out of sin through conversion to "the capture of the soul by God" and "the soul in the presence of God." It is not only keen in its psychological analysis, but is also a practical aid in the Christian life.

(11) *Rational Living*, by Henry Churchill King, President of Oberlin College (The Macmillan Co. $1.25), applies psychology to the whole field of life, treating of the relations of mind and body, of the intellect and emotions and will in their relation to life, and making practical "suggestions for living" of the highest value.

(12) *Principles of Education*, by Frederick Elmer Bolton, Ph.D. (Charles Scribner's Sons. $3.00). This large volume is an elaborate treatment of the whole subject of education from biological and psychological points of view. It is a very illuminating work and it is of special value to the minister as well as to the teacher.

INDEX

Allen, Prof. Alexander V. G.,
his biography of Phillips
Brooks, 314.

Ames, Edward Scribner, his
*Psychology of Religious Ex-
perience,* 380.

Apperception, 29-30, 35.

Arnold, Matthew, on nature of
religion, 88; on the meaning
of *metanoia,* 155; on philosophy, 338.

Arnold, Dr. Thomas, his methods of teaching, 369.

Astronomy, value to the minister, 329.

Associations, mental, their nature, 32-35; their laws, 34;
how they multiply under attention, 49; intensify temptation, 118-119.

Athanasius, referred to, 283.

Attention, primary form of the
will, 48; involuntary and
voluntary, 48-49; its selective
power, 175-176.

Augustine, quoted, 93; referred
to, 283.

Badè, Prof. W. F., quoted, 91.

Balfour, A. J., on prayer, 237.

Baxter, Richard, referred to,
136; on childhood conversion,
189.

Beauty, sense of, as root of religion, 98; in worship, 254-
256; in literary style, 306-
308.

Beecher, Henry Ward, quoted,
277, 327; his humour, 311;
his imagination, 313; his style
of pulpit delivery, 324; referred to, 343, 348.

Beethoven, referred to, 245.

Begbie, Harold, his *Twice-Born
Men,* 149-152.

Bible, the, as source of religious psychology, 23-24;
grew out of experience, 90-
93; its pedagogical method,
201-202; a storehouse of religious truth, 208; how it is
spirit and life, 212-213; full
of song, 243-244; of imagination, 263, 366; humour in,
310; a contemporary book,
367.

Bolton, Frederick Elmer, his
Principles of Education, 381.

Bourne, Rev. Ansel, case of,
147.

Brooks, Phillips, his sermon
topics, 295; his illustrations,
308; his imagination, 314; referred to, 343, 348; his reserve power, 361.

Browning, quoted, 16, 108, 178,
193-194, 228; referred to,
274; his imagination, 313.

Bunyan, John, referred to, 136.

Burns, quoted, 264.

Bushnell, Horace, on the Christian nurture of children, 187-
189; his sermon on " Unconscious Influence," 292.

Cæsar, referred to, 346.

Caird, Dr. Edward, on nature
of religion, 88.

Calvin, referred to, 283.

Carlyle, his conversion, 144-145;
quoted, 318; referred to, 335.

Carpenter, Senator, quoted, 320-
321.

Categories, the, 29, 31.

Chalmers, Thomas, quoted, 156,
242.

JAMES H. SNOWDEN, D.D.

The Psychology of Religion

8vo, cloth.

Psychology is one of the most rapidly advancing of modern sciences, and Dr. Snowden's book will find a ready welcome. While especially adapted for the use of ministers and teachers, it is not in any sense an ultra-academic work. This is evidenced by the fact that the material forming it has been delivered not only as a successful Summer School course, but in the form of popular lectures, open to the general public.

WILLIAM HALLOCK JOHNSON, Ph.D., D.D.

Professor of Greek and New Testament Literature in Lincoln University, Pa.

The Christian Faith under Modern Searchlight

The L. P. Stone Lectures, Princeton. Introduction by Francis L. Patton, D.D. Cloth.

The faith which is to survive must not only be a traditional but an intelligent faith which has its roots in reason and experience and its blossom and fruit in character and good works. To this end, the author examines the fundamentals of the Christian belief in the light of to-day and reaches the conclusion that every advance in knowledge establishes its sovereign claim to be from heaven and not from men.

ANDREW W. ARCHIBALD, D.D.

Author of "The Bible Verified," "The Trend of the Centuries," etc.

The Modern Man Facing the Old Problems

12mo. cloth.

A thoughtful, ably-conducted study in which those problems of human life, experience and destiny, which, in one form or another, seem recurrent in every age, are examined from what may be called a Biblical viewpoint. That is to say, the author by its illuminating rays, endeavors to find elucidation and solution for the difficulties, which in more or less degree, perplex believer and unbeliever alike.

NOLAN RICE BEST   *Editor of "The Continent"*

Applied Religion for Everyman

12mo, cloth.

Nolan Rice Best has earned a well-deserved reputation in the religious press of America, as a writer of virile, trenchantly-phrased editorials. The selection here brought together represent his best efforts, and contains an experienced editor's suggestions for the ever-recurrent problems confronting Church members as a body, and as individual Christians. Mr. Best wields a facile pen, and a sudden gleam of beauty, a difficult thought set in a perfect phrase, or an old idea invested with new meaning and grace, meets one at every turn of the page."—*The Record Herald.*

P. WHITWELL WILSON *of the London Daily News*

The Christ We Forget

A Life of Our Lord for Men of To-day. 8vo, cloth.

A book with scarcely a peer in contemporary publishing. The author, an English University man, brilliant journalist, and sometime member of Parliament, writes the story of Jesus of Nazareth in a wonderfully arresting fashion. His book is utterly free from theological terminology or conventional viewpoint presenting a picture of Jesus which while actually new is astonishingly convincing.

EDGAR YOUNG MULLINS, D.D. *Pres. Southern Baptist Theo'l Sem., Louisville*

The Life in Christ

"Dr. Mullins has recognition throughout the country as a great teacher. This volume shows him a preacher of intellectual and spiritual power. Excellent models for the growing minister, forcible, intellectual, spiritual."—*Christian Advocate.*

FRANCIS E. CLARK, D.D. *President United Society Christian Endeavor*

Christ and the Young People

12mo, cloth.

"A study of the Life of Jesus in a quite unusual vein. The editor has seldom during his life been so helped by the printed page. It is indeed a remarkable presentation of the life of Jesus, sincere and impartial."—*Zion's Herald.*

JAMES M. GRAY, D.D. *Dean Moody Bible Institute*

A Picture of the Resurrection

12mo, boards.

A plain, unadorned examination of the historical fact of Our Lord's Resurrection, of its indispensable prominence in the faith of the Christian and of the power its acceptance exercises in buttressing his belief in a physical resurrection from the dead, and the attainment of life eternal.

A. T. ROBERTSON, M.A., D.D.

The Divinity of Christ in the Gospel of John 12mo, cloth.

"A fascinating study of the Gospel of John. The book is not a full commentary on the Gospel, but an effort to develop the thesis of the book with brevity and clearness, so that the average man may understand the book better as a whole in detail."—*Christian Observer.*

HENRY C. MABIE, D.D.   *Author of "Method of Soul Winning"*

The Unshaken Kingdom

12mo, cloth.

Treats of the fundamentals of the Christian faith, against which the storms of time beat in vain. There is a fine missionary spirit running through the book, which finds a special expression in the chapter entitled The Ultimacy of Christian Missions.

DAVID BAINES-GRIFFITHS

When Faiths Flash Out

Essays in Spiritual Replenishment.

"Thoroughly health-giving, evangelical and consequently hopeful. The author possesses the power of felicitous expression, and gives us many helpful illustrations."—*Episcopal Recorder.*

ADOLPH LEHMANN, D.D.

The World to Come

The Progressive Manifestation of the Kingdom of God Among Men. 12mo, cloth.

Points out that Christ's Messianic Kingdom, when completed, will be followed by that of the Father, and indicates what the Bible teaches concerning this Dispensation, and its place in the development of the Kingdom of God.

DAVID A. MURRAY, D.D.   *Author of "Christian Faith and the New Psychology"*

The Supernatural : or Fellowship with God

12mo, cloth.

"Virile and will stimulate earnest thinking and vitalize flabby faith. The author sends his earnest message from the mission field. It will prove an effective weapon against prevelant naturalistic tendencies in Bible interpretation in the homeland."—*Christian World.*

DAVID J. BURRELL, D.D.

Why I Believe the Bible

12mo, cloth.

Does anyone knowing the author doubt his ability to give in clear, concise and convincing form his 'reasons' for a definite faith in the Book of Books. The work will confirm faith, cure skepticism and convert the honest enquirer.

ESSAYS AND STUDIES

CHARLES L. THOMPSON, D.D. *President of "Home Mission Council"*

The Religious Foundations of America

12mo, cloth.

A survey of the religious elements which from various European sources went to the making of America. The Reformation principles, which are the very springs of her national life, are traced to their original Old World channels, and their culminative influence in the New World measured and appraised.

EDGAR WHITAKER WORK, D.D. *Author "The Fascination of the Book"*

The Bible in English Literature

12mo, cloth.

Dr. Work believes that English-speaking people possess the Bible in the blood. When men bare their spirits to God, one sees the naked soul of humanity in the creative literature of the race. A volume of singular freshness, to be read with delight and to be studied with profit.

WILLIAM JENNINGS BRYAN

Heart-to-Heart Appeals

12mo, cloth.

The cream of Mr. Bryan's public utterances, selected from the principal speeches and lectures delivered by him during his eventful and picturesque career. The topics treated of include the following: Money; Imperialism; Labor; Trusts; Income Tax; Peace; Religion; Pan-Americanism. etc., etc.
A New Booklet by Mr. Bryan.

The First Commandment Boards, net 35c.

GEORGE McCREADY PRICE *Professor of Chemistry and Physics, Lodi Academy, Cal.*

Q. E. D., or New Light on the Doctrines of Creation

12mo, cloth.

The author, an acknowledged conservative, has in his several former volumes, found hearty approval and cordial endorsement from Professors Sayce, Parker, Wilkinson, Johnson, and many others. The work is reverential but scientifi frankly calling in question many recent popular hypotheses.

RICHARD L. SWAIN

The Real Key to Christian Science

12mo, cloth.

"The author's experience with 'leaders' of the Science Church, his defining of them of their own faith, the approval by them of a large part of his analysis, together with the unanswerable conclusion is commended both to converts to, and critics of, this rapidly growing system of ethics. The work is unique—unlike any previous study of the cult."

BIBLE STUDY

EDWARD AUGUSTUS GEORGE

The Twelve : Apostolic Types of Christian Men

12mo, cloth.
"Under his living touch the apostles seem very much like the men we know and their problems not dissimilar to our own."—*Congregationalist.*

PROF. W. G. MOOREHEAD

OUTLINE STUDIES in the NEW TESTAMENT SERIES
The Catholic Epistles and Revelation

In One Volume. *New Edition.* 12mo.
Containing James, I and II Peter, I, II and III John, and Jude, and the Book of Revelation.

ALEXANDER CRUDEN

Complete Concordance

Large 8vo, cloth.
New Unabridged Edition, with the Table of Proper Names entirely revised and mistranslations in the meanings corrected, many suggestive notes.

WILLIAM SMITH, LL.D.

A Dictionary of the Bible

Its Antiquities, Biography, Geography and Natural History, with Numerous Illustrations and Maps. *A New Worker's Edition.* 776 pages.

NEW THIN PAPER EDITION

The Boy Scouts' Twentieth Century New Testament

Officially authorized by the Boy Scouts' of America. New Thin Paper Edition.
181. 16mo, khaki cloth.
182. 16mo, ooze leather, khaki color,
Contains an introduction by the Executive Board, the Scouts' Oath, and the Scouts' Law.

HENRY T. SELL, D.D. (Editor) *Author of Sell's Bible Studies*
XX Century Story of the Christ

12mo, cloth.
From the text of The Twentieth Century New Testament, Dr. Sell has completed a Harmony of The Gospels which, while studiously avoiding repetition omits no important word in the fourfold record of the earthly life and teaching of our Lord. He has done his work well, and the result is a compilation specially designed and adapted for the use of the average reader.

BIBLE STUDY AND DEVOTIONAL

A. T. ROBERTSON, M.A., D.D.

Paul's Joy in Christ

Studies in Philippians. 12mo, cloth.

A study of Paul's unfailing optimism and spirit of rejoicing. Prof. Robertson brings all his expository skill to the presentation of this fact. The result is a new evidence of the value which may be set on the work of this accomplished New Testament scholar.

JAMES H. DUNHAM   *Dean of College of Liberal Arts and Sciences, Philadelphia*

John Fourteen

The Greatest Chapter of the Greatest Book.

"Will be welcomed everywhere by earnest students of the Bible. On every page is revealed the keen discriminating mind of a scholar, who ever exalts Christ and magnifies the Word of God above every other message."—*Baptist Standard.*

WILLIAM HIRAM FOULKES, D.D.

Sunset by the Lakeside

Vesper Messages to Young People. Boards.

Under this general title, a number of devotional messages such as are eminently suited to Young People's Conferences, are brought together in attractive and useful form. Into these brief addresses, Dr. Foulkes introduces some really choice, reverential thoughts such as cannot fail of proving helpful to everybody into whose hands they come.

YOUNG FOLKS' BIBLE STORIES

LETTICE BELL   *Author of "Go-to-Bed Stories," etc.*

Bible Battles

Israel's Victories Retold for Young Folks. 12mo, cloth.

Commencing with the victories of Joshua, a stirring panorama of Old Testament battle scenes is here presented. The narratives are all simply and effectively told in language peculiarly suited to juvenile readers.

ADA R. HABERSHON

Hidden Pictures

Or, How the New Testament is Concealed in the Old Testament. 12mo, cloth.

In a series of delightfully-drawn pictures, Miss Habershon presents some of the most arresting and salient incidents in the history of ancient Israel. These she employs to show how wonderfully they foreshadow and pre-figure the coming of Immanuel, as related in the Gospels.